EVERYTHING I NEVER WANTED

EVERYTHING I NEVER WANTED

A Memoir of Excess

BARBARA SANTARELLI

She Writes Press, a BookSparks imprint
A Division of SparkPointStudio, LLC.

Published 2017

Printed in the United States of America

Print ISBN: 978-1-63152-258-1
E-ISBN: 978-1-63152-259-8
Library of Congress Control Number: 2017942674

For information, address:
She Writes Press
1563 Solano Ave #546
Berkeley, CA 94707

Cover design © Julie Metz, Ltd./metzdesign.com
Cover photo © TK
Interior formatting by Katherine Lloyd/theDESKonline.com

She Writes Press is a division of SparkPoint Studio, LLC.

Names and identifying characteristics have been changed to protect the privacy of certain individuals.

Contents

For my mother, Charlotte Payne,

who gave as best she could and more

than she ever realized.

"The greatest thing in the world
is to know how to belong to oneself."

— *Michel de Montaigne*

Prologue

GRATEFUL FOR GRAY

The same biting cold that stole the leaves and colors from the trees is now stinging my eyes and numbing the tip of my nose. It's January; colorless, cold January. The trees are in a winter coma, but resilient enough to weather the misery. I'm giving resilience my best effort. It's just a matter of counting down and keeping distracted. At the moment, I'm actually counting time. In just six minutes our train will arrive. No winter coma for me. Unlike trees, human coma often precedes death. I'm not ready for that. I have other plans.

We are waiting for the southbound 10:15 Harlem line train to Grand Central. It's off- peak for the one-hour express ride on this Sunday. My husband, Nick, and I are huddled closely in the January cold. "Whose idea was this anyway?" he asks.

"I think I remember it was you who said, "Let's grab *The Times* and a train to the city this morning," I remind him. I was content to spend the day in the house watching TV or reading and not bothering to change out of my weekend uniform of sweatpants with frayed edges and a few stains.

We take temporary shelter in the glass kiosk meant to protect commuters from rain, snow, stinging sleet, and brutally cold temperatures like today's frigid sixteen degrees. Inside the glass rectangle, I feel like a human trapped in a fish tank. The little cubicle only serves to cut the day's biting wind, which comes in gusts. "How many days till May?" I ask. I get a dirty look in response. Wearing a thick knit watch cap and wool scarf that covers his nose and mouth, all I can see are Nick's eyes. Even with just that inch of his face exposed, I know it was his dirty look. The sarcasm is okay. We are both tired of spending cold Sunday mornings drinking too much coffee and waiting for spring. We feel a bit self-congratulatory this morning for breaking the pattern of Sunday stupor. We have forced our sluggish, bulky-clothed bodies out of the house and onto this platform. We think of the train as a magic bullet we will step into, knowing it will eject us into a beaux arts building throbbing with life in only an hour. This plan rarely fails or deviates. First, we will spend only ten or fifteen minutes in the grand space of the main concourse. Usually we are as still as the painted pale-blue heavenly sky above. Tourists and travelers will swirl around us in constant deliberate motion. We will plant ourselves instead and collect their energy. This vast space connects to platforms, passages, and tracks that move the others away as if pumping blood through vessels and feeding the city.

Next, we will go below to the market. Why is food so much more important in winter? Today, I will buy smoked paprika for turkey chili. The spice stall is crowded with stainless bowls brimming with colorful flavors from exotic places we will never visit. I think of the palette of colors as art. The sight is visually intoxicating. Next, the food court. We will look at the menu, but I know beforehand that we will share a panini of smoked turkey and brie. A glass of pinot will make it festive and special. Relaxed, we will then watch the purposeful people and play a game of guessing who they are, what they are named, and where they are going. The wine warms our brains and stretches our imaginations. We check the schedule because we are ready now to return. We have fought boredom, fat, and the status quo of marital inertia. Our arsenal includes sixty-five combined years of marriage. The last fifteen of those years have been together. Obstacles are our allies.

A woman and what appears to be a teenaged granddaughter walk toward our glass box. The elder woman casually opens the door, and they step in. The door closes softly behind them. Just good timing, I think, as just minutes before, the gusting wind challenged Nick's ability to pry the same door open. We squeezed quickly through a narrow opening and were unceremoniously smacked on our backs when the wind claimed the door's intention and shoved us forward. There are four of us in the fish tank now. Together, we wait behind glass.

She appears to be sixty something, like me. We are women of "a certain age." We are contemporaries. Well, maybe not. She is absolutely elegant in her winter-white melton wool knee-length swing coat. It flares perfectly from the funnel neck to a gentle bell curve, dipping an inch or two longer in the back to ensure a graceful silhouette. The hem ends an inch above spidery-thin legs clad in black tights. The sleeves also end in gentle bell curves. Each cuff has a single, beautifully finished bound buttonhole. It is finely tailored. I imagine she would not expect me to know about these details. The buttonholes are there to embrace two domed, jet black, honeycomb-faceted buttons. Her slim wrists and small hands are covered in fine black kid gloves. They are unadorned. She wears the softest, rich, black suede boots over the black tights. They are so slim, encasing her spider legs. I am sure she is an AAA-width shoe. The narrow point of the boot extends several inches unnaturally beyond her toes, lengthening their appearance. Perhaps it is this shoe gear that helps her to hover and glide rather than seem to take real steps. Perhaps this is why she was able to sail through the same door that held us back. Her hair is a cool, soft blonde in a windswept, carefully casual, ear-length style. That little bob easily costs $400 to trim and maintain every five to six weeks, I'm sure. From head to toe, I know she is always perfectly stylish. I dislike her easy elegance. I've decided to dislike this perfect stranger.

I cannot see but imagine that under the coat is a nicely textured wool bouclé tweed pencil skirt. I imagine it might be cranberry and charcoal with just enough nap to offset the fine-gauge dove-gray cashmere turtleneck above it. The skirt has French seams and a hidden zipper. Absolutely not any extra fabric over pencil-thin hips. God forbid! Without the benefit of actually seeing her clothes, I know exactly how she is dressed. The look is a perfect choice for an afternoon in the city with Amanda or Skylar or Chloe or whatever the girl's name is. It is a perfect choice for shopping, theater, or dining. Everything about her is perfect. I absolutely don't like her.

She is self-confident, and probably smug. I imagine she is pampered. Our paths will never cross. We will never have a conversation. That opportunity will never present itself because I believe I am invisible to her. Invisibility is painful for me, never having overcome that last vestigial childhood scar. Perhaps understanding it should be enough. I allow myself the luxury of fondling and stroking my now-smoothed-over-but-still-present little keloid I've almost forgotten is there. Elegant, confident women remind me it is still there. Self-assured people remind me of the years spent wanting to belong, to fit in. There were too many years spent on the outside watching people who never questioned their own value but ignored mine. That self-assurance triggers a response as immediate and invisible as pollen that prompts a sneeze. It is reflexive. I am irritated in their presence. I am uncomfortable. It may even be an allergy. Yes, an allergy. I have shaky self-esteem and insufficient immunity to arrogance. It is less of a problem now that I understand it.

Our eyes meet. Being women (of almost any age), we assess each other. I am convinced that it is dominant genetic trait found in females. It is the human equivalent of dogs sniffing each other's rears when they first meet. We look at and dismiss each other unceremoniously. She is a delicate, fog-gray, fine-boned greyhound in cashmere. I am an interesting, but mostly invisible mutt. Unclassifiable, unimportant, dismissed. My own choice of wardrobe begins with gray flannel clogs. These are my favorite. They are warm and wide (D width) and sturdy. They are a little pilled, but God are they comfortable. I love them. My jeans are Gap, and they're too tight. The top button is opened, a very bad sign at 10:00 a.m. The crotch is tightly wedged, with no drape anywhere. Over these I wear a plain, ribbed, charcoal turtleneck, not cashmere or even a nice merino wool. Perhaps a sturdy acrylic blend. My jacket is a warm but ubiquitous black down from L.L.Bean. It is not a Moncler, but fits well and is super warm and goes with just about everything I own.

My gray alpaca gloves and headband coordinate well. All set for my own day in the city.

The train arrives and the four of us choose seats on the same empty car. We sit at opposite ends, but all facing forward. For sure, by now I am totally erased from her thoughts, perhaps never occupying space there to begin with. As the train pulls forward and away, I still consider her spidery legs and pointed boots. We pass Goldens Bridge and Bedford and Katonah, and before the Mount Kisco platform she is tucked away as one more reference point in my collection of elegant, smug, dismissive people I can't help but dislike. I tuck only her details away someplace in my mind.

By the time we approach Chappaqua, Nick and I are huddled comfortably, sharing an actual hard copy of *The Times* and making plans for a lovely day. I've dismissed her almost completely from my thoughts. I've quelled the anger of feeling invisible and dismissed her slight as inconsequential. I've kept the details. I've enjoyed the details she has unknowingly shared with me.

Chapter One

IMMEASURABLE DETAILS

I've spent most of my life carefully observing details. I love detail. Sometimes, I form an imaginary frame within my field of vision. Within a twelve-inch frame I can reduce the sky to a single wisp of gray cloud or the side of a building to a single window with a crooked shade. I wish people were as enjoyable to frame. Imagine setting the frame over a benevolent smile or a soft gaze and trusting the image as real? I will stick with clouds and rocks and spider webs. I am rarely observed in return, or even noticed. Most people are more preoccupied with imagining how they appear within other people's frames. Overlapping, interlocking, tangled, and stacked frames that distort the truth and which I discard. So few are special at all. They are too often transient, fading illusions not worthy of a frame. Images are worthy of framing because they are special, unique in some way, if only momentarily, to another person. Those smug, self-satisfied, sneeze-provoking people are dismissed by me. Sorry, no frame from me unless I think you are worthy. I have complete control and pleasure in my private art gallery. I decide who gets framed and who gets left out.

Nick calls me a scorpion in an eagle's nest. He means this as a compliment. I am not sure if I am flattered, but it feels right. I was born under the November horoscope sign of Scorpio, whose traits include being passionate, exotic, and strong. He knows that I am passionate. Strong and exotic may be a stretch. Like the eagle, I observe details others may dismiss as unimportant and savor the potential importance of trivia.

That is how I happen to know about French seams in a world where French crullers are more revered. Growing up in a family unlike most of the others in my neighborhood was sometimes isolating. Ours was a single-parented Jewish family of three in an Italian Catholic neighborhood with robust-sized families of five or six. We ate Swanson TV dinners and had quiet holidays. We didn't go to church. I was aware of being different and was tentative when making friends, as I feared they would reject me. There was often time alone. Those larger families had gatherings and events and endless chores and church and homes that ate up time. I had time alone to observe and consider things that normally go unnoticed. I learned to enjoy details as if they were companions. I confirmed my own existence and value by becoming a critic of the value of everything around me. It was initially a survival mechanism. By qualifying and quantifying a world that placed me apart, I could navigate well.

By the time I was nine years old, I understood the difference between cumulus and nimbus clouds. I had memorized and visualized the poem "Trees," by Joyce Kilmer. I knew that the large gray owl with brown stripes across its chest that lived in the dead oak close to my bedroom window was a barred owl. He had a low voice that called, *Hoo . . . hooo . . . hooo.* It sounded to me a lot like the sound of a hollow wood flute. I thought he may be lonely also.

I knew that the neighbors preferred not to socialize with us or include my mother in the casual banter and chatter other neighbors shared. I somehow understood they thought us different and unworthy of including. I guessed that maybe we were if they thought so.

No matter, from my vantage point of isolation and nascent anger, I became a critic extraordinaire. I entertained myself by qualifying and quantifying my surroundings. Each detail offered escape and understanding that brought comfort. I became self-schooled in appreciating things that others never noticed. I had discovered an alternative to friends and belonging. Instead, I ingested and absorbed minutiae and thrived in what otherwise may have been a void. I enrolled in the School of Immeasurable Details. It wasn't the three-story redbrick public school building we went to. It was the empty space where I had the freedom of observation and thought that ultimately formed me. It was the breathing space I am now most grateful for.

My "finishing school" started early in life in an ugly railroad apartment shared with my divorced mother and my older brother. The lime-green, shingled, three-story house was the ugliest on Amundson Avenue, a dead-end street in the East Bronx. We were the only renters on a street of old, small private homes inhabited by Italian and Irish working poor, aspiring to the middle class. In the early 1950s, the still-unpaved street was a combination of gravel and tar and had two empty lots to play in. Not much had changed since 1947, the year I was born. My favorite lot was the one with lots of broken glass. The glass pieces were green and blue, and occasionally amber. There I found small pieces in shapes that could look like precious stones, and I imagined the fine rings or necklaces they could be set in.

I collected them in an old jelly jar and saved them to consider their possible futures. I also liked the tiny weeds that had sprigs of pink-lavender clusters. They grew no more than two inches high and sometimes sprouted up between spaces of cracked asphalt and gravel. This microenvironment was a place I liked to be when I was alone. This lot was where I first discovered the pleasure of details, and how they provided me the ability to escape within them. The tiny weeds were gathered into miniature bouquets tied with a blade of grass. Collectively, they were no longer weeds but floral arrangements for the weddings of black or red ants that lived in the gravel and soil.

In 1945, when my parents moved to Amundson Avenue, they felt fortunate to find housing in the postwar shortage. The young married couple recognized its ugliness, but this was to be a transitional and short stay. It was a stepping stone to something better in the near future. Charles, my father, an NYU graduate with a degree in civil engineering and a new job at a fledgling architectural firm, was moving up fast. He was well paid and sent on jobs in rural New York and Pennsylvania, where office buildings and hotels now cropped up to accommodate new communities and postwar optimism.

Charles and Charlotte, then twenty and twenty-two years old, settled in and looked to the future. Amundson Avenue, after all, had a decent history. The Edenwald neighborhood was developed by early Swedish immigrants. It was originally known as Swedenwald, and was, a generation before, a place where Jonas Bronck himself would have been comfortable. There were still families named Johansen and Petersen, but mostly now it was names like Cerbone and Colondona, first-generation Italian-Americans happy to have a first home. My parents bought one expensive chair as a symbol of their imagined future. The French provincial chair cost two weeks' salary. They had two children within their first three years there. My brother, Stephen, was born first. I was born exactly two years later on November 1. My half-Jewish, well-educated father and his twenty-year-old, first-generation American wife were optimistic. My mother, fluent in the Yiddish she spoke to her Russian-Polish parents as well as in the language of ambition, was destined to be different even before the divorce. Perhaps their differences were insurmountable. My father, Charles Payne, III, proudly identified with the paternal ancestors believed to have arrived in this country on the Mayflower. His Polish-Jewish mother embraced that history as well. The marriage was conceived in cultural imbalance with the scales tilting heavily toward failure.

By 1951, Charles met an attractive married cocktail bar singer as he toiled on a project that took him to Poughkeepsie for days at a time. He left us shortly thereafter, and the three of us spent the next twelve years trapped in the ugly apartment in a shabby transitioning neighborhood. We were the only renters, the only family touched by divorce (rare in the fifties), the only Jews in a solidly Catholic neighborhood. We were also the poorest family, since my father rarely sent child support, and my mother did not work. He left a black 1948 Studebaker that saved us from a totally bleak lifestyle. It had a pointed "nose" and round glass in the back. I thought it resembled a rocket. We used it to escape.

"Stevie, Barbara, where do you want to go?" my mother would ask. When neither of us would answer, she decided for us. "Let's just get lost, okay, and see where we end up." We took turns yelling "right, no, left" and ended up in strange neighborhoods. Eventually, the black rocket could not go in reverse, and Mom was forced to find convoluted paths to navigate and park. No big deal, she managed.

Today, I own that French provincial fruitwood chair that held so much promise. It has a graceful undulating frame at the top. There is a delicate fruitwood gallery connecting the legs that reflects the undulations above. The chair and I are both in our sixties, the chair perhaps a year or two older. Like me, it is unique, a bit different in style and dimension than other chairs of its time. The chair and I have seen some strange fashion trends. Its original gray-green matelassé cover had faceted nail heads holding it to the frame. In the sixties it wore striated, orange velvet and had the nail heads removed. In the seventies, it donned a subdued beige fabric with a boring blue stripe. Today, it hosts an ill-chosen but well-intended green-and-brown paisley, the color of baby vomit. The frame was refinished at that time. The upholstery shop owner suggested that the collection of DNA embedded in the wood may not be healthy! I was swayed, wiping all forensic evidence of Charles and Charlotte from the chair that I had inherited when my mother died. I like to think of that chair as a half-sister, we share DNA and history. I believe that all my sloughed-off epithelial cells imbedded within the rich wood grain and delivered in liberal doses of lemon oil into the chairs own cellular structure qualifies as shared ancestry.

My earliest memory is linked to this chair. I can recall my father sitting cross-legged in it. The smell of the pipe he smoked is embedded in my gray matter. I am sitting at his feet and admiring his fancy shoes. The shoes are woven leather oxfords, a variation of a Huarache. The left foot swings slowly back and forth. He wears a sock of dark brown with a clocking stripe of gold. I believe this is my earliest memory, and possibly was his last day at home. Even then, at just three years old, my attention to detail was forming future memory. An intrinsic sensitivity to my surroundings would bring comfort and challenge in the years ahead. There would be no shortage of adjustments or details to consider.

Change seemed to be everywhere in the next few years. Johnny Mathis, Elvis, and doo-wop music replaced Patti Page, Teresa Brewer, and even eclipsed Sinatra's popularity. Amundson Avenue sported a new row of attached brick houses. My very first kiss happened in the still–under-construction row houses, in an unfinished living room smelling of wallboard and wet plaster, next to an unfinished baseboard heating unit (very modern) in what would be the model apartment. His name was Louie Greco and I hated the idea of someone's spit on my mouth. Eventually, a first friend, Alexis Colondona and her lively family occupied that very space.

My mother, burdened with high ambition, great intellect, and few resources, set her ambitions for us quite high. While Alexis and her older sister played "In the Still of the Night" by The Platters, sounds of delicate flute and tinkling piano keys fought for our attention. Surely, she thought, "Peter and the Wolf" and the "1812 Overture" would have more appeal. Our home even sounded different than our neighbors. I couldn't understand how she thought the instruments were the voices in a narrative about animals or history. Couldn't we just listen to someone sing real words?

My mother's chosen vocation was a quest for culture. She filled bookcases with children's and adult classics. *The Red Pony, Alice's Adventures in Wonderland,* and *Grimms' Fairy Tales* shared space with her books. The seventy-eight records, in their colorful cardboard jackets containing classical music, were stacked on the bottom shelf. None of the moms in our neighborhood worked, so I never considered an alternative for my own mother. The fact that she only had a high school diploma may have been a limiting factor. Her own childlike belief that wishing for a dreamed-of future entitled her to having it was more a factor. Somehow her original trajectory had created the illusion that she was still upwardly mobile. Her imagined future did not include working. She waited for a future that would be elusive. She clung to the accoutrements of the imagined future as if they were life preservers. The finer things in life remained important. She was a snob by proxy.

Alexis had two sisters, two brothers, and a tall, angular bleached-blonde mother, referred to as "Beauty" by her husband. I envied her home. It was inherently superior to all other homes since it had been the model and was the end unit in the row of houses. That status included extra light from windows on the side of the structure. Her mother had furnished it lavishly from Roma Furniture, an importer of grotesquely ornate rococo reproductions. Brightly gilded baroque frames matched the heavily padded and tufted hunter-green chairs and sofa. Anything upholstered was sheathed in heavy plastic. A round glass coffee table held Capodimonte bowls filled with silk flowers and completed the set. I completely understood the need for a velvet rope held by brass poles guarding the opening of the room. It clearly stated that all routine traffic should flow directly down the long hallway paralleling this room.

My mother scoffed at this innovative tactic. "Oh my God, a movie-theatre rope to guard the plastic-covered funeral-parlor furniture." She was obviously not as impressed as I was. Since most of our furniture had origins in the Salvation Army store, I had reservations. The Salvation Army did not import from Italy or allow you to match pieces. Most of our dishes and our record player came from there; I knew fine furniture was a rare find. My mother still pointed out the finer points of our own furniture. "Barbara Ann, that chest on chest is constructed of tiger maple. See the lovely burled wood, and let me show you how the drawers have dovetailed joints." I learned about wood grains, furniture construction, and furniture periods.

I still thought the plastic-coated matched furniture was more special. I didn't care that it may not be solid wood at all. My mother spit out the word *"composite"* when describing their furniture, as if she might choke on it. The steel trap of my young mind registered and stored every word my mother ever said. Children of single parents have an intrinsic need to listen, follow, and trust the one person they must depend on for everything. Somewhere in the dark reaches of my brain I stored my mother's wisdom. I believed her. I trusted her opinions even as I was beginning to form my own. If nothing else, my love of details and of my mother made the information important. My mother was determined to impart her knowledge of finer things to me. If I liked their furniture or music or clothing, she said, I needed to learn and value what she knew was better.

I struggled with homework after dinner most nights. Sitting on the sagging faded plum-colored sofa next to my mother, I observed her ritual of plucking her perfectly arched eyebrows with more dedication than I had to my math. A large round magnifying mirror balanced on her folded knees as Rachmaninoff's Second Piano or Tchaikovsky's Ninth Symphonies competed with the numbers of a long-division problem for my attention. Occasionally, the high-pitched warble of Mario Lanza's operatic voice was a reprieve from the monotony. "Mom, do you think that Elvis is today's Mario Lanza? I think his voice is even better." Her newly plucked and now pink right eyebrow raised in response. She carefully and deliberately laid down the mirror on her lap and sighed heavily. I knew that sigh. I knew what was coming, a lecture right after a snarky chuckle. "Humphhhhh.

The only thing Elvis and Mario Lanza have in common is not their vocal chords." I got the innuendo. I understood Elvis would not be sharing homework time. I was resigned to the reality of homework with classical music. I knew Elvis was not up to her standards. While she waited for better, her displaced dreams would become my own. I began to believe in the power of superior knowledge. If my mother was a snob by proxy, I was her sycophant. I decided to love Elvis even if Mario was, of course, the better singer.

Her interests were not limited to furniture. Literature, art, and architecture were peppered into the cultural stew. I learned about mansard roofs, coffered ceilings, cupolas, and corbels. I saw uninteresting black-and-white self-portraits of Ben Shahn. I heard about Norman Mailer's themes and German opera. It was a haphazard tornado of facts that seemed to blow around her as if driven by a personal storm. Those winds blew the delicate seeds of her dreams away as if they were feathery dandelion seeds snapped from a fluffy globe. Her task, now mine as well, was to capture and collect them. By holding that knowledge of finer things, we could own them. If most of the seeds of her own dreams were lost, a few might safely land and germinate in a next generation.

I am sure Beauty had never heard of Tchaikovsky or Beethoven. We had bookshelves with French and American fairy tales that had detailed pastel illustrations. We learned about Currier and Ives, and every week at the supermarket we got the next letter in the *World Book* series. We took turns randomly picking a page and reading an obscure fact. The white leatherlike volumes eventually became a complete set and had an annual supplement that took up two shelves in a tall, golden, oak bookcase that also held my mother's hardcover novels, *Reader's Digest* condensed books, and a gruesome and graphic large version of Dante's *Inferno*. I would have preferred afternoons in the cultural vacuum of the Colondona home. In spite of a full diet of enriching details, hanging out with a friend was more important than what my mother could offer me. Everything my mother wanted me to learn was starting to become a burden. I felt conflicted because I enjoyed Alexis's family and their things, and I started to question whether things had to have a hierarchy as my mother seemed to insist. Why did Mario Lanza have to be better than Elvis? It was fun to be in a house unburdened by learning. They seemed to have already achieved whatever status they wanted. I don't think Alexis had a bookcase, but she had a white cabinet with dolls and stuffed animals that I would happily have traded for any book on those shelves. Alexis's father was tall and dark and had a thick moustache. Beauty said he looked like Clark Gable. He owned a pizza place near White Plains Road and brought home delicacies every day. I was already, at eight and ten years of age, totally uncomfortable with my friends' fathers or other men. I understood there were different rules and behaviors reserved for them. Those were skills I didn't have. All the books and new knowledge could not provide this fundamental human experience.

Mimi Cerbone was my other friend on Amundson Avenue. Like Alexis, she was also one of five children. The family owned a bakery and pastry shop. On a good Sunday, I would help stuff cannolis in the back of the shop. I loved the smell of almond paste, vanilla, and powdered sugar. Their old and shabby single-family home housed three generations as well as an aunt, uncle, and two cousins. There was constant conversation, fighting in both Italian and English, and unsupervised children running everywhere. An open box of pastries was always on the kitchen table. Cookies with powdered sugar and my favorite, lobster-claw pastry, sat on a countertop as casually and permanently as the salt and pepper shakers in my house. I rarely ignored the freedom of helping myself to a few cookies.

The chaos and activity of both homes included drama and events that were only statistically possible in families of large size. The more fascinating of Mimi's two bothers was Marco. By the age of ten, he was well-known to the police and had what was then called a JD record. Marco threw rocks at passing cars, stole from small shops on Dyer Avenue, did little to no school work, and was basically shunned by other children and parents on the street. He had a special relationship with my mother. Marco was neither feared, nor shunned in our house. "Charlotte, is my face dirty?" was a question he would ask almost daily. "No, Marco, your face is clean. Want a banana?" He was fixated on having a clean face. Sometimes I thought he just asked because he wanted someone to just look at his face, to see him. Other than scolding parents and outraged motorists, no one really looked at Marco. My mother always looked, and smiled. She would go on to admire his curly hair and send him home. Marco would stop by every day for a banana and reassurance that his face was clean. There was never discussion among us about Marco. Perhaps he was, like us, an outsider.

One day, Marco arrived with Mimi, both of them very excited. "Grandpa died last night. . . . Want to see him?" Mimi and Marco were rarely a team. Today, however, they sprinted together with flushed faces and breathless excitement. They seemed anxious to share some good fortune.

"What do you mean, want to see him?" I asked.

"He's in the dining room! Come on!" Marco could barely speak. I joined them and sprinted to their front stoop. Normally by that point in the approach to the Cerbone house, there would be yelling, but the two youngest children, Pasqualina and Pepe, sat quietly at the top step. At five and seven, they would normally be busy breaking something or going missing long enough that an adult would be screaming their conjoined names in anger. Today, they were silent sentinels at the entrance to a house of death. I knew it was going to be a big deal. The last time all the kids acted like this was when Madeline, the oldest sister, announced her pregnancy at age fifteen. The younger kids were banished that day and understood the need to be quietly absent. Today, kids were included. We entered together. We walked in single file, Marco first, me last.

There in the center room off the kitchen lay Mario Giuseppe, Sr. He was in a dark suit, on what I think may have been the dining room table, placed in front of the sliding pocket doors, behind which Aunt Lena, Uncle Mauro, and their two children normally slept. Aside from an opened, sweet-smelling box filled with my favorite almond-pignoli cookies, I had never felt more drawn to a site. He stayed in that place for two days, and I made visits as often as possible to marvel at death, to observe the family's quiet acceptance of a dead body in their dining room, and, of course, to eat as many pignoli cookies as I pleased. My mother did not visit the dining room to pay her respects. "We do things differently," she said. "Jews get them buried the next day." I preferred their custom of remaining at home a while and smelling cookies till the very last minute on earth.

Chapter Two

JESUIT JUSTICE

Death touched Alexis's family, too, in a more tragic and dramatic way. The last two of the five Colondona children were towheaded boys named Nicholas and Alexander. They were treasured as the youngest and only boys after three girls. My mother took the opportunity of their names to teach us a bit of Russian history. "Let me explain about Russian czars and get out the *World Book* so you can see where Russia is."

An unusual decoration in their home was a gold shadow-box frame with a wrinkled colorless object folded and floating above the image of the Blessed Virgin. This "treasure," according to Alexis, was the birth caul covering Nicholas's face as he entered the world. It was, I was told, a rare sign of blessing and good fortune. It seems, most often the embryonic sac is lost or expelled at birth. The frame hung discreetly in the corridor opposite the living room entry and beyond the velvet rope. I asked my mother to explain this mysterious object. "Pagan and disgusting," was her short response. Confused, I dismissed its importance and the greater mysteries of childbirth. Frankly, both the caul and childbirth were a bit creepy. I usually avoided looking at it as I followed the velvet rope to the kitchen.

I didn't like that shadow box, but thought Nicolas was a handsome and lucky boy. The blessing of that caul came with a limited warranty in Nicholas's case. His good fortune had run out in spite of any magic he was born with.

The sound of screaming and wailing carried across the still-vacant lot between the window of that end unit to the second-floor window of our kitchen, which faced Alexis's house. I imagine it carried to every house on the street and beyond. A police car was parked in front. Nicholas and Alexander had wandered off to play. No one knew for sure if the accident happened close to the Dyer Avenue station of the elevated train we affectionately called "the dinky," because it was just two train cars long, or somewhere else along the tracks. What did happen was that Nicholas had stumbled on to the third rail and was instantly, irrevocably gone. Life was forever altered in their home. A somber quiet replaced Elvis and doo-wop and laughter. I struggled to understand how a beautiful boy, born with a blessing from God, was unlucky enough to die before he was ten.

The subject of God became, from that point and forever after, a source of discomfort and skepticism to me. I noticed that the shadow box had disappeared from its prominent place on the wall of Alexis's house. There was a tiny hole in the wall where the nail had been removed. I thought about the image of a smiling Blessed Mary that shared living space in that shadow box. Did she feel as betrayed by God as the rest of the family? Maybe she just got buried in her shadow box in the larger box that held him in his grave. That seemed fair. She should at least keep him company forever. I took an inventory of the other religious artifacts in their home. Since we had none, and they were not part of our cultural repertoire, I was fascinated by their importance to others. The large wood crucifix still hung over her parents' bed. Jesus looked down on them, His suffering obvious. Maybe it helped them to accept their own misery. He obviously understood better than anyone the meaning of misery. Alexis still had her pearly-white plastic rosary beads hanging in the corner of her wall mirror as always. God still seemed to live in their home. They didn't seem to be mad at God. Signs of Jesus's importance were still in place. Their faith seemed to be intact. I wasn't so sure I would have been as forgiving. They were as sure of Jesus as they were of themselves.

They still went to Church on Saturday for confession and again on Sunday for Mass. They didn't question God, and they never spoke about Nicholas. There was something not right about this trade. God got to stay, but Nicolas didn't.

Every Wednesday, Mimi and Alexis and lots of other kids in PS 68 left early to go to "cat-a-kiss-em." Catechism was something else Jews didn't do. I was left to complete the day until regular dismissal time and to think about the good Jesus-related arts-and-crafts projects I was missing. When I asked my mother what they did there, her response was, "They teach kids that Jews killed Jesus Christ." That filled me with a combination of anger and fear. The few Jews I knew were family members: aunts, uncles and my grandparents. My uncle Walter couldn't even stand up to his wife let alone kill Jesus.

Mimi and her Catholic cohorts made first Holy Communion without me. This was worse than catechism, because they were going to get to dress up in white dresses and wear bridal veils. I consoled myself by positioning our fine sheer simple curtains over my head and looking through the blur to a mirror to see how I would have looked. Our curtains were of the finest Batiste. They had six-inch-deep hems. I knew they were really good curtains, but they looked just ordinary to me and made an uninteresting veil. I was not happy with being Jewish. I wanted a veil and communion.

Mimi, Alexis, and others in their families never spoke about religion. It was simply just part of their lives. For sure they had many artifacts in their homes (in addition to Nicholas's birth veil), but those were also just accepted decorations. The only thing beside the communion veil that I loved was a rhinestone cross Alexis wore every day. It glittered and, on sunny days, gave off rainbow-colored reflections. A small glass droplet sat at the intersection of the glittering bars.

"Look inside," Alexis invited. "See that little splinter? It is a real piece of wood that came from Jesus's cross."

"You mean the one in your parents' room?" I asked. I lodged my head under her chin and craned my neck to the right. I looked inside the bubble with my right eye. Sure enough, a little brown wood splinter could be seen.

"So that is the real piece of wood from the real cross that he died on before he became God," Alexis continued. I looked again for traces of blood that might prove that. I didn't doubt the authenticity of the artifact or the story. This was hard evidence. I thought it special to own something so beautiful and sad. It marked her as a member in good standing and worthy of sharing how God was born. She was a legitimate member of a mysterious and elite religious group. I tried not to think about what my mother said about Jews killing Jesus.

Most Saturdays I would accompany Alexis to church for confession. Our Lady of the Blessed Nativity was, at that time, a small, wood-framed, Tudor-like structure. It reminded me of a Swiss chalet. I could go inside and wait. There were more mysteries. People kneeled, bowed, crossed themselves, and whispered.

There was holy water and candles, an elaborately carved "telephone booth" with a heavy grate and burgundy velvet curtain. There were crying life-sized saints, and of course a larger-than-life suffering Jesus on a cross up front. The pious demeanor of my friends was reassuring. If they seemed calm and happy, it must be all good. I was really okay to sit this part out. They knelt and crossed themselves. I took a seat on a bench and rested my feet on a velvet kneeling platform. I was not taking part in any ritual. I was watching and waiting in respectful silence as they confessed. I felt guilty just breathing in the strange scented fumes of constantly dying votive flames. Was I receiving an infusion of Catholicism by just breathing? My mother had no idea where I was on Saturday mornings. I knew she wouldn't be happy, even if I was just waiting inside the church.

My mother became more aware of the need for Jewish identity as I spent more time at friends' homes. We did have God and prayers as informal requests for special things, like enough heat on extra cold days or for the car to start when it acted weird. The Ten Commandments were cited from time to time if ethical questions arose, but now we added prayers before bed. We recited the "Now I lay me down to sleep, if I should die before I wake" prayer. Surely any kid with half a brain of any religion hates that prayer. It is a first consideration of mortality and good reason to hate sleep. On Friday nights now, we lit candles and thanked God for everything we had and asked for his blessing in the coming week. I tried to think of new reasons for gratitude. I hoped that God really paid attention, but thought he would listen to Catholics first. Candle lighting each Friday was something we did that was special. I loved the flickering candlelight that lasted through dinner. I was 100 percent sure that God saw us on Friday evenings. I hoped he liked our candles. Even though our home was missing the symbols, my mother made a benevolent God a presence. She reinforced that God was good and watched over everyone. If this was true, I thought, he must watch me all the time. I hoped he wasn't angry that I went to church sometimes. I thought maybe he was okay with any recognition.

By the time I was ten and my brother twelve, my mother committed even more thought to religious identity. We had Passover Seder with Grandma and Grandpa, and my mother researched synagogues in Jewish neighborhoods in other parts of the Bronx. None were close. I had now spent almost two years on the sidelines of Catholicism. I was comfortable with any religious ritual. There were more Catholic than Jewish ones. If the Jesuit saying, "Give me the child for seven years, and I will give you the man," holds any truth, my mother had already missed the opportunity to indoctrinate us as identified Jews. There were those first years of a near-religious void followed by a crash course saturated with Catholic icons, symbols, places, and a community of people that shared membership in their common beliefs. Then there was a belated effort to bring a Jewish God home. I didn't long to be Catholic or not to be Jewish. I simply longed for real membership in either of those theisms. It was confusing. Some years we had a live, but small Christmas tree. This, of course, offered another educational opportunity. There were Norwegian pines, Norway spruces, and the most elite of all Christmas conifers, the Douglas fir. We did not have a Douglas fir. Perhaps another aspiration in life? Our tree was strung with bubble lights that glowed and featured sparkling bubbles that looked like carbonated cherry cola. We had a menorah every year. We dutifully took turns lighting a twisted waxy, anemic pastel-colored candle. The challenge was to find one that wasn't listing to a side or already showing splintered cracks. We were happy to get small and mostly practical gifts for eight nights.

One memorable Christmas, we woke up to discover a set of Schwinn two-wheelers under the tree. The Salvation Army was again a treasure trove for mom. Steve's was a hastily repainted cadet blue, but mine was a nearly new bright-red beauty. My mother had given us a special gift and me a poignant lifetime memory. There is another vivid memory linked to my mother. Her closet was small, but offered escape and dress-up choices. I especially loved a three-tiered iridescent purple half-slip. If I hiked it up under my arms, it became a strapless ball gown. A pair of very high kelly-green heels with ankle straps completed the outfit. I was a movie star or a princess. Where would my mother ever have worn such flamboyant things, I wondered? It was fun to pretend. Christmas trees and menorahs and kelly-green high heels were all just that: pretend things. I wasn't a princess any more than I was Jewish or Catholic. Religion was another empty space in my identity which would need to be reconciled in the future. I thought that religion might be a form of imaginary playtime for grown-ups. For the time being, we were playing catch-up. The Jesuits were correct. Religion was now another piece of the puzzle where pieces just never fit in easily. Three years and five years beyond the Jesuit cut-off line, we were introduced to an Orthodox synagogue. This was the only one willing to offer complete scholarships and no membership fees to us. The altruistic act was well intended, but too late.

My brother, Stephen, was forced to take a crash course in Hebrew at the Orthodox synagogue to become a bar mitzvah. He was then, and remains, brilliant. He caught up the four years he had missed, and then excelled and performed to the delight of my religious grandfather and proud mother. He was fluent in reading and writing Hebrew. He memorized prayers and ultimately a long Torah portion he would read at his bar mitzvah. He was, unfortunately, an unwilling participant, who took no personal pleasure in his immersion. Joining late and performing beyond expectations had only made him an outsider to the other boys. He couldn't wait to not return. Within a month of completing his official induction as a Jewish man, he resigned. It wasn't a formal resignation, but a declaration that he simply wasn't returning. That let me off the hook as well.

I had been signed up for a girls' class in Hebrew school. In the 1950s, girls did not get bat mitzvahed. I was to learn prayers for candle lighting and Shabbat, and special songs and rituals. Also a latecomer to the social construct, I went once and refused to return. Unlike my brother, I was considered less intelligent and less in need of confirming my religious identity. We continued to live in religious limbo. I decided I believed in God but liked him best in my thoughts or outside in pretty places. God belonged in clouds or even a starlit sky. Take God into a building, and I became uncomfortable. I didn't belong there. I remain, even now, uncomfortable and always eager to leave the confines of most religious "houses." I can deal with God better without so much ritual and distraction. One to one just makes sense to me. I didn't fit in with either religion and didn't see God in any of those inside places. Having never really belonged in either of those houses, I have chosen to respect them all but to avoid non-essential exposure. Today, I practice little more than a pantheist belief that some supernatural and benign force governs all of nature and the universe.

That said, who can resist the beauty of a Christmas tree or the taste of a Hannukah latke? Religion is an arena that serves to separate and stratify. My earliest exposure was of religious isolation. I can claim credibility in reciting an "Our Father" as convincingly as the "Shema" (the centerpiece of all Jewish prayer). This literacy is proof of my good effort to belong. God forgive me my lack of conviction in believing that he loves some more than others and is more present in a big building. That void in faith sustains my belief in something better. I am brought to tears each and every time I hear John Lennon's iconic song "Imagine." It speaks to me and brings the peace I never found in a house of God. I believe God was present in the Salvation Army the day my mother must have hunted for those two bikes. I believe that deeply.

Chapter Three

ALTERNATIVE UNIVERSE

The same year I was released from formal religious education, a new house was constructed on the last remaining building lot on our street. The newly constructed solid brick cube was different from any existing house. This freestanding home looked across at the attached row houses opposite and seemed, from the onset, to assume superiority. A flight of concrete steps led to a main entry that was grand. A fancy wrought-iron scroll-work bannister led to a front door flanked by false colonial columns and a formal pediment above the door with an urn at the center. A narrow concrete porch ran across the front and was set below a huge plate-glass window. There were louvered shutters framing the window. It made Mimi's house to its right look like a poor relative. The old wood-framed house with gray shingles was suddenly shabby. The stark difference of the home matched that of the new inhabitants. The new family tilted the existing balance of the neighborhood.

The Coughlins were Catholic, but otherwise unique. Kathy,

the only child, attended St. Ann's school. The family also worshipped at that parish. Her father wore a suit and drove Kathy, in her Catholic school uniform, to school each morning. Kathy didn't walk with us to PS 68, and she didn't go to catechism but somehow, she managed to meet the three other girls that she played with on weekends. Her mom was tall and thin, and wore ballet flats and ladies' pants with a crisp crease. Mrs. Coughlin was very quiet. My mother said she was reserved and seemed to be full of herself. She seemed content to sit on her front porch and read a book, if she was ever seen outside. Reading was a perfect guise for her real purpose, which was to evaluate her new neighbors. When she wasn't on the porch reading, she could be seen looking out the large plate-glass window. In those places, she had been able to take inventory and was not comfortable with what she saw.

First of all, there were no other Irish families. The first time she heard the screams of "Pasqualina-Pepe," she must have cringed. The men in the neighborhood wore polo shirts or button-up shirts with no ties, and none wore suits. They all seemed to grow tomatoes and basil somewhere on their lawns. The children seemed unsupervised at play and were loud. She was an efficient intake coordinator and also discovered that one of the little girls Kathy had befriended had no dad at all. That family also didn't go to Our Lady of the Blessed Nativity. A little sleuthing revealed a worse problem. They were Jewish. That was a serious social shortcoming.

We played together nicely for several weeks, most often in front of Kathy's house. She had a perfectly paved driveway and a front porch that seemed the equivalent of a luxury penthouse. Her mother could monitor our play and conversations easily from either the porch or window. Mrs. Coughlin was cautious in her new surroundings, perhaps anxious for Kathy to have friends. She watched and listened carefully. She frequently called down to the group with a reminder to be careful or even to offer a snack. She needed to let the girls know she was there.

Kathy obediently followed her mother's prompts. If her mom made Toll House cookies, Kathy presented them proudly. Perhaps being an only child made her mom's opinion as important as being the child of an only parent. She parroted her mom's words often when we played.

"Your mother is a prostituter!" Kathy said one day, out of the blue.

"She is not," I said, not quite sure what that was, but sure it wasn't a good thing.

"She is not."

Mimi and Alexis had no idea what that was either, but came to my defense. "That is not true. Take it back," said Alexis, somehow knowing it was not a nice thing.

"Kathy is so mean," I told my mother over that evening's dinner. "And anyway, what's a prostituter?"

I don't remember getting an answer. All she said was, "Just don't play with her again. It must be that great Catholic school she goes to."

There were only four little girls on the block, and the others were not targets of name-calling by Kathy. One day, we were playing double Dutch on the street when Kathy's mother set up a huge blow-up pool with clear blue sides.

A voice from the other side of the street called out to us. It was Kathy. I stopped, turning to see Kathy in her latest bathing suit. The bathing suit was a beige loopy terry cloth. At the chest, was a puffy faced puppy in dark brown. The puppy had soulful eyes and long floppy ears that hung freely and swayed playfully when she walked. Her mother walked out to stand next to her and then called out, "Alexis, Mimi, come on, the pool is full. Get your bathing suits on." Without hesitation, the girls dropped the rope and ran across the street. I took a step forward, drawn to the sad-eyed puppy more than by the path my friends were taking. "Not you," said Mrs. Coughlin. "The pool is too small, and you are too fat."

"Yeah, you can't come in my pool, because all the water will come out," Kathy added, her hands planted on her hips. "And beside that, you'll make it dirty."

Mrs. Coughlin smiled approvingly at her daughter.

The red, wood handles of the jump rope I gripped became red-hot extensions of my hands. I held them tighter. The handles and my red-hot shame grew into heated anger. Mimi took a tentative step into the aqua-blue oasis in the driveway. Her heel caught the edge of the inflated vinyl wall and a trickle of water spilled out onto the hot concrete. I was without voice or thought to consequence. I saw Mrs. Coughlin watching the scene from her perch above. The red wooden handles felt like they were burning my hands. I dropped them to the ground and thought I might cool my hands only in the pool water. But my hands had their own plan. They grabbed Kathy's limp and damp ponytail as she leaned against the plump inside edge. They held the mousey-brown string of hair that belonged to her head. With both hands, I yanked her surprised and unresisting body over the bouncy edge of the pool.

I noticed that as she bounced off the pool's edge, the floppy ears of her bathing suit dog lifted up in surprise with her. With both hands, I brought my enemy to the still unpaved and gravel-coated street. I turned in wild circles, dragging her along in the hopes of propelling her into flight. She was a shot put. I think I heard her mother's voice in the distance. My hands released her and retrieved my new jump rope. I went home. There seemed to be silence as I walked.

Not only was the assault violent, but it was inflicted by a timid, complacent, previously well-behaved, pudgy, little girl. The same child who'd always said please and thank you, and always made certain she did nothing that would bring attention to herself or the fact that she knew she was different. My mother was not at all angry. "The little shit deserved it. Stay away from that anti-Semitic shanty Irish kid from now on." There was no punishment and no discussion of anger management or hurt feelings. "Did you remember to bring home the jump rope?" she asked. My mother was pragmatic.

While Kathy may or may not have been learning about Jews killing Jesus in Catholic school, the rest of us walked up the hill of 233rd Street, turned at the corner of Seton Avenue, where we waved to the pharmacist and thought about what candy we might buy on the way home. The half-mile walk to PS 68 went by quickly. I liked my school and routine. There was a bologna sandwich with mustard most days, and five-cent pretzel rods bought on Fridays from a big, round tin. Girls Scouts met every Wednesday after school. There were a few highlights, like winning the Hula-Hoop contest after school and a school dance in fifth grade. I won a poster contest for Brotherhood Week. My poster of a staircase with costumed and different-colored children took first place. The logo "Brotherhood, Stairway to a Better World" was written up in a local paper. I credit the *World Book Encyclopedia* as my single resource for costumes and clothing of other countries and photos of people that looked different. There were no different-looking or colored children in the school. Everyone was white and, I assumed, Catholic. The teachers were mostly pleasant and expected little from me. Being the younger sister of a brilliant older brother, who skipped grades twice and was always in Special Progress classes, could have been a challenge. Not so for me. A quiet demeanor and mediocre academic performance placed me squarely in the low-middle range of any class I took. Most teachers were sweet or stern versions of every other adult I knew. They were our parents in absentia, but there was one who was more like Kathy's mother.

Mrs. Wilson was my teacher in fourth grade. She wore below-the-knee straight skirts and matching suit jackets, which, in spite of a tightly nipped waist, were masculine, no-nonsense business suits. She wore clunky high heels and had salt-and-pepper hair with one broad white streak carefully dipping in a pompadour above her chalky-white forehead.

Mrs. Wilson was stern and fastidious. Her classroom reflected a desire for order, rank, and precise function. She would have made a perfect Nazi. Every morning, one monitor would be assigned to inspect the neat line of robust geraniums lining the back windowsill. They could prune dead leaves and then carefully measure and water each plant. Those geraniums were obediently in constant bloom. Every two weeks that person would rotate the plants for even sun exposure. Another monitor would take out the clothes brush from the long, built-in oak closet that was her personal closet. That person would brush lint from her outer coat and then the jacket she wore. They would return the brush without speaking and return to the front row. Another "front row" student would take out a special shoe brush and polish her shoes. Mrs. Wilson was then ready to begin teaching. Her solid rectangular desk of dark wood would hide her shoes and lower body. She rarely stood. Occasionally she would rise to take the long pole with a hook at its end to open a transom window, some twelve feet up, for fresh air. She even held it as if it were a bull hook with greater potential should the need arise. Mrs. Wilson had about thirty students in her class. They, too, were carefully named and placed in appropriate rank.

Directly across from her were the first six desks spanning the width of the room; that row was aptly named "cream," perhaps the cream of the mediocre crop. The next two rows of six desks were "milk," predictable, manageable, solid students with questionable worth, who presented little challenge for a teacher. The fourth row, "skim milk," were slow or lazy students that hovered precariously between a designation of milk (if they would ever awaken to her talents) and the dreaded last row "water." Students in water were deemed by Mrs. Wilson and their classmates to be hopeless. They were called retarded from time to time, and mostly languished unbothered by anyone for the better part of the school day.

I was placed in skim milk and feared that I may slip further down to end up sitting next to either "snot-nose Lee," who spent his days staring out the window and managing a constant viscous rope of green goo that eventually encrusted his lower left shirt sleeve, or next to Louise DeLong, whose head lice were even more active than Lee's left hand. I did my homework, paid attention, and never raised my hand for fear of a wrong answer. By this time, I was also painfully aware of looking different. A Toni home permanent had somehow triggered both frizzy hair and a new case of psoriasis. My arms, legs, and scalp not only itched but sported reddened, scaly plaques in unpredictable sizes and shapes. "What's the matter with your skin?" asked adorable little Cookie Corrado in the third row. "Ugh, is it catchy?"

"It's not catchy, just an allergy, a kind of skin condition," I recited by heart, a response that would be repeated for the remainder of my life.

We were learning how to tell time that year. Directly outside the classroom and about six feet above my head was a large clock encased in a heavy oak frame. It dared the wall to support it. At different times each day Mrs. Wilson would unexpectedly chirp, "Who would like to go outside and tell us all the time?" First-row hands flew up quickly and rigidly, assured in the air. Jackie Kemp, row one, middle seat, front and center, waved wildly to be picked. A few tentative hands rose from milk-row three and one faltering timid arm in row four. In rows five and six not a single hand moved. I sat with arms neatly and squarely folded on my desk. "Barbara Ann, please go in the hallway and tell us the time." I had not mastered the skill, and she knew it. An ah-ha moment for Mrs. Wilson.

I left the room and faced my enemy . . . the dreaded clock, with its little hand on two and big hand on the eight. I headed back in with my guess. "It is ten minutes before eight!"

"No it is not, go out and try again." My second and third guesses would most often be wrong, and I would be allowed to sit, while Jackie Kemp or another smart-ass would head out and return quickly to announce the correct time. Every now and then, fortunately, I was met by the principal, Mr. Tully. Mr. Tully was old and stooped; he had white hair and walked slowly. I think he was happy to have an excuse to stop and rest for a moment. "Hello, Barbara Ann. It is twenty minutes past ten. You can tell Mrs. Wilson that." I imagined he hated her too, but wasn't sure why he would. I wasn't even sure why she hated me. She didn't like anyone in row five. She might have hated row six, but mostly she didn't look at anyone in either of those rows. But she did look at me. She looked directly into my eyes when she commanded me to tell the time. Her eyes locked and stayed on mine and pinned me in place. I felt as pinned as a prized butterfly about to be stuck under glass for perpetual display. Her stare was disabling. It scared me and made me feel helpless. "Go out there now and tell us the time," she said. It was hard to move when paralyzed with fear. Did she hate me because I was Jewish? Did she even know that I was Jewish? Did she hate the scaly pink skin that I hated too? It wasn't my fault. Anyway, I thought it was better than Louise's head lice or Lee's green snot. She never asked them to tell the time.

The fear became anger, and the anger became my ally. It allowed me to move my legs, to move, to walk. This was not the thoughtless, visceral, reactive rage that moved my hands to Kathy's wet hair. This was thoughtful anger. New synapses crackled to life in my brain. The new connections formed words and thoughts—an alternative language that was exclusively mine. Unexpressed words were silently remixed into soothing thoughts. The revised thoughts used language rich in anger, irreverence, and even humor. They became mindful mantras that empowered me. Internal words were my private weapons. When asked by Mrs. Wilson to return to the hated hallway clock a second or third time, humiliation was transformed to a private dialogue that placed me respectfully complying and walking past the clock, and out of school without taking a hall pass. I imagined her inability to explain to the principal how I'd vanished. I imagined her sputtering and afraid. At age nine, I'd learned the language of coping. I embraced preferred thoughtful outcomes and brought that coping skill with me as a lifelong friend.

We were preparing for a May Day event. All the local schools had a maypole, with streamers and flowers representing school colors. The streamers were to be woven around the pole in a festive circular dance until they were tightly braided around the pole. Our class was making flowers out of pipe cleaners and pastel tissues. Row by row we were called up to take a handful of either blue or white tissues from the tissue boxes safely stacked in

Mrs. Wilson's personal closet. After what seemed like a very long wait, Mrs. Wilson called on row-four skim milk. "Row four, you can go to the closet and take white or blue tissues to your desks." I stood up and followed the five others in my row. I was the last one to reach into the closet and select the colors I wanted.

THWACK—a fierce sharp pain in my left wrist—from where? Mrs. Wilson stood next to me. How strange that she cut the line, I thought. "Do not touch anything in my closet, not with that skin. Get out," she shouted. Shocked and in pain, I returned to my seat empty-handed and holding back tears. This time, I could not grab her hair or hit her or throw her as I had Kathy. I could do nothing. It was the start of a new daily ritual for me. The only thing I could do at age nine. I thought of my hatred and desire to escape Mrs. Wilson. I thought and somehow knew I would never return to her class. I would find a way. *I think I won't go back until next year. Maybe by then she will get run over.* The thought was pleasant.

I had no choice about going to school, but I could avoid seeing Mrs. Wilson. "Bye, Mom, see you later," I'd say as I left the house. When it was raining, she dropped me off at the front door. The old building had a wide flight of steps going into a double-doored maw, which swallowed us up and in. I'd give a last turn and wave, go through the doors, and stay right there until I was sure it was safe—one, two, three, four, five, six . . . up to twenty—then I'd finally go through the same doors. Other children were still coming in. It was easy to slip out unnoticed in the noisy chaos. The ritual was the same every day. Straight down Monticello Avenue, which led directly to 233rd Street. Turn left, cross the street and into the park. Seton Falls Park seemed vast to me. There were familiar parts where I felt safe. A large rock with a wide crevice sat at the edge of 233rd Street. Set back about thirty feet, it was a neighborhood spot kids played in after school. I could sit there a while and simply watch cars pass by. Venturing farther into the park was not possible.

When we played in groups of three or four, we courageously ventured through rough paths and uncultivated overgrowth toward Dick Tracy rock. The rock was a sharp-edged vertical edifice. The resemblance to the cartoon character was hard to miss, difficult to climb, and a great perch to throw acorns from if you made it. I would never go there alone. We had all seen suspicious men hanging out in the depths of the park. We knew it was not normal for grown men to be hanging out alone. After an hour, I walked toward Dyer Avenue to safer, more familiar territory. Surely no perverts would dare be hanging out near Our Lady of the Blessed Nativity. No way I would enter alone; I walked the periphery a few times and headed to the stores on Dyer Avenue.

The only one of interest was the Pickwick card shop. I entered, twirled a display case holding fake jewelry, and saw where Alexis's mysterious rhinestone crucifix had its origins. A moonstone ring caught my eye. The kaleidoscope of fractured colors replaced my desire for the miraculous glass droplet holding a piece of wood. This was something I could hope to own. Not wanting to be asked if I needed help, I left. Realizing there was more time until the walk back to school and dismissal, I headed toward the drawbridge over Baychester Creek. Hunger was not a problem. My brown paper-bag lunch had a bologna sandwich on dark-brown bread with mustard . . . my favorite. Two Fig Newtons wrapped in wax paper were a pleasant surprise. I ate lunch watching the drawbridge rise twice to accommodate passing oil barges and headed back, slowly.

Aware of the need to not be seen on familiar streets, I circumvented the usual route and enjoyed looking at nicer homes on streets bordering Mount Vernon. The neighborhood was close to Westchester County . . . a step up. These houses were mostly brick or fieldstone. Some were older frame houses but had pretty front porches with hanging plants and lacey wood trim. There were sidewalks here and separate garages for the cars. It was lovely and different. No detail escaped my notice as I walked ever so slowly back to PS 68. The ritual lasted only three days. A call was made on day three to my mother to ask what was wrong and when I would be back in school.

"I am not going back to school. Mrs. Wilson hates me. No one cares if I don't go. She looks at me like she really, really hates me," I was crying. I rarely cried.

"For God's sakes," my mother rolled her eyes at me. "She looks like a mean old crow. Don't look at her, and she won't look back at you. Everyone probably thinks she hates them." I continued to cry. I had her attention because this was out of character.

"Well maybe she looks mean to everyone, but it was just me who she slammed the closet door on." Her interest grew. I elaborated on the incident.

"Did she actually call your skin disgusting?" Mom's voice was now softer and kinder. "I'll be going to school with you tomorrow. Let's see how ruffled the crow's feathers are tomorrow when I get there and speak to the principal.

"Bitch." My mother spit out the curse word. Now, I could feel her anger.

Her anger only made it worse. My mother's plan to confront a formidable enemy unnerved me. I believed Mrs. Wilson would hate me even more now. "It's okay, Mom. Just send a note telling her that it's not contagious," I offered.

"No, I don't think so. I think maybe I'll let Mr. Tully know you were assaulted by that bitch." She was more thinking out loud than speaking to me. This too was now out of my control.

"Let me see your arm," she ordered. I held out my arm, grateful that there was no evidence of physical harm. I was happy enough with my thoughtful alternative universe. Imaginary clocks or cars or trains, disabling or destroying her was enough gratification. My mother's bravery and resolve seemed pointless by comparison. I went to bed fearing the next day's events. I imagined my mother kicking Mrs. Wilson in her backside. Thought: *Mr. Tully gave Mom a quick wink as he pretended not to see*. I fell asleep in that alternative universe.

Mr. Tully met with my mother the next morning. "I think she must be exaggerating, a teacher would simply not do that."

"There are no bruises, but I suggest you ask the teacher and other students what happened," was my mother's logical reply.

Mr. Tully promised to follow up and personally escorted me back to Room 120. I could not hear the short conversation between them but did notice that Mrs. Wilson's normally chalk-white skin had colored to a rose-pink flush.

She continued to ignore me and never again asked me to go in the hallway for the time. The damage was done. I hated school. The ritual took on new form. I now entered the building, walked toward the classroom, past the classroom to an exit at the far end of the hallway. A fast descent down one flight and out the side entrance of the school. My new route down Strang Avenue was a short-lived escape. Mr. Tully started to follow me on foot the first few days. He was old and slow, but eventually would yell my name, and I would stop. Every normal fourth grader in those years would have been terrified of disobeying the principal. We returned to school, and I was escorted back to my enemy. Usually there was complete silence from my classmates, who seemed to take a perverse pleasure in the scandal.

After a week of this problem, my mother was asked to meet with the principal. "She is really a problem. This is a safety issue for the school. I need you to speak with her," Mr. Tully solemnly stated. "Perhaps some consequence for the behavior should be considered. This cannot continue." The principal looked grim as he spoke.

"Actually, Mr. Tully, with all due respect, I believe it is the teacher who should be blamed," my mother countered. "This child has never challenged authority before. Why would she suddenly take risks and behave so differently?

"I am inclined to believe Barbara Ann. You will simply have to transfer her to a different class if you want her to attend school."

"Mrs. Payne, that is impossible. It is the last week of May. There is no way she will be helped by putting her with a new teacher and all new classmates."

"Then, I imagine you should be prepared to follow her everyday so she doesn't walk into traffic," my mother replied quickly. "If you would like, I can take my car and meet you so you won't have to go on foot," mother offered in saccharine-sweet tones. I returned to school the first week of June and completed the year in Mrs. Burke's class. I was invisible. No longer able to flee, I discovered a refuge and a friend. Why had I never seen the school nurse before?

With just four weeks left in the school year, the twenty students and teacher unfortunate enough to pick up a new student were committed to ignoring the intruder. I was quietly compliant. The only respite left were the bathroom visits I timed like coffee breaks. Two wood rectangular blocks that had been poorly carved in "shop" class rested on the wood ledge, which also held chalk below the huge chalkboard. In choppy relief, the word GIRLS was crudely sculpted. This was my focal point.

Clutching the block of wood, I took my time. Although I had not, even then, conquered telling time, I knew that I could safely stay out in the amount of time it took for the big hand to go between any two numbers. The old enemy framed in oak was now my ally. I depended on the clock to maintain a safely timed absence from the room.

I walked past the clock and swiftly passed Mrs. Wilson's and another fourth-grade class. I continued down to the end of the corridor, which ended in an alcove housing two small rooms.

One door had the words Book Room stenciled in gold. It was always closed. I imagine the other door read Nurses' Office. That door was always open. Sunlight often spilled out and a hanging plant looked healthy. Behind a desk, a fat black woman wearing a navy-blue cardigan sat. She was always sitting it seemed. She was the only black person in PS 68. I'd never spoken to a black person in my life. This was strange territory. The first few passes at her door were met with a smile and a bit of tilt to her head. At some point, maybe after a week, she spoke when she saw me. "Hello, want to come in?" Her voice was soft and very low, almost a whisper.

I moved closer to be sure I had heard her. I felt like a parakeet suddenly offered an open cage door; risk or reward? Did she know I was the runaway girl? I risked it and entered.

Soon, I visited every day and stayed little more than ten minutes each time. I watered plants and read books as she continued to sit quietly and write. I learned that her name was Mrs. Bridgewater. I don't recall a conversation. I simply knew I was welcomed in her room. She was different, and I was different. She smiled a lot and sometimes for no reason. She was a happy and kind person, there when I needed kindness most. I was able to finish the school year with that thin thread of human kindness and connection. I held onto that as fiercely as I held the block of wood that said GIRLS in rough relief. The bathroom pass was a golden ticket.

Memories of both Mrs. Wilson and Mrs. Coughlin are as

deeply carved in my mind as the crude letters on that bathroom pass. Mrs. Wilson and Mrs. Coughlin were well-dressed, well-camouflaged haters, who left their mark on my already-frail self-esteem. They were salt in the wound that became that smoothed-over scar that troubles and surprises me still. Mrs. Bridgewater was there to show kindness. I spent so much time with her. I am grateful for her kindness, but there is a perverse gratitude to the other women who fostered my newly articulated anger. Anger that had its own language and plans.

Nothing was ever the same after my year with Mrs. Wilson. I was different. Now, after fifth grade my old friends were going to Catholic school. I would be going to a newly constructed middle school that served a minority population living in the forty building low-income housing project that was uncomfortably close to our neighborhood. But if I didn't have friends, I had a newfound ally. I had wrapped myself in the protective armor of the uniquely measured, thoughtful, and at times entertaining ability to vent and convert anger to internal dialogue and loneliness to loneness. Loneliness is the feeling of isolation, abandonment and rejection. Loneness is different and better. Loneness offers enjoyable, cryptic, and soothing thought. Loneness is reflective, pain-deflecting, humorous companionship. Loneness is self- soothing mindful comfort food. Loneness is good. Loneness exists as a creative alternative universe.

I wore my anger and loneness the same way I wore the training bra that covered my newly budding breasts. I was aware of its newness, its restrictive and sometimes irritating quality, its foreign-body quality. I wasn't sure I liked either, but knew I needed them. Both had the ability to make me feel secure. Both gave covert support others couldn't see. Both were part of the physical and psychological wardrobe I was taking with me to middle school and well beyond.

Chapter Four

VACUUM-PACKED LUNCH

I was an easy target in JHS 142. The only white girl, I was as invisible as a black dog in freshly fallen snow.

"Hey, princess. What-ya-doin?" An anonymous voice, a group snicker, and a sharp finger flick to the back of my head. I walked faster. *Yeah,* I thought, *right, that's me, a princess.* No reason to turn. This princess was not stupid. I looked ahead down the flight of concrete steps. I wasn't angry. I was an intruder; I didn't belong here. I wasn't angry at them. I was angry at myself and my mother for allowing me to be there. I could recite Catholic prayers with ease, but I was not Catholic. My mother would consider a Catholic school alternative an abandonment of Judaism. There was no reason to consider that. I am sure other private school options were as foreign to my mother as they were to anyone in our lower-middle-class neighborhood. There was often not even enough money for new shoes. There was no one to blame, but I was angry anyway. It was simply unfair. I was angry at this helplessness and inability to fit in. I resigned myself to life on the sidelines. There was no way out. This was different from Mrs. Wilson. This time Mom wasn't bailing me out. She was as helpless as I was.

This was a new kind of scared. This assault wasn't personal, it was simply territorial. I needed to find safe ground. I thought of that barred owl that used to live in the tree near my window. During daylight, his patterned feathers became camouflage. He seemed to disappear into the thatched tree bark, his feathers indistinguishable from the bark. The owl in that tree was a safer bet than the white girl in the black school. Camouflage was out of the question for me though. Speed was the only alternative. That owl would fly. I wasn't a princess at all; I was a speed queen. Always the first student seated in the next scheduled class, even algebra!

Some classmates were friendly, but the friendships ended the minute we left the classroom. I honed the skill of appearing invisible. No one really wanted a token white friend. These were poor kids from the projects. Life was hard and fast and well-defined. I was an anomaly.

Lunchtime transfers were safer. Anxious to eat and play, there was no time to taunt the white girl. The basement cafeteria built on a hill at the edge of Seton Falls Park had windows facing the woods. I took comfort in knowing the flat sharp plates of rock that formed Dick Tracy Rock were near. I remember lining up for lunch when there seemed a safe place. I grabbed a faded pink plastic tray and slid it along the triple steel railing that faced the steaming food behind glass.

There was mac and cheese, so thick the serving spoon stood straight up when the lunch lady stuck it in. She served up brown-gray discs that passed as hamburgers. A group of three girls were ahead of me and in animated, curse word–flecked discussion about someone named Kendra. "Girl, I'm gonna kick that jacked-up girl's ass later. Thinks she's all that." The large girl in front of me rolled her eyes and looked to her buddies for affirmation. She pivoted her head toward me. I felt compelled to nod in agreement, but decided it was safer to remain invisible. *Jacked up,* I thought. *What part of speech did that term come from? Save me from these imbeciles, and let me get through lunch.*

I was adopting my mother's air of intellectual superiority. I was indeed her sycophant. I was superior to others in my knowledge, after all. As long as I knew more, I was as good as and even better than those who rejected me.

My inner dialogue distracted me from the reality of bad food and no friends. Next in line were two boys. Mac and cheese their choice for lunch as well. The burgers were destined for the dumpster today. The boys were talking also. The words faded into the background. The cafeteria smelled strongly of cheese doodles and mac and cheese. It reminded me more of stinky feet than food.

I scanned the room for a seat. "Ugh." It was crowded this lunch period, and there wasn't one empty table available. It would only have made me feel conspicuous if it were. I would have looked lonelier, whiter, more like a loser, certainly not invisible. I saw a table with two fat girls more engrossed in lunch than each other, and a boy who may or may not have been with them. It seemed safe. I sat at the end and faced the window and landscape. The four of us sat together and processed lunch silently. The quiet at the table was strange in a vast space otherwise filled with noise and voices. I took out a pen and began writing on a napkin. I made a list of things in view from the window: Tulip tree, Manhattan schist, oak tree, stratus clouds, Fordham gneiss, gray squirrel, jewelweed, golden slipper, and mourning dove. I looked busy rather than rejected. I was the camouflaged owl. I observed the flora and fauna of the park and recorded my knowledge. Things I knew that the other kids didn't. So many things my mother taught me. They were things that made me feel superior despite being invisible. I began to enjoy the solitude and task at hand.

Soon the lists were expanded. Creating lists had become a daily ritual. I challenged my memory. I included other voices to drown out the din of background noise. Silently, I worked with my grandmother's voice to recall and record as many dirty words in Yiddish that I could think of. That was most enjoyable of all. I could imagine Grandma saying the words: *dreck* (shit), *putz* (person without value, fool, or penis), *schmuck* (idiot or penis), *gae cocken* (go shit), etc. That list was long and most fun. My mother's voice prompted names of presidents, types of wood; and my own voice, the names of my favorites on *American Bandstand.* I can't say I was bored. Other people shared the solitude. I was enjoying loneness. I was embracing it. These years of junior-high solitude were ultimately empowering. I filled the social void with facts instead of friends. If thought and silent words were my weapons, knowledge and details were the bullets and ammunition I stored in my arsenal. Details were tangibles; friends were transient.

At the end of the school day, huge numbers of kids would exit the building and head across the street to the projects. Some would head toward stores on Baychester Avenue. I was the one white girl, who would head out and turn in the opposite direction. At the corner of 233rd Street, I headed east and walked the length of Seton Falls Park, my old haunting ground. The challenge of avoiding an occasional exhibitionist lurking behind a tree with his exposed penis in hand or a tough group of kids looking for a little fun after school kept me alert. Just like navigating the long school corridor. I always made it home in record time, *American Bandstand* and Dick Clark waiting for an hour's escape before homework and dinner, if I was lucky. Sometimes my mother had other plans.

"Good, you're home, let's go." My mother's welcome-home greeting was brief. "We're going to Mary's house, but just for an hour, I promise." *Not true,* I thought, *and not fair.* In the absence of real friends, the regular teenage dancers on *Bandstand* were important to me. I followed the dancing and dating of Justine and Joe as if we knew each other. "Mom, why now, couldn't you just go before I got home?" It made no sense to me that two women without jobs had to ruin my afternoon when they had all day to themselves. "Mary doesn't even have a TV downstairs so I'll miss my show," I reminded her. Mary and my mother had a no-fail secret weapon. "She's making you a special pizza. It's in the oven already." The secret weapon was fully deployed now. My resentment dissolved with thoughts of yeasty, warm crust and melted mozzarella. Sorry to Justine and Joe, but nothing trumped Mary's pizza. I was an easy target. We left for what would be more than the promised one hour.

Twenty years my mother's senior, Mary offered life support to Mom's feeble, final agonal breaths of social climbing. Firmly planted in the ugly apartment and unwelcoming community for seven years, she had, by now, all but abandoned those original dreams. Mary's husband, Eugene, had been my father's boss at the prestigious engineering firm they worked in. Until recently, Mary had been the boss's wife. Within two years of the original business association, Eugene had died suddenly from a massive heart attack, and my father succumbed to a massive bout of marital infidelity. He pursued his libidinous quest for love in Poughkeepsie. Neither man was able to return.

Mary and Mom were now firmly joined in an unlikely

friendship based on the indignity of having been so unceremoniously left to fend for themselves. I was unwittingly brought along as a less-than-interested participant. I was as helpless to escape as a fly trapped on the windshield of a traveling car. I was released into an alternative universe of the trappings of culture. There was not a plastic cover on a single piece of furniture. My mother admired and spoke about the furnishings and collectibles with a reverence I'd never witnessed before. "The house just oozes culture and travel," she'd repeat all too often. My benchmark for impressive decorating still rested on the reference points of velvet ropes and fake flowers at Alexis's house.

Mary fit into Mom's construct of higher aspirations. The widow had four adult children. All were launched into adulthood except an only son, Eugene, Jr. He had shortened his name to Gene. He was an incredibly handsome young art teacher, who still lived with his mom and escorted her to the opera, ballet, and annual trips to Europe to enjoy better opera and finer food. He spent little to no time at home otherwise. Mary was an accomplished seamstress and supplemented her widow's income by making designer dresses for wealthy matrons in Mount Vernon or Bronxville. These were our more fortunate neighbors just beyond the Bronx border.

Mom was undeniably impressed with Mary's dossier. She owned a classic fieldstone single-family home just a block short of Westchester County . . . almost out of the Bronx! She held season tickets to the Metropolitan Opera. She traveled annually to Italy or France and attended fashion shows featuring famous designers. She spoke three languages and dressed impeccably in couture reproductions that clung to her ample bosom and hourglass body as if meant to be worn by her alone. She had widow status as well, preferable to being the dumped divorcée. Mary got something out of the relationship, too. She basked in my mother's adoration and availability to fill long, lonely hours.

Early evenings and weekends were spent playing endless games of Scrabble. Mary and my mother played Scrabble by strict rules. Although a dictionary sat on the kitchen table, it was rarely consulted. These two had an agreed-upon list of obscure words that were acceptable: words like adz (alternative spelling for ax), pi, zoa, and countless others memorized and embedded in their minds' rulebooks. Occasionally a questionable spelling would cause a spirited debate and unpleasant tone. "Taxis is the plural of taxi."

"No, the only acceptable spelling is taxies."

"Absolutely not, one is a plural noun and the other a verb!" A dreaded trip to the dictionary would resolve the issue. Both left feeling a bit diminished by the need to consult the final arbiter of language use. Mostly I didn't pay attention, hoping the debate would signal a final game. The Scrabble words were absorbed occasionally. Words and language mattered to my mother, and so they mattered to me. The word vitriol has a basic point value of eleven. I learned that vitriol dominated their lives in spite of its modest point value.

They discussed Mary's underperforming sons-in-law and the emerging horror that her only son, Gene, seemed to prefer the company of men. "Fairy, I swear he's a fairy. If his father were alive, it would kill him." This statement from Mary was accompanied by a triumphant claim to a sixty-five-point single-word score. Her ability to form seven-letter words and utilize triple-point markers emphasized the power of her words . . . both spoken and played. Words were nonnegotiable. "The fairy has a new friend, Jesus; I think he's a Puerto Rican. Someone from his school. I hear them on the phone speaking Puerto Rican to each other so I can't understand." Of course Mary knew the language was Spanish, but she thought Puerto Ricans spoke an inferior version. "Yeah, well, I understand too much. All that education wasted. "Quartz. That's forty-four points. I got rid of the Z and Q. Your turn." Mary shifted her ample bottom from side to side in her chair as if she were itchy or uncomfortable. I sat across from her in the kitchen enjoying the last bit of thin crust. She reminded me of a dog shaking water off itself after an unwanted bath. After her bottom settled into the seat, she moved her shoulders from side to side, almost shuddering. I thought that this Puerto Rican thing was something like an allergy for her. I sat as a silent spectator hoping the reaction would pass and that I might be offered a second slice of pizza.

Mary listened patiently to my mother's endless concerns about money and continued rage at being left to manage unpredictable and insufficient child support payments. I wondered if they ever listened to each other, or just ruminated as they shuffled the little wood tiles around on their individual holders. Their voices and the low clank of wood against wood blended into the fragrant atmosphere of oregano, basil, and, Mary's favorite scent, Abano bath oil, which permeated her skin. I silently absorbed it all.

I loved Mary's home. Although I rarely ventured beyond the first floor, I knew and loved every inch of it. By the time I imagined that I had missed that day's *Bandstand*, I settled into the much-revered living room and used my old trick of finding inanimate companions to entertain myself. There was no television and lots of time to do homework, read, or examine each and every foreign object in my sight. Her home offered primary evidence of exotic world travel and mysteries well beyond the Bronx.

As they played a second or third game of Scrabble, I wandered every square inch of space, simply looking. A fireplace of heavy stones dominated one wall and was flanked on either side by built-in bookcases. Floor-to-ceiling books and small pieces of sculpture filled them completely. We had many books, but not books that climbed walls on shelves built into the walls. I couldn't remember a single book in Alexis's home. The object I loved best was an elaborately enameled bust of Nefertiti, and below her a tiny replica of King Tut's sarcophagus. It was both amazing and weird to my young mind to imagine those dead Egyptians. I looked them up in the *World Book* to learn about their lives. A silk Bokhara rug covering most of the dark wood floors was a lovely place to sit and read. The blocks of burgundy and navy became a lovely nest and was where I sat to do homework. Mary's bedroom had a feminine, pastel-colored Aubusson rug. I knew these facts because Mary was proud of them and delighted in sharing the provenance of her possessions with my easily impressed mother. I continued to absorb facts as if I was a human sponge. I absorbed and stored the information because it was better than long-division homework. My silence may have looked like boredom, but I was absorbing the accoutrements of culture.

My favorite place in the room was a small, three-tiered mahogany corner curio shelf. Tiny Venetian and Murano glass miniature animals inhabited that place. My favorite was a black skunk with a thin white stripe. The skunk stayed in my hand until it was time to leave and be reluctantly returned. I considered stealing it more than once, but understood it was not an option. "Mary, what kind of glass is the skunk?" I asked, more interested in alerting her to my desire to own it than to learn of its Italian roots. What followed was a narrative on both Venetian and Murano glass. Great, but not what I was hoping for.

"Mom, I finished my homework. Can we go home now?" I sat across from Mary and admired my favorite painting on the wall above her head. A few oranges in a cream-colored bowl . . . one orange was partially peeled and revealed a lacey net of rind. I could smell that orange if I tried. I could imagine the slightly sticky delicate netting on my thumb and forefinger. Gene painted that, and it was reason enough to love him.

"Barbara, if we play one more game, I promise to make your Revlon doll a new outfit." Now that put me into a position of power I liked. Mary always had fabulous scraps of fabric and remnants left from her wealthy clients. Her doll creations were miniature versions of couture designs. My doll and Mrs. Coates (her best customer) would have matching outfits. I was left with pattern packets with drawings or photos of dresses and skirts by Balmain or Dior on the cover. The next time I came over the outfit would be sitting on the kitchen table waiting for me. My favorite scent was that of Mary's sewing machine. Yes, it had a fragrance. When she brought it to life by turning one small knob, a tiny light on its underbelly flicked awake, like a heartbeat. It soon whirred into action, and there was the smell. The smell of electricity when it meets lint and thread and bakes its own delight. It is like the smell of ozone, which some people can detect during thunderstorms or on rainy days. I always know it when it's there. I first learned that special scent in Mary's workroom. I love the smell of sewing machines and steam irons over cotton fabric as much as any expensive essential oil in perfume.

Every other Saturday, we made a special trip to Jack's Fabric Shop. Mary and my mother in the front seat of Mary's Volkswagen Beetle and me and Prince, Mary's small black mutt, always crowded into the back. Jack Goldstein, the third generation of

Goldstein's to own the business, boasted hundreds, or what seemed like thousands to me, of bolts of fabric laid out on long tables or towering and slouching vertically to hold each other up against every inch of wall. There were also tables holding folded stacks of remnants. This twice-monthly trip was to purchase the perfect fabrics for Mary's custom orders. I enjoyed sitting with Prince and having a chance to look at what was a lush exhibition of patterns, colors, and textures that might ultimately become a doll dress. I also enjoyed the bumpy and noisy ride of the tiny foreign car. Prince and I enjoyed the same status as silent passengers. We were equally content to have a change in routine.

Walking past the remnants or through the catacombs of fabric that had traveled from China, New Zealand, India, or Scotland to live humbly together in Goldstein's shop was a treat. There were silks so light they felt like whispered breath when touched. Fine wools that would softly and smoothly yield to form invisible seams and hems. As I wandered unnoticed, Mary, Jack, and Mom would engage in banter about price. My mother had an important role as foil. Jack Goldstein knew and loved that Charlotte, like him, was a Jew. She was also divorced, beautiful, and flirtatious. All of these finer points were called into play while Mary negotiated the price of fine fabrics.

Only now do I think of Mary as my mother's official fabric pimp. Mom, at five feet eight inches and a lean but shapely one hundred and thirty pounds, was stunning. Her thick straight chestnut-brown hair, hazel eyes, turned-up nose, and chiseled features routinely caused heads to turn. To Jack, she looked completely like a *shiksa* (Christian girl), but could spout irreverent Yiddish phrases to his utter delight. The banter and outcome varied little from week to week.

"Here they are. It must be Saturday. My favorite *shiksa* and her *bubba* (grandma)." Jack's face lit up at the sight of them.

"How is my favorite *gonif* (thief)?" was my mother's sharp reply.

Mary would go into action, selecting the best fabric for the coming weeks' commissioned skirt or dress while Mom flirted with Jack.

"Jack. Are you for real?" Mary would suddenly pipe in. "Eighteen dollars a yard for this plaid? A joke, right?"

Then Jack would be redirected to business. "Mary, that's merino. If I give it to you for less I'd be losing money on it." Now Mom rolled those soulful eyes and chuckled, "Jacob, *az di Bubbe volt gehat Beytsim, volt zi geven mayn Zeyde.*" Translated from Yiddish that meant, "Jack, if my grandmother had balls, she'd be my grandfather." I knew and loved that expression. It was one of my grandmother's favorites. She delighted in translating and explaining it to me just a few years before.

Mary waited. "Okay, I'll give it to you for $16.00." He sighed in resignation. Not good enough. My mother was the daughter of *hondlers* (bargainers). She had work left. She looked directly into Jack's eyes now. "Fourteen, Jack. *Tokhes oyfn tish.*" (Put up or shut up, or, more literally, put your ass on the table.) But she always spoke with beneficent innocence. "Okay, okay already, no profit today." Jack's final price. Mission accomplished. A quick kiss on the cheek and almost imperceptible body brush and they were ready to return triumphantly to the waiting dog.

Prince, Mary's ugly little mutt, was welcome respite from the company of the fabric pimp, fake Jew, and proprietor of homeless treasures, which I later came to call them. At the time, I only knew that I was uncomfortable and embarrassed by the interaction between my mother and Jack. I was relieved to be away from the man that transformed my mother so completely when she entered that store.

The feisty terrier was relieved to be able to stick his panting face out the rolled-down window. As we passed black kids tossing balls or riding bikes near the car, Prince barked ferociously at the moving objects. "Prince, stop that now! Do you know you're also a little black boy?"

Mary was delighted with the comparison. "It's hilarious; the dog is a bigot. Doesn't even know he is a little nigga-baby." My mother was silent. Her face fixed and posture stiff. I could sense her anger. I waited for her response. I held my breath and waited. "Mary, the dog is reacting to being cooped up in the car too long. When we get back, I need to get back home. I have a headache, my mother whispered." I was sad and angry and more eager than my mother or the dog to leave the car.

After that, the Scrabble games became less frequent. Mom spoke less and listened more. From the quiet vantage point of Mary's living room, I felt as if the house had somehow tilted. Everything looked the same. The little glass animals weren't sliding off the shelf and Nefertiti looked as calm and aloof as ever. Sometimes when I did listen, I expected to look at the famous face and see her kohl-lined eyes roll in her inanimate head, but they didn't. She and I listened in silence as the point value for the word vitriol increased.

"That faggot never comes home on weekends anymore. He's with the spic every weekend." She paused. "Charlotte?" she asked, as if my mother's silence was approval rather than disgust, "can you believe he'd rather be eating bean dip on Orchard Beach this weekend instead of seeing Maria Callas perform? The two of them trotting around in their Speedos, showing off their wares." I wondered why she just didn't ask my mother to go with her. My mother liked opera almost as much as she loved symphonies.

One day, the room itself seemed to tilt. The house seemed to shake on its foundation. The Scrabble board enjoyed its final play and could not be righted. It was one thing for Mary to take on the niggas or the fags or the spics, but this time it was Jews.

"Charlotte, I can't believe you feel sorry for those kike spies." Mary said the words so casually it may have been possible to not even hear them. "They sure got what they deserved. Good for those two kikes." The famous trial of accused spies Ethel and Julius Rosenberg was in the news. They had been sentenced to death and would leave their two young sons without parents. It was a controversial American case and especially important to outraged American Jews. Few approved of this much muscle-flexing by the government.

Was it Mary's use of the word kike, her indifference to her friend's religion, or the plight of two orphaned boys? Was it the decision itself? Maybe it was because at the end of that final game she found herself with an awful set of letters and a losing score. I imagine that she was stuck with a high-pointed "J" and "W" without an "E" in her hand or on the board to spell the word Jew and just leave. I knew without her needing to tell me that Mom was done playing Scrabble that day and forever with Mary when we left. I would miss pizza, Princey, and Nefertiti. I had had my fill of fine tailoring and fancy words and was happy to return to Dick Clark and *American Bandstand* after school. I understood that the finer things in life were a lot like religion. They offered good hiding places for bad people. I thought that was why dogs didn't go to church or care about clothes.

I did not appreciate the concept of benign neglect during those years spent in silence or isolation creating diversions from my reality. Now, I am almost grateful. The absence of friends that should have helped me to become socially competent helped me instead to become more curious. The deprivation of peers that should have provided laughter and identity provided self-reliance in their place. In the absence of friends, I embraced what was offered and what could be salvaged. In Mary's house there were the accoutrements of culture. In middle school there was the natural world outside—and a large plate-glass barrier that was a window. These became my insensate friends. There were also my own amusing thoughts as I challenged myself to recall words and facts that became lists. Was that a form of interaction? There was an intimacy with the collected details that replaced the need for intimacy with people. The assemblage of details and facts and pleasure from my love of them sustained me. Before adolescence, I had acquired a collective base of knowledge and thoughts many adults never achieve. It was an inverse learning curve. It would take almost a lifetime to retrieve the skills I'd need to learn to love or value people as much.

Chapter Five

MAYONNAISE AND MEN

My mother met her next best friend by chance. In the absence of words on a Scrabble board, her hours were now filled catching up on words in best-selling books. Summer reading was especially pleasant outdoors, often on a bench in Seton Falls Park. On one of those warm afternoons, she shared a bench with another reader and future best friend.

It would be impossible not to notice or be curious about the rotund woman dressed in denim, sky stone, and silver, who took up more than her share of bench space.

Elaine's physical presence was a spatial, visual, and even auditory phenomenon. With each inhalation her large breast lifted and heaved a long Navajo squash blossom necklace into motion. The close-set delicate flower petals tinkled in slow rhythm. Her wrists and fingers were wrapped in cuffs and circles of all shades of turquoise. Her denim pants stretched across her melon of a belly. In 1959, denim pants were called dungarees or overalls and were worn almost exclusively by young children and farmers. Her short heavy-boned legs ended in wide feet wrapped in crisscross-leather-strapped sandals. They swung freely, several inches shy of meeting the ground.

I sat on a large flat rock about twenty feet behind them. My mother and I were generally alone at this edge of the park. The exceptional heat of that July day must have driven the oddly dressed woman into the shaded park. We had never seen her before. I was distracted from creating a chalk garden on my rock. Along the fissured sides, I drew green chalk vines that climbed to the top. I paused to watch the intruder from time to time. In between drawing each floating purple three-petaled violet, I'd steal another glance. She was like a human peacock. The violets I drew floated between wispy white clouds. Sometimes chalk dust blew freely around them, making them seem real and windblown. I noticed in between clouds that a girl about my age sat silently reading on the next bench. I guessed she belonged with the brightly clothed woman. I was captivated by the sight of the almost clownish peacock-woman but less interested in the girl. Two new people had intruded on our normally private place.

Elaine spoke first. "What are you reading?" she asked. My mother was reading *Exodus* by Leon Uris. It was a best-selling title but may also have been a reflexive choice in response to her recent bout with anti-Semitism. She was absorbed in the dramatic story of Israeli statehood.

"And you?" she asked in polite response.

Elaine smiled and turned to fully face my mother. "Ahh . . . ahhh . . . I am enjoying *Lady Chatterley's Lover*."

Indeed, this woman was different. That book was still considered to be scandalous erotica by most Americans. My mother had told me about the very sexy, "dirty" book that she wasn't going to read. I had paid little attention to her choice then but years later would learn it was one of a trio of erotic books that then had been released after years of litigation involving several countries and courts. D. H. Lawrence had written the first edition more than thirty years before Americans could purchase it. That year, it was on the best-seller list. "I'll lend it to you when I've finished it," Elaine offered. Hope you don't mind all those dog-eared pages. You actually may want to read those first, or just those altogether." She now laughed out loud and waited for a response. She had taken a calculated risk after all. The pretty young woman might have politely excused herself and left. Elaine could not have known that the divorced, lovely young woman was lonely, socially liberated, and as much a misfit in the neighborhood as she was.

"That's an offer I can't refuse," my mother said, returning the smile. I realize now that Elaine would not have cared about being a social misfit. In fact, it might have pleased her.

The pendulum had officially swung to the far left. Gone was the dull brass, conventional and predictable measure of time with Mary. It was about to be replaced by a turquoise encrusted, erratic, oppositional, pleasure-seeking keeper of my mother's spare hours, that had little regard for convention or time itself. My mother was venturing into a new rabbit hole. I held on for the next set of life lessons. I had little choice and unshakable trust.

It wasn't long before we shared weekends with Elaine and her biracial, illegitimate eleven-year-old daughter, Diana. That silent girl I observed on the next bench that first day was, like me, listening carefully and curiously to our mothers' conversation. It was good to have a friend for both my mother and for me. Finding this exotic family, which included an ever-absent grandfather, was like finding sea glass in Kansas. They were as misplaced in this colony of conformity as we were. My brother spent almost as much time with our new friends, because their house captivated and delighted both of us. The often-absent grandfather spent almost all of his time working and living with artists like himself in Greenwich Village. He made only rare and begrudging visits to his daughter and grandchild.

Kyle Ross, Elaine's father, had spent almost a decade designing and crafting the arts-and-crafts treasure just one block from our ugly house on Amundson Avenue. His challenge was both creative and practical. He hoped to provide security for his forty-two-year-old daughter and his granddaughter. In spite of having a master's degree in social work and a secure job as a New York City caseworker, Elaine showed little desire for domesticity. Kyle had left his beloved artist colony in San Miguel Allende, Mexico, to build the house on a cheap lot in the East Bronx. Once the house was complete, he preferred life in the city and traveled between the Village and Mexico, supporting himself comfortably with occasional sales of his work to high-end art dealers and galleries.

Ultimately, the treasure existed hidden by overgrown weeds, tree roots, and any uncultivated shrubs thriving exclusively on tenacity. A sturdy wood pergola holding large, gnarly-trunked wisteria vines further hid the home. In spring, the fragrance and soft lavender clusters might give the hidden secret away. He had furnished the interior of the home with a decade of the landscapes and seascapes he'd painted in Mexico as well as a few beloved animal sculptures. Hand-crafted and secondhand Mission oak furniture filled the rest of the space. Outside the house sat Elaine's 1955 custom-painted turquoise Plymouth. The custom paint job doubled the car's cost. Like Elaine, there was not another one like it.

I was primed to appreciate oil paintings by those lacey orange rinds and the cream-colored, highly glazed pottery that were the subjects of the painting I loved across the table at Mary's house. I was now mesmerized and visually addicted to Kyle Ross's landscapes and seascapes. They seemed to hang on every wall, and the uncovered multi-paned windows delivered changing light that brought them to life. I marveled at his ability to create shade and shadow with subtle color. As the light shifted, it seemed as if the clouds moved, casting longer shadows, and the water caught light differently on ripples. Boats actually appeared to bob in the water. A very special place in the beamed living room was an alcove with built-in benches that surrounded a heavy stone fireplace. It was a cozy place to read. The hearth that the stones rested on was squares of moss-green Rookwood tiles with pine cones in raised relief. The benches ended in half walls that declared this space special and apart from the large room. A blanket strung between these walls sometimes created a stage curtain for plays and shows produced by Stephen, Diana, and me. We understood this house was unique and wonderful. Elaine and Diana and their home were unlike anything we knew.

Unlike Mary, Elaine's pedigree had its origins in a socialist, free-spirited home. Raised by liberal, progressive, unconventional parents in Greenwich Village, she was a self-proclaimed "Bohemian." Mary's elegance had worn thin as it became obvious that the trappings of culture were little more than a thin facade that hid a rotten infrastructure.

Elaine's bold and bawdy persona provided a breath of fresh air to my mother. Socialism was not foreign or frightening to her. My grandfather embraced the concept as a factory worker involved in union growth and protection in the 1930s. Elaine's landing in this tightly woven, conventional neighborhood was again a matter of finances and fate. The tornado that had taken my mother's original dreams and spun them out of reach had somehow yanked this Greenwich Village Bohemian from her roots and planted her in Seton Falls Park, sharing a bench with a receptive audience.

I sometimes wonder if I can fault Mary for my own persistent adult distrust of perfectly dressed women. That niggling little visceral anger and possibly unjust belief that the perfect exterior is just a disguise. My gut reaction is to dislike or dismiss women that spend so much time looking perfect. The rational grown-up me understands this is short-sighted and a flaw. But still, it reminds me of strong perfume that helps to hide the unpleasant scent of sweat. Now, there was her antithesis. Elaine, in denim and pounds of silver jewelry—an inelegant, obese, irreverent woman that was preoccupied with romance and good times. What gifts and baggage would she leave me with?

Elaine's work clothes were an assortment of ill-fitting, boldly colored and patterned, clingy-knit jersey shifts. They ended above her heavy-boned, massive knees and bowed legs. My mother marveled at the size of her knees. "Her knees must weigh forty pounds apiece. She really should wear longer dresses," Mother would say routinely. Elaine's knees offended my mother's aesthetic senses. I had never before considered the size of knees or weight of individual body parts. I did know that I would happily have settled for thirty-pound knees free of ugly and itchy psoriatic crust. I knew my mother was proud of her long, thin freckled legs. She loved wearing shorts as much as I hated wearing them. Elaine's curly salt-and-pepper hair was short, unkempt, and oily. She may have been as dirty as she was different. If Elaine's colorful and bold choices failed to catch the attention of neighbors, her daughter's looks certainly would. Long stares, curious whispers, and side glances accompanied Diana wherever she went.

Biracial children were rare even in Greenwich Village in 1959, but in this part of the Bronx, they were uncommon and scandalous. If it was difficult to be fatherless and Jewish here, it was impossible to be both of those and look like Diana. She was fodder for shunning, but I was happy to have her as my friend. Fate could not have dealt a child a crueler hand. Not only was her lineage, legitimacy, and race questionable, but she was decidedly ugly.

My mother, not one to sugar coat her words or refrain from creative imagery, described her as a ten-year-old embryo. Her large head was supported by a spindly neck. Her abdomen was huge and rounded and connected to spindly limbs. Her skin was pale, translucent, and had a waxy, yellow pallor. It was my mother that called her skin "high yeller." I understood she was referring to the pale-yellow undertone of her skin. Her kinky hair and flat broad nose suggested a Negro father. Thin blood vessels traced visibly through the skin on her arms and legs. Her eye color was ungraciously described by my mother as dead-fish green. Her crowning glory and the final insult was a grayish-brown head of Afro hair. Because Elaine was lazy and disinterested, she lacked motivation to learn the special care her daughter's hair would require. It was simply easiest to keep it close-cropped, which only emphasized her exceptionally high forehead. In an effort to clarify her gender, Elaine routinely affixed a squashed pastel bow to the side of Diana's head. "Jesus, Elaine," my mother would say. "Can't you even find a decent bow? That looks like a Christmas package someone left under the tree too long." The bows were not changed.

Just as I hadn't known at the time that the term high yellow was an offensive and outdated racial slur, I hadn't thought much about my mother's insensitive language. I understand from the vantage point of history that the ugly term was a way of socially stratifying black people by the preferred shades of their skin. But in 1959, the civil rights movement was just beginning. I give my mother a pass on that one, although I think her language was casually cruel. I have come to treasure the important unintentional lessons my mother gifted me. Her rejection of Mary's friendship demonstrated her intolerance of bigotry and homophobia. These were my earliest lessons on those subjects. Now, she would demonstrate the importance of empathy toward Diana, in spite of her colorful descriptions. I had learned my own first painful lessons of callous behavior before meeting Diana. Now, my mother would demonstrate compassion. I learned empathy then, even if I am not always able to extend it to well-dressed women today. I am grateful for those early lessons in compassion that seem to exist intrinsically, if imperfectly, in me now. Observing my mother's response to Diana and her mother's indifference instilled a more objective thoughtfulness in me and gratitude for my own mother. Accepting the shortfalls that she would soon exhibit took longer to reconcile.

Over the next few years, Diana, Stephen, and I would spend lots of time together as our mothers pulled and tugged at their own friendship. It should have been good to have a friend. A friend just eight months older would logically be welcomed in the absence of other friends. How could I be grateful for this silent girl who preferred books and food to fun or friendship? She soon became more burden than friend.

Diana spent so much time at our house on school days, we began to see her as an unplanned, unwanted sibling. "Mom, when is she leaving?" Stephen would ask. "Does she have to eat with us again?" This would be in earshot of Diana, who appeared to be engrossed in a TV show less than five feet away.

"Stevie, be pleasant. It's not her fault. Her mother should be here very soon. Now just do your homework." Elaine rarely showed up before dinner. Most often, Diana would eat with us and return to the television before Elaine made a grand entrance well after dark. Elaine had after-work dates and dinner with friends almost every evening. She rarely even explained whom she was with or where she was. It was simply a routine that was insidiously established within a few months of becoming friends.

"Pushka, pussy, pussycat, I am so sorry. Did you eat? How was school? Come, Pushka, let's go home." Diana would sheepishly and silently follow her mother home. We were happy to see them leave.

Elaine's abuse of my mother's friendship eventually prompted Mom to confront her behavior. Elaine enlisted a backup babysitter for Diana somewhere near Tremont Avenue, a woman known to her through Social Services as a client. This now enabled Elaine to go away on weekends or stay out later on weeknights. She made no secret of a new boyfriend who was in the process of moving to Indiana. Elaine often flew out on Fridays and returned late Sunday. Diana spent some evenings with us and was with Rose otherwise. Although silent and withdrawn, Diana did voice her preference for our home. She told us that Rose's ten-year-old son and eight-year-old daughter hated her and called her names. She said she hated Rose. We heard but didn't really listen or care, I suppose.

One evening, we got an angry phone call from Rose. I could hear her loud voice through the phone receiver held inches away from my mother's ear. Elaine had failed to return by nine p.m. as promised on a Sunday evening. "Where the hell is she? I have to get up early tomorrow," Rose complained to my mother. "She had a fight with my kid, and I slapped her. Pick her up or else." It was cold and dark and late that fall evening. Steve and I were in pajamas but not yet asleep.

"Let's go. Barbara, Stevie, get in the car. We have to get Diana." Neither of us would protest. We both felt responsible for her misery. If we hadn't complained, she could be with us.

We were overjoyed to see her. Our joy perhaps more rooted in salvaging our guilty consciences than in rescuing Diana. We were overly solicitous, and she silently joined us in the back seat. Three unhappy children on their way home for two of them.

I now believe that my mother's habitual acquiescence to friends was based in her own insecurity. Both Mary and Elaine were years older and inherently more authoritative. She was in awe of Mary's cultured life. She was both awed and jealous of Elaine's academic superiority and credentials. A higher education was one more thing she spoke of often and believed she was cheated out of. Both these friends designed the structure and rules of play in their relationships. Maybe she thought them superior and deserving of that privilege. She was childlike in her need to please them.

It was not until I was an adult that I questioned and resented her intellectual inertia and martyred acceptance of being a victim. It was only then that I began to question why she didn't work. Why didn't she go back to school? Why was she single or sad or poor? Was it her own fault? Was it Steve's and my fault for hindering those options? Mostly that is what I believed until adolescence, when I began the process of differentiating myself from her, and when I began questioning everything and stopped caring as much. Before that, her unhappiness, like everything else I trusted about her, was simply fact and belonged to me as legitimately as all her knowledge and opinions did. Because that unhappiness was linked to single parenthood, it was my fault. I was happy when she was happy. This was symbiosis in action. She was happiest with friends, and so our own roles were as unbalanced as her friendships. She was my beautiful, brilliant, funny, all-knowing, omnipresent mother-child. And sometimes it was simply good to escape the complexity of that relationship.

Fortunately for Diana, we were reaching an age where being

alone after school was safe for a few hours. She was free to not be a burden to anyone. Most days, I would let my mother know I was going to Diana's house until dinner. Still miserable in middle school, we shared stories about hating it. I was both duty bound to be with her but also happy to be in her house and away from home.

"Want a sandwich?" she would ask.

"Nuh-uh, no thanks." Her favorite after-school unsupervised passion was making mayonnaise sandwiches on white bread; mine was silent observation. We were like two comfortable, contented cats coexisting without connecting. She stacked the sandwiches on a dull green melamine plate. The mayonnaise knife was orange Bakelite. Even these everyday things were different. Other people had stainless flatware and glass plates. Diana licked the last remnants of mayonnaise as daylight faded. I pulled a chain on one of the mica-shaded lamps and noted its effect on the closest landscape. As the paintings receded, wood sculptures of whales and nudes seemed to take the stage in shadows. It was time for me to leave. I was sad to leave her alone, even in the company of so much beauty. She seemed unaware of things beyond Nancy Drew mysteries and mayonnaise sandwiches. I left her alone, waiting for her mother to return.

I left before it was completely dark and walked home quickly to avoid complete darkness. I hurried up the narrow staircase of our ugly hallway in the ugly house to a small apartment with one faded large print of a nondescript beach in the living room. Tonight we were having beef stew for dinner. The house smelled good even if it didn't look good. Our dinner was an improvement on mayonnaise sandwiches. I was happy to see my mother and grateful for her imperfect presence. There was a short time of innocent gratitude for the status quo and many enjoyable distractions from looming changes I would not accept as graciously in the next few years.

But at that time, weekends were different and most fun of all. If Elaine was home, we would have dinner with them and a special "show." The fireplace alcove was ready. Our props lay on the benches, hidden by the hastily taped curtain.

"Diana, you have to hold the flashlight higher," I'd command. "No one can see my head! Keep it still; you're shaking it so much. . . . And Steve, you have to hold the curtain until I say to pull it."

"And now directly from her last performance at the Bolshoi ballet is Mme. Barbara doing a pirouette, a plié, and five foot positions." Diana's scripted, flat voice announced my part.

In my black ballet shoes and a silk-fringed shawl belonging to Elaine, I twirled, squatted, and positioned my feet. Followed by applause, I introduced Stevie next.

With Ed Sullivan as our inspiration, we were ready. "Directly from his last sold-out performance is Stephen singing 'Anywhere I Wonder' by Julius La Rosa." Steve always sang this song; he loved it. Predictably, it brought my mother to tears. She would later say it was so bad she had to cry. We thought she loved it at the time. Diana did not perform. She was the stagehand and helper, but never a star. When the play was over, Elaine would build a fire, and we would enjoy roasted marshmallows. She made a perfect fire and prided herself on being an advanced Girl Scout. We were a family of five. There was not another family like ours in the neighborhood. It was a time of transition from unquestioning innocence to curiosity and change.

In spite of Elaine's deficiencies as a mother, she was an incredible source of information on all flora and fauna. She was fearless and curious, and took the three of us on nature hunts when she was not searching for romance. We rode our bikes to what seemed to be exotic places, salt marshes and estuaries and beachy coves. Before Co-op City was built and before City Island was overbuilt with restaurants, these places were swampland and brackish woodlands. Everything was noted and identified; spike grass and cat tails, Queen Anne's lace and goldenrod, golden slippers and fiddler crabs, red-winged blackbirds and bobolinks. We learned and loved them all. She had an amazing ability to make you see details no one else did. She was a magician. She was a Girl Scout *par excellence!* Her wanderlust and desire for adventure drove her to abandon rules and reasonable behavior. We slugged through mud in our shoes and walked on slippery algae-covered green boulders to get better views. We abandoned well-worn footpaths to explore uncharted areas thick with thorny bushes and poison ivy (which she carefully identified), that might reveal a rarer species of bird. She was more adolescent than adult. Her knowledge and abandon almost redeemed her flaws. She opened the mysteries and beauty of the natural world to us.

In Mary's home, I acquired an impressive vocabulary, and an understanding of the accoutrements of culture. I also learned to dislike well-dressed women. Elaine provided the foundation for a lifelong love of art and nature. Her love of the natural world and sexuality were a routine part of conversation, but she never considered her students' receptivity. My own perspective on the subject of men was one of wariness and discomfort. Mine was a world populated with strong, if flawed, women. As much as I enjoyed outdoor ventures with Elaine, I cringed when men were the topic of conversation. She talked about men and sex with enthusiasm I could not understand. Elaine, like Mary and my mother, was a woman who left me a mixed legacy of gifts, including love of art and nature and words and beautiful things without nurturing a sense of my worth as well. None were skilled at nurturing. I was audience and student. I existed on the sidelines. These strong women succeeded in imbuing me with knowledge, curiosity, and appreciation for many things, but I needed more. They nurtured deficiencies and doubt in me rather than confidence or social skills. My thoughts remained mostly unspoken. The rich inner dialogue persisted. I longed for the comfort of belonging to the world of mundane, mediocre mainstream life. Belonging was elusive.

Elaine, so much like an adolescent, seemed to have hormones and a libido that were in overdrive. This seemed a permanent condition in her case. As Stephen, Diana, and I chronologically approached puberty, our mothers seemed to be testing their boundaries more than we. Elaine had always had a "love interest." There was Herman, a huge, Turkish man with a leather factory in the East Village. Foreign-accented, longhaired, heavy, old, and weird, he was not one of my favorites. Although their relationship was enjoyed mostly in his warehouse (the probable love nest), or apartment, or a coffeehouse, we met him occasionally in her house. I wondered why anyone would want to be anywhere near him. I had little interest in knowing him. He had even less interest in knowing us. After Herman, there was a boyfriend in Indiana. The distance resulting in more frequent weekends away. Elaine talked openly about sex and again, we ignored her descriptions of good kissing, great sex, and longevity as it applied to both erections and relationships. She was simply being her. More like a badly behaved teenaged sibling, we dismissed much of her chatter and enjoyed her irreverence at times. Sometimes, we laughed to disguise our embarrassment or discomfort. Going forward, most men and any well-dressed woman would challenge my more rational ability to reason. I gave little slack or benefit of doubt to either. Some of the curriculum taught by mom, Mary, and Elaine would need to be unlearned.

Always looking for men, whether weeknights after work or weekends away, she was driven by her lusty libido. Elaine had convinced my mother it would be a good strategy to find men as a team. Parents Without Partners was a fast failure. "They all just want to get laid," was my mother's analysis.

"What a bunch of ugly losers. Ugh." This was Elaine's rating based on a single meeting. Some of that could be valid, but they were men and women acknowledging they had children that were important in their lives. Not exciting enough for sure. They planned a childless vacation together to Block Island, apparently thinking that they could widen the field.

Block Island in 1958 was a poor man's paradise. Elaine had spent her own childhood summers in Martha's Vineyard. She knew that Block Island was saltier, shabbier, and a haven for recreational and commercial fishing. The Ocean View Hotel, a turn-of-the-century, huge hotel had seen presidents and grand people in its heyday. By the 1950s, the roof sagged, floors sloped, and linens were musty. No matter, it was cheap and had a veranda that overlooked the beach from its hilltop perch. It had a huge wraparound bar that stayed open all night and attracted a rowdy crowd. The perfect backdrop for adventure. My mother and Elaine sent the three of us to an inexpensive Jewish Federation camp in Upstate New York where we could be safe, happy, and away for two weeks. They believed they deserved a little vacation and that we would just love sleep-away camp. A little religion certainly couldn't hurt us.

We arrived in Narrowsburg, New York, on a Friday afternoon. My duffel bag contained a bathing suit, some clothes, and a new pair of red-soled, white buck oxfords, my mother's idea of sturdy hiking shoes. The shoes never left the confines of the duffel bag. Nobody wore shoes like that, nobody! Luckily, I had a pair of Keds. "Okay, everybody, put on your bathing suits. We are going to test your swimming level. When we finish, time for a nap and change your clothes for Oneg Shabbat. We will all introduce ourselves then," a khaki-clad teenager shouted in too loud a voice.

I wondered, *What is Oneg Shabbat? Something about an egg, one egg?* I'd never heard of it. *What am I supposed to know that I don't?* We trudged down to a brown-green lake with a small wood dock. Luckily, Diana and I were together so far. Her body tightly encased in a shiny green-and-white-striped bathing suit, her huge belly and skinny veined legs were already drawing glances. I had to contend with the psoriasis on my own legs, but her presence drew all attention away from me. That was no consolation. I always felt protective of her. I understood the misery of being different. I watched the rest of the group to see where the stares were going. Everyone was new and unsure of themselves; the looks were limited to furtive glances. I was ready to protect her. There had been enough times that cries of "fuzzy, fat horse" were shouted at her in my presence. I could relate to being victimized. Looking back, I'm not sure if she was as humiliated as I was for her. Her failure to respond annoyed me. I imagined she might have also created a protective inner dialogue or maybe she just believed she was deserving of the treatment. I just wouldn't let anyone get away with that in this place also.

We took slow steps into the uninviting lake. It was slimy and muddy under our feet. It was cold. No one was anxious to put their heads into it. One by one, we got a swimming grade and ran for our towels. We headed back to our new home, a wood bunkhouse with six cots. Everyone put on skirts, blouses, and shoes. Apparently the "egg" ritual was a more formal thing. Diana and I had shorts and pedal pushers and a bunch of short-sleeved polo shirts. Thank God we were in the same boat here. Did our mothers get a required clothing list? For sure they did, but if it said something about Oneg Shabbat they would not have connected the dots. Not part of their vernacular for sure. The appeal of the camp was most probably cost and not the cultural curriculum.

The assembled group sang songs and did prayers. We had never heard any of them before but did a fairly good job of moving our lips enthusiastically. We stuck together like glue that night and for the next twelve nights. By the end of the stay we could recite a blessing for bread. That one motivated Diana the most. No mayonnaise in sight but really good challah. We survived without being teased or noticed. I have no memory beyond the muddy lake and the first Friday night prayers. We understood that our partnership as outsiders was key to that survival.

While we became initiated as real Jews, our mothers enjoyed being single girls. Elaine had been right; the duo attracted lots of men. Actually, my mother was the magnet and Elaine benefitted when it was a group. They enjoyed the beach but enjoyed the onboard parties at Old Harbor more. After a hard day of fishing, there was a hard night of partying on the boats. Most boats were large and had room on deck and below to relax. Many of the sportsmen traveled in groups. Business clients, coworkers, fishing aficionados, and best buddies were all out for a great time—for a man's weekend. Occasionally, a family would dock. Mostly the boats with families or quiet people docked at New Harbor on the other side of the island. Live music from Ballard's Inn carried out to Old Harbor. It was festive, and hopping from boat to boat the ultimate summer fun. Elaine and Mom had a wonderful vacation. This was the first real vacation my mother ever had. This was also the first time in more than a decade she was child-free. Now, carefree and with a friend hell-bent on fun, they focused on men. In spite of the other insecurities in her life, my mother was completely confident in her beauty and ability to attract men. Perhaps she deluded herself into believing that asset could be used to restore her hope and dreams for a better life. Did she think some rich guy out on a fishing trip would save her from life on Amundson Avenue? I wondered even then if being pretty had hurt more than helped her. In later years, I came to believe her beauty was as much a handicap as a gift. It was a nebulous cloud that overshadowed and stunted the growth and potential of that wonderful intellect.

Flirting with Jack to finesse the price of a yard of fabric was small game. Wealthy sportsmen were higher stakes. I was old enough to understand that. She returned from that vacation in high spirits and with stories that I would rather she had not shared. I listened patiently as she described strings of party lights along the tall masts of the boats or tuna towers that were even taller, and the lush interiors of the boats. Always the student, I learned new nautical terms. I imagine knowing words like scuttle, stern, or starboard was interesting to her, or at least good Scrabble fare. I listened as patiently to her as any mother would to humor her child. I was the grown-up, worrying about her safety and judgment. I resented being in this position, but never expressed a word to her about how I felt.

A week or two after returning home, my mother began dating. She had tried a few dates when we were younger, but they were isolated events. I cried miserably when she went out on those evenings. The insecurity of having my one parent go out at night terrified me, so she stopped. Now, with older children and Elaine's encouragement, she was eager to have men in her life again. She dated two men she had met on vacation. She was smitten with both and often had weeknight dates with one or the other. It occurred to me that weekends were probably family time they could not spare or explain to their wives and children. The men knew and cared little about us, but I learned plenty about them. I learned that Sal owned not only a forty-three-foot fishing vessel, but a Buick agency and a lovely home in Babylon, Long Island. Bill, the second man, hailed from a well-known jewelry manufacturing family in Providence. He traveled extensively and had homes in both Newport and Providence. They were wealthy, handsome, upstanding, and, I assumed, respected family men.

For as long as I could remember, my mother had told us, "No man is interested in dating a woman with children. You two are the most important thing in my life. If men don't want my kids, then I will be alone; it's fine." This was a mantra we accepted as truth. Why was I beginning to think that we really weren't the most-important things in her life anymore? We felt responsible for her being condemned to a life alone and a life of poverty. We always wanted her to be happy, since she had sacrificed so much for us. If she did not have us, we believed, she would be free to remarry and start over. Her happiness was important. If dating someone's husband and father now made her happy, then I thought I should be happy as well, but this happiness felt wrong. My mother seemed to prefer Parents With Existing Partners to Parents Without Partners. That thought made me sad. I knew that she would still be alone and still be poor. I knew these men would not change that.

For the first time in my life, her happiness unsettled me, because I could see that it came at a cost. My guilt for being responsible for her unhappiness was as great as my anger at the men I believed were deceiving her. Neither man emerged from their cars to see her home or meet her children. Just how much did they care about her if they couldn't give just that little bit of courtesy and respect to her? Meeting her children would have extended the circle of guilt to include them. I was sure they lied about their intentions, and she believed the lies. Her dates could not have coincided with a worse time in my own emerging interest in dating etiquette. I imagined that an almost two-hour drive from Babylon to the Bronx was based on favors exchanged. I also believed the exchange would not be to her advantage. I felt deceived by my mother also. How could someone so smart be so stupid? Was it enough for her to just be flattered by their interest? Why weren't we enough for her anymore? I hated her behavior. I was old enough to understand that beauty was used as barter. Her dates were laden with unspoken, covert sexuality and thoughts I quickly repressed. I recalled Elaine's crude sexual discussions, not meant for my ears. I felt almost nauseous. At twelve, I was becoming sexually aware. My own body had changed dramatically. I had begun menstruating the year before, had graduated to a real bra, and had my own surging hormones creating awareness and curiosity about boys. I did not want to think about my mother's boyfriends.

While a flashy new Buick waited outside, my mother would put finishing touches on her hair or makeup. "Barbara, look at that gorgeous head of thick black hair. He reminds me of Anthony Quinn," Mom babbled as she hurried. That year, the actor had won an award for a popular movie. My mother sounded silly. I resented being treated like her friend and confidante. "Yes," I answered flatly, not bothering to tell her I hated this man. Always more competent in inner thought than expressive language, a simple "yes" would do. My inner voice was louder and more honest.

You have a better chance of marrying Anthony Quinn than this lying Long Island cockroach in his big ugly Buick, is what

I wanted to say. I hated knowing about his split-level home, spoiled wife, and smart children. I hated that all I could ever see or know about him was a long-distance view of jet-black hair through a car window. I understood my mother was living vicariously. She was enjoying things she couldn't have for real.

I was annoyed at her lapse in judgment. Her self-assured intelligence had always been a source of pride and comfort to me. It was the one thing that helped offset the things in life we were missing. We were more intelligent than anyone who may have had things we didn't. No one was as smart as my mother. She was, I believed, all-knowing, and she gifted me with her knowledge. Now, she seemed innocently ignorant. The gift was diminished, tarnished.

I began the painful process of needing to differentiate myself from her. In my need to do that, I blamed men for corrupting her. Men had previously been mysterious creatures existing on the sidelines of my life. I knew them as the principal, the pharmacist, the president, my doctor, and my friends' fathers. They never lived with us or shared my life. Now, I wondered why I had ever blindly trusted or respected any of them. I believed few of them could ever be trusted. I thought that when I got older, I never wanted to depend on any man. I would be smarter than my mother for sure. Maybe, I thought, I was even grateful for the lesson and anger that took me from the vague tomorrow of childhood to an ambitious, focused independence from men. Until now, I had no ambition beyond middle school. Now, I knew that men would never be my means to an end. My mother was prettier than I. I knew I had to be even smarter than she. Differentiation later gave birth to self-direction. I would never depend on a man. I would design and control my own life. I would definitely be a working woman. I sometimes thought about what job I'd like. More often I just thought about what I enjoyed now.

I knew all the things that I loved and treasured. I loved books and art and birds and strange weeds and foggy days and beautiful homes and fine furniture. I loved pizza and pumpernickel bagels and spaghetti. I loved words and how they comforted me when I thought things I couldn't say out loud. I loved my brother and my mother still, but I did not love men!

I was beginning to see the world through the critical lens of adolescence. It should have been a remarkable time of sexual awakening and an opportunity to belong, but instead I was starting off with some serious handicaps.

Chapter Six

A FEW GOOD MEN

There was only one man I knew I liked. I believe I loved my uncle Walter. Throughout my childhood, he hovered on the sidelines of my real, everyday life. The Sundays of my childhood were given over to a flimsy facade of and attempt at an extended family. For exactly three hours most Sundays, Uncle Walter, his wife, Aunt Dorothy, and cousin Mark visited us. Occasionally we would reverse the pattern and visit their garden apartment in Alley Pond Park, Queens. Uncle Walter was mild mannered, seemed perpetually middle-aged, soft, and slouchy. He was like the comfortable old sweater you enjoyed knowing was there if you needed it. He looked very much like my mother and grandfather. I took pleasure in this biological link to a grown man. This, I realized, was the closest I'd get to having a father.

They'd arrive at noon in an always late-model, always charcoal-gray Oldsmobile or Buick. Aunt Dorothy toted a crumpled shopping bag and a grease-stained white bakery box with hastily re-tied, red-striped, knotted string. Uncle Walter held a stack of month-old *Life* magazines that were gratis copies from his job at the Ogilvy & Mather advertising agency. Finally, chubby, sullen, spectacled cousin Mark, a month younger than I, trudged slowly in last place. He had a thick book firmly tucked under his arm. He seemed to instantly vaporize as he entered the apartment and retreated to the one bedroom of our apartment. His own bedroom was filled with beautiful Ethan Allen maple furniture. He had his own bookcases and a desk with a matching captain's chair. He had dark-wood, louvered shutters on the windows. I loved how adjusting the slats could change the light and mood at any time. I don't believe he cared about any of those things. My unsociable, erudite cousin had the onus of only-child success resting squarely on his soft, round shoulders. His vision was limited to a narrow twelve-inch field of distance, which ended at a book.

Aunt Dorothy, always in charge, would herald the official start to the visit in her loud nasal voice. "Charlotte, I brought a large can of tuna, dig up another can of tuna, mayonnaise, and ketchup. I have onion rolls and marble rye." I believe Aunt Dorothy traveled with a six-ounce can of chunk light tuna or Season-brand sockeye salmon as religiously as other women carried lipstick.

My mother slapped six mismatched plastic placemats on the table. It soon became an indoor, inelegant "picnic" of unwilling participants. Steve and I hated the sloppy pink fish concoction we were obliged to be grateful for. Mark was called from his reading reverie to retrieve a sandwich before being given the grace of returning to his solitude. Because he was so sedentary, that fishy mayo appeared to move right to his fat thighs. He was sent to a private fat kids' camp in Maine each summer and always returned slimmer for a few months.

"Wally," she continued, "take an onion roll, they're delicious." She chose Uncle's clothes and even his choice of bread.

He sat obediently and ate heartily. The pink mushy fish salad made slushy, clucky mouth sounds as he chewed without ever closing his mouth. I loved him but hated those sounds. The usual banter about Mark's grades or our grandparents' health filled the hour. Lunch over, my mother and Dorothy began a contentious game of Scrabble. Dorothy was as self-assured and cocky about Scrabble as she was about everything else. My mother was an amazing adversary, however, and Dorothy was no match for her. Once again, intellect was our currency, our only wealth. The poor, divorced younger sister of her husband had every advantage in this arena. The underlying sentiments of resentment were palpable. This was no game. This was ego warfare, advantage Mom! My mother's voice was heard continuously correcting or criticizing Dorothy. "Mase, M-A-S-E, is not a word, Dorothy. You can't keep looking up words to use your letters, that's not what the game is about. It is a game of skill and vocabulary." The leaden innuendo landing a one-two punch to Dorothy's ego. "If you have to look up words that you don't know, you shouldn't be using them," my mother let loose her final thrust.

Dorothy, now offended, countered, "Charlotte, do you still see that disgusting woman Elaine?" It was an obvious attempt to distract Mom from the issue of the dictionary by reminding her of her social status and unconventional friend. Walter, the mediator, the man in the middle, and the master of corny jokes, would distract with his version of humor.

"Dot, I saw you turn that letter over. Not fair, the other blanks are out. Ha, ha, ha."

I realized he was afraid of Dorothy's anger. He was a man who'd been cowed by his wife. He used humor like Mom used her excellent vocabulary. These were weapons of defense. He rarely claimed more than a hoped-for distraction from her wrath, never a victory. Uncle Walter's most amusing habit of writing, then reading aloud "throwaway" letters was my favorite part of their visits. I imagine he spent lots of time ruminating over why he was angry. His written words were carefully, deliciously chosen to be ambiguous and cryptic. His letters read with the rhythm of a benign greeting card. Toward the end of a visit, the letters helped everyone to transition to a lighter mood. As the Scrabble tiles were being plucked up and returned to a canvas drawstring bag, he would announce the reading of his weekly, unpublishable, unmailable letter. He cleared his throat ceremoniously before beginning. He waited a few seconds for dramatic effect as we waited expectantly. His letters made irreverent references to the nuts, tits, asses, and ignorance of political figures, his office staff, Dorothy's friends, and neighbors. Almost anyone might be the subject. Anyone but Dorothy, of course. There was always a double entendre. He'd laugh convulsively, crumple and crush the paper into a tight ball, and toss it overhand across the room into a trash can. He rarely missed his mark.

Dorothy tolerated the outburst with a sardonic, parental, patient grin and then the air was cleared. I think that it was his version of my own angry inner conversation. We shared interesting coping mechanisms, even better than a biological link perhaps. We both understood written or thoughtful inner words were wonderful weapons where a voice given to them might be dangerous.

After his reading, the final trump card was played, "Let's have dessert," which meant the game was over whether it was finished or not. The grease-stained cake box was presented by Dorothy. Leftover and crumbled Danish pastries and cookies, a wedge of soggy apple crumb pie, all the sweet remains of Thursday's mah-jongg game. Surely, Bea, Florence, Sylvia, and Dorothy (the mah-jongg group) had their fingers all over this offering. Instant coffee in mismatched mugs marked the end of the visit.

"Wally, Marko, time to get going!" Dorothy called out. All decisions were hers to make. Aunt Dorothy was the engine that powered the train. Authoritative, opinionated, and smug, Dorothy called the shots. I recognized that power. I both hated and admired her strength. Uncle Walter liked to end the visit on a positive note, but he walked on eggshells.

Humor would suffice when he may have preferred an expressed opinion or sentiment. "Okay, hernia, ready to go," he'd quip. He liked to call her hernia instead of honey. She'd give a long-suffering look at him and begrudging smile. Calling her hernia, I'm sure, was his funny way of letting us know she was, in fact, a pain. A charcoal-gray-sweater-covered arm would give me a quick hug as they left. I loved those hugs and him. I wondered if my cousin knew how lucky he was. More than that Ethan Allen furniture, I envied him his father. I wondered if there could be other men like him.

The sound of their car motor starting would signal a safe time for my mother to explode. The charcoal-gray sedan would not even have begun to roll before Mom was yelling. "Jesus Christ, she thinks she is still the head nurse, for God's sakes, and my poor Caspar Milquetoast brother is scared shitless of upsetting her. Well, it's been a long time since she cracked the whip on the ward. Time to give it a rest."

Dorothy was extremely proud of her nursing career that had ended with marriage. She delighted in telling dramatic and graphic tales, which I enjoyed hearing. I looked forward to these stories; they redeemed her in my mind. This was my introduction to gory amputations and enemas and death. It was complete drama, and she was always the heroine. It was hard to reconcile the image of the nurse heroine with the woman reduced to left-over cake and made-up words. I did consider how good it might feel to be that self-assured and that powerful. She was omnipotent in her home. She was almost as powerful in our home. It is easy now to link her strength and successful nursing career to my first nod to future plans. Dorothy was not as smart or as beautiful as my mother, yet she had successfully attracted my wonderful uncle and enjoyed the status and excitement that I thought only existed in my Sue Barton nurse novels. Her stories from Monmouth Memorial Hospital were as exciting as those in my *Cherry Ames, Student Nurse* or Sue Barton books. I never questioned my uncle's happiness. Even if he was simply an accessory, their marriage seemed strong. He knew how lucky he was to have married this nurse. If nothing else, his safety in her hands was assured.

Aunt Dorothy was lucky, too. She had both Uncle Walter and a wonderful father. Sometimes, when we visited at Alley Pond Park, her dad would visit also. We loved Mr. Singer because he smiled constantly, told great stories, and gravitated to Steve and me during his visits. Mark, preferring books and solitude, missed out on his wonderful tales. I thought Mr. Singer liked us more than his own snooty grandson. His right arm lived a flaccid paralyzed life in a sling. It had been crushed in a work accident many years before we met him. That handicap only made him more exotic and special to me. Having only one arm and a constant smile was a winning combination. Al Singer was a hard-working, self-made man. His recycled crate and box business provided nicely for his family. He was as fond of children as he was of animals, and enjoyed being at his daughter's home when he knew we would be visiting. Steve and I listened with delight to his stories about the two pets that went to work with him every day. Pete the parrot and a poodle named Princess had jobs. "Pete knows how to open envelopes for me; opens all the mail." He waited for Steve and me to laugh each time he said this.

"Princess is in charge of traffic. When the trucks pull in, she announces them." While Mark read in his room, Steve and I peppered him with questions and laughed at his stories.

"Charlotte, hi, Al Singer here." A rare phone call on a Monday morning from Mr. Singer. "I would like to buy Stevie his bar mitzvah suit. He is such a good boy, so smart. It would make me happy if I could do that." My mother was so grateful and so relieved. The cost of the event was weighing heavily on her. There was a small donation to the synagogue that had given him a full scholarship to attend Hebrew school. There was the cost of refreshments for a small party to follow the ceremony. The cost of clothing for all of us was just one more stress point.

"Thank you so, so much; that is so generous and will be even more special coming from you," she said. But then the next evening the phone rang again.

"Hello, Charlotte, listen, I feel terrible but about the suit. But, well, Dorothy is carrying on about it. She seems to think Mark will be jealous. I don't think he knows or cares, but you know how she is. She gave me hell. She said I should have asked her first. Anyway, I am sending you a check for $100 for the suit. Just use it, but promise me this is just between us. I don't want her to know. Don't even tell Walter."

Of course my mother accepted the offer; she needed the help. She thanked Al, but she was completely enraged at this humiliating situation.

"That bitch, begrudging Steve a decent suit. Amazing how she can even strong-arm her poor father." My mother slammed the phone down. The check arrived; the suit got purchased. The bar mitzvah was a lovely understated celebration. My smart and handsome brother made us all very proud. He entered manhood in a cheap, secretly purchased suit surrounded by proud family and few friends. Elaine attended wearing a garish-colored jersey dress that was tighter than usual. Diana had a new pale-pink bow clenching plastic pearls at the center that matched a new pink cardigan. I thought she looked pretty. Aunt Dorothy sat many rows away in a camel-colored chenille suit. I suppose it was smart, but I thought she looked like a camel-colored plush toy dog. I have no memory of my own clothes or emotions on that day. This milestone began a change in the frequency of Sunday visits with my aunt and uncle and would coincide with other big changes for our family that were on the horizon.

We saw them once a month or less. Visits were often combined with visiting grandparents. The ritual weekly visits that provided indelible memories slipped away at some indeterminate time. There were no more Scrabble games. There was still crumbled cake, instant coffee, and Dorothy's opinions on everything. My mother once told her she was too opinionated.

"Thank you" was her response. "Grown-ups are supposed to have opinions."

I thought about that statement a lot. I liked it then and practice it now. Knowledge and opinions are invaluable assets. Opinions, expressed or repressed, nourish and gratify me. They comfort and delight me and surpass any savory pleasure my palette has ever known.

I thought about Aunt Dorothy's confidence. She could intimidate her husband and father, and they stayed. She threw insults at my mother without remorse and indignantly fielded criticism. She seemed always able to have things her way, from revoking gifts given with love, to unfinished Scrabble games, and hated mushy pink tuna every Sunday. What was the source of her confidence?

In my young mind there was a link between her power and self-confidence and her career. She had been a head nurse, after all. She faced life and death and misery and pain and made it all better when she could. When she couldn't, she showed courage and resolve. She commanded respect and received it without question. So what if she was bossy and humorless and not really as smart as my mother? I believed that nursing was at the core of her confidence. How else to explain her entitled status? She was neither pretty nor pleasant, but managed to corral and keep the love and respect of the only two men I knew I loved. I understood this. Nursing was what I would do when I grew up. Nursing was that job I knew I wanted to have. Nursing could guarantee me that same self-confidence and entitlement. This invaluable lesson from Aunt Dorothy motivated me. Passive unintentional lessons were how I learned best.

My formative years were spent surrounded by women. Men were never a big part of the minutes and hours that made up daily life. They were not a part of the years that formed me. Men were an empty place; they existed as negative space. Negative space that defined me as significantly as the full-blown female forces that were more concrete. There was no man in my life to confront Kathy's mother or Mrs. Wilson or Mr. Tully. My mother taught me to ride a bike and bait a fishhook with a writhing, squishy worm without flinching. It was my mother who was with Steve and me in a rented rowboat, learning to row and fish and discover. There had never been a man at the dinner table. Why would an envisioned man be included as I looked to the future? In the variegated packet of seeds that included many women, the "man-seeds" were missing. They couldn't germinate in my future if they were missing.

Now 1960, I was almost twelve, but I was like a five-month-old infant discovering my own detached but amusing hands as I considered the future. My awareness of full potential was sadly stunted. Those missing man-seeds crippled normal development. When I considered the future beyond nursing, there were only vague thoughts of someday. Someday, I might also have a home and beautiful things in it. Maybe I'd own a nice car and have a family. Maybe that family would include a man. I hoped all these things would be mine. I hoped there were a few good men like my uncle, that maybe I'd find a man like him. But at the time, there was only the delight at contemplating a narrow future. Like the infant, I was happy with what I could clearly see. What was merging into sharper focus was that I needed more than what my mother had settled for. All her knowledge and culture had only enhanced her frustration and made her miserable. I had been a perfect neophyte. Now, as I considered the future, I rejected her present. I needed control. That control did not include men. It would be decades before I learned and embraced the words of the famous French writer, philosopher, feminist Simone de Beauvoir. Before I knew her articulated words I believed them and felt them: "I am too intelligent, resourceful, and demanding for anyone to be able to take charge of me entirely. No one knows and loves me completely. I have only myself."

My plan did not include a man to either facilitate or impede it. Men were part of a foggy future. I realized that I would collide with that future at some point. I might contemplate men later. I hoped by then there were a few other good men to be found.

I thought my brother might become the third good man I knew. According to Jewish law, my brother was now a man.

Of course, not only was he still just a boy, but he was also my brother. It was impossible to think of him as a grown-up. It was beyond impossible to imagine him in any sexual context. Still, in the very small world of a family of three he was my projected self as a boy. Siblings often share an intimate and privileged knowledge of their childhood unknown to others. He could understand me in ways no one else would. He would be a man someday. How could I ever not love him? I would always love him, even when he became a man. Someday I might want to love another man. For now, he was still a boy and other men were unimportant. I was happy just knowing my future was a career in nursing. I could continue to love my brother and forget about men completely. They weren't all that important at all.

Chapter Seven

VIVA VILLA AVENUE

The bar mitzvah marked my brother's "manhood," as well as thirteen years now spent on Amundson Avenue. Somehow Steve not only survived, but thrived there. He had several good friends that lived closer to PS 68. He had made friends that lived on other streets, too. They built models, went biking or sleigh riding, and went to Boy Scouts together. They were all solid students, but Steve was the acknowledged smartest. Theirs was the last class to graduate after eighth grade, because after his class they restructured the New York City school system. Beginning in 1959, middle school began in sixth grade. My class was only the second to enter JHS 142. Steve had been spared my middle school experience. He was the only one among his friends going to the prestigious Bronx High School of Science in September. His peers went on to good Catholic high schools or to a large public high school. As I struggled to remain invisible in middle school and not fail algebra, Steve began to commute to Science High. The trip involved taking three busses, followed by a very long walk under the elevated train tracks of Jerome Avenue and crossing the parklike divider of Mosholu

Parkway. Most of the walk was through commercial properties specializing in car repairs and customization. Only one area was really an obstacle. The last part of his trip was a walk across a notoriously rough street, Villa Avenue.

In this otherwise solidly upper-middle class, mostly Jewish residential area of six-story prewar apartment buildings, one street was unique. Villa Avenue looked and was different. It was the buffer that divided the commercial properties from the middle-class residential neighborhood. Villa Avenue was a remnant pre-dating the densely packed canyons of apartment houses. Its small, wood-framed single homes had never been more than poor people's dwellings. The houses stood shoulder to shoulder in a decrepit display of solidarity. The poor Italian families living on the street were equally close. They drew tighter as the neighborhood saw a trickle of black families buying in during the early sixties. Many of the original owners could be identified by statues of the Blessed Virgin enshrined in concrete hoods that stood protectively on the small patches of front lawn. We referred to them as, "Mary on a half shell." Plastic flowers bloomed behind chain-link fences regardless of season. This was their territory. Young and old alike were protective. This was a neighborhood with bluster. This was a street where newly emerging men took a certain pride in the need to bully. Name-calling and fist fights were part of its "culture." These same bullies walked past the Blessed Virgin unapologetically to a hearty dinner and close-knit family.

Steve always left school immediately after his last class at 2:40 p.m. every day. Getting from the easternmost to the westernmost part of the Bronx took more than an hour. Unless it was snowing, he never missed a transfer or arrived home more than fifteen minutes late. He arrived home just before 4:00 p.m. daily. While I maneuvered quickly around the demons that may have lurked in Seton Falls Park, which was my own unpleasant ritual at dismissal, he was choreographing his trip home. By 4:00 p.m., I was already watching *American Bandstand* at home or at Diana's house, watching her stack up a sandwich or two.

I remember the April day clearly when my brother failed to come home by four o'clock. By four fifteen my mother checked the time. Fifteen minutes later, she asked, "Did Steve tell you he was going anywhere after school today?"

I was watching TV but becoming aware of the time also when the phone rang close to five o'clock.

The phone call was the beginning of changes I never imagined. My mother's voice was loud and, I thought, maybe angry. "The police?" she shouted. "Police? Where is he? When did it happen? Barbara, get in the car, your brother is in the emergency room." She was shaking and pale. We ran to the car. I had never seen my mother frightened before. I'd seen her angry, but not scared. Now I was frightened also. Neither of us spoke. She ran every red light on the way.

When we got to the emergency room, Steve already had stitches near his right eyebrow. I remember thinking that they looked too thick and too black for skin, a poor choice. His nose looked huge and strangely bent to the left. His hair was still sticky with dried blood. He was silent, and whiter than my mother. I felt weak and nauseated and frightened. When he realized we were there, he tried to speak. The nurses and police told him to rest while they explained to my mother what they could glean from Steve and a single witness who had seen most of the encounter from her bedroom window. He came home with us that night, but it would be two days before he could finally speak. His voice was low when he finally recounted the horrifying details.

He had walked down the sidewalk outside the school, crossed over the rail yard overpass, and waited for the light. When the light changed, the few kids not being picked up by parents headed toward the Bedford Park stop of the number-four train. Most were headed to Grand Central and good neighborhoods in Manhattan or north to Woodlawn and Westchester suburbs. As they turned left, he headed toward his first stop, one block past Villa Avenue. Alone now, he hurried for the bus.

That's when his assailants approached him. He recounted his story in a low, flat voice.

"Hey, asshole. Hey, genius. What's the rush?" a lone black-T-shirt-wearing teen asked. Steve didn't answer. He was not just book smart, he was people smart. He told us he began walking a little faster then. Steve saw the boy was not alone. At least four friends stood behind him and added their own taunts. He sensed the danger. "I knew I had to walk faster and get off that street," he said.

"Fuckface, I'm talking to you. Come over here. What's the big rush?"

Faster now. Not quite running. *That shows fear,* he thought. "I knew it would be worse," he said, "if I acted scared."

"Yeah, well I am in a rush. Got a bus to catch . . . sorry . . . gotta rush."

"Did you say sorry? Yeah, you are going to be real sorry. Get off my street, asshole."

"Happy to oblige," he said, and then he ran. But they were faster. They had closed ranks and were forming a circle that was closing in on their prey. They were inches away. "No way I could outrun them," he said, "but I tried. I started to run when they were really close."

But not fast enough. From nowhere, he felt a weight hit his back, forcing him to fall forward. Books fell beyond his face.

The heavy biology and English textbooks he held and needed for homework flew past him and scattered on the sidewalk. His nose hit the pavement and bounced off. Now there were voices and laughter. "This prick thinks he can walk on our street just because he's so fuckiiiiiiinnnng smart. Say you're sorry okay . . . apologize and we'll let you go home and study. Say it."

Steve was too stunned and afraid to speak. He said nothing. It's possible an apology would have provoked more abuse. They took turns banging his limp head into the pavement, kicked him once or twice, and left, laughing.

Eyes and ears are everywhere in a tight little neighborhood. It might have been a frightened old lady or protective mother or a new black neighbor, but someone called the police.

I knew it couldn't have been the Blessed Virgin in her concrete hood. Obviously, the concrete prevented the transmission of cosmic messages to a God that should have intervened. Instead, a regular lady watched and hoped my brother would escape. She called when she witnessed the inevitable begin.

Whatever was previously wrong with Amundson Avenue had not been enough to motivate my mother to move. My lack of friends or misery in middle school hadn't been enough. Her acknowledged hatred of the landlady or insufficient heat in winter hadn't been enough. Our designation as cultural outsiders wasn't enough. But now an intolerable event had occurred. The hour-long bus ride and need to walk across Villa Avenue created a tipping point. We were moving. I was leaving my childhood in the East Bronx behind.

Without a single discussion, her plan took shape. I was leaving behind my childhood home and everything familiar to me. Now, the memories which were coined in those years are stamped with negative images. Most were ugly. I was happy to leave. The apartment was cold. The thick and cracking walls had never once been painted. They were a dirty tan color. The narrow railroad flat had no interior doors to formally separate kitchen or living room from bedroom. The nasty landlady hated us and stood silently scowling whenever we entered "her house." My friendships were few and frail. I was aware of my family's inferior status. I envied almost everyone for something I didn't have. The hallmark of those years was yearning. I wanted a pretty home, friends, a normal family, a father, I suppose. I wanted a religion to belong to and a God I understood. It was a constant state of reasonable want. Only now, from the vantage point of age and distance, would I consider using the word deprivation to describe it. It was another negative space. But negative space also boldly defines what exists within it. There is that clarity now. The good byproducts of those bad years were moving with me. I learned to love art and nature and books. I learned to enjoy adventure. I honed the art of inner thoughts and stoicism. I learned to love language and words. These were found treasures and salvaged resources in negative space that I am grateful for. I may not have savored and embraced these unintentional gifts without the deprivation. They formed a part of me I value even today.

The two most important people in my world were moving with me. So, snaillike and efficient, I carried only myself in a protective and permanent shell. Anything most important existed in that tight, convoluted shell of thoughts and knowledge and hope. I never experienced belonging in those years, and wouldn't miss anything tangible. Anything important to me fit snugly in that shell.

Snails are known to hibernate until they can safely thrive. It was time to transport myself to a more hopeful environment. The move west was a wonderful change. I happily left those years behind.

Chapter Eight

THE NUMBER-FOUR TRAIN

"I can't go back to yesterday because I was a different person then," Lewis Carroll writes in *Alice's Adventures in Wonderland*. In Carroll's story, Alice follows the White Rabbit into a rabbit hole. Seeing a beautiful garden she wishes to enter, she must turn the key and fit through the door. In this effort, and to her horror, she shrinks, she grows, she constantly changes. When she is not changing, her surroundings change and distort without warning. Her journey seems endless. She cries great tears and the tears pool and become a sea. She is carried forward. "'I know who I was when I got up this morning,' says Alice, 'but I think I must have been changed several times since then.'" I understood completely. A similar sea carried me forward.

My mother's narrow target of just a few blocks in the Norwood section of the Bronx was carefully chosen. The neighborhood was bordered by Mosholu Parkway and Gun Hill Road running east and west and had Jerome Avenue as its horizontal axis. It was at that point in time still solidly Jewish but about to change. It was walking distance from the High School of Science, and Steve didn't have to cross Villa Avenue. It was as much a simple reflex to the incident as it was a long-standing goal. It took the sight of her sutured, swollen, and humiliated son to galvanize all the fragments of possibility into a cohesive plan of action. It wasn't an accident that if you turned your back, literally, on Amundson Avenue and walked in a straight path, this is where you would be.

It was an alternative universe and a dramatic change. Beginning with the early 1960s, this and many similar Bronx neighborhoods began to decline. As newly arriving Puerto Ricans discovered the Bronx, the Jews were usually the first to move. They moved to the newly constructed Co-op City, which was previously the marshland we explored with Elaine. If they were young professionals, they found entry-level homes and co-ops in lower Westchester. The most financially sound moved first, leaving old people and nonprofessionals behind, at least initially. This decline was our good fortune because it meant the rents slipped a bit and credit checks were relaxed. We could afford to make the move. It would take a full decade for the neighborhood to complete its erosion from middle class to poor, and that was just enough time to carry us to young adulthood.

We had followed our own White Rabbit down this rabbit hole. Everything and everyone was strangely different here. Everything seemed somewhat distorted. We were off balance. We were disoriented. The new world was vertical. People lived behind doors in stacks. They were shelved like groceries in a vertical structure. Our apartment was accessed by stepping into a small elevator that creaked and complained as it ascended six stories. We were used to living on the second floor of a private house in a neighborhood where all homes only reached as high as two stories. Now, we lived on the top floor and took the elevator up and returned back down to an expansive granite-floored lobby, which always smelled of cooking. The cooking smells were foreign to me. We'd left a neighborhood of Italian families. There seemed to always be a sauce pan simmering with tomatoes, basil, and oregano. An undertone of sautéed garlic married the scents and permeated the air of my friends' homes. That was not the olfactory essence of this lobby. Even the basic scent of garlic was displaced by onion. I wouldn't associate this with the smell of Jewish food until much later.

I understood that these simple smells signified a fundamental difference about the neighborhood. The majority of residents were still Jewish. I would later learn to love the smell of a savory Friday night brisket or warm-from-the-oven onion bagel or bialy. I couldn't imagine the new Puerto Rican families would dislike the flavor of this lobby. The adjustment to new foods and defying gravity were just some of the differences.

Because the decline was so gradual, ours was decidedly still a Jewish neighborhood. The stores reflected this. During this decade, there were a documented hundred and fifty kosher delicatessens in all of New York City. The single block of Jerome Avenue between Mosholu Parkway and Gun Hill Road had three. There was enough business for Schweller's, Katz's, and Epstein's to do very well. The proximity to a large hospital (Montefiore) guaranteed a wait at any of them at lunch.

The bagel factory and kosher bakery did robust business as well. A small supermarket with a respected "Appetizing" section was teaming with people. I was not sure at first if "Appetizing" was an adjective or a noun. The foods there were new to me. People stood with serious expressions, aggressive body language, and held tiny numbered papers announcing their turn. Occasionally there was an argument about the numbers and accusations of cheating. They were waiting to buy lox or nova or other delicacies. Behind the curved-glass display, rows and rows of perfectly aligned gold, whole whitefish with dead eyes looked up at the anxious customers.

I wondered what the whitefish were thinking about the badly behaved adults. The fish were lovely. They could easily compete with a showcase of fine jewelry.

All these stores stood beneath the inelegant canopy of the guano-encrusted support beams and tracks of the Jerome Avenue number-four train that stood above Jerome Avenue. One block west was our neighborhood. The apartment houses were as neatly and tightly packed as the whitefish in Olinsky's. The people were different here. They were friendly and open and seemed pleased that we had joined them. There were questions, of course, but we spoke English and that was good enough for them, reassuring in fact.

The women all pulled or pushed two-wheeled shopping carts to and from Jerome Avenue. They looked like they all had reluctant dogs on taut leashes. More people walked than drove cars. Although there were no Mad Hatters here, there were *yentas*—chatty, nosy women who watched everyone as if it were a paid profession. Old people sat in folding-aluminum beach chairs in front of the buildings. How strange it was to see beach chairs placed on cement instead of sand or grass. They reminded me of the pigeons that lined up under the horizontal beams of the elevated tracks. Their heads turned in unison when people passed by. When the subject of their observation was out of earshot, opinions were shared and debated. The place was "curiouser and curiouser" than we could ever have imagined.

The neighborhood wore its people like clothing. This was a wardrobe of old and young, garish or going-to-work people. Accessories were walkers and beach chairs and transistor radios playing static Yankee games to be shared. There were tennis shoes and orthopedic shoes walking constantly. People walked from lobbies to stores and laundromats or parks and subways. From dawn until dusk they were out there, always visible. They covered the neighborhood in a cloak of thriving, brilliant life. I left a place that existed in quiet privacy. People lived mostly in solitary backyards and small homes. They hid from exposing the intimacy of their mundane lives. They cloaked themselves in sheltered private lives, which weren't readily shared. It wasn't an easy place to find belonging. Now, I lived in a neighborhood where everyone belonged. Everyone was a bit of texture or color of the neighborhood, even me.

Apartment 6E may once have been a highly desirable choice. High floors in the city are typically quieter and more expensive. But 6E faced the back of the building and had a questionable view. The single bedroom (shared initially with my brother and later with my mother) had one window facing an interior courtyard of brick. A second window, with a fire escape, faced Jerome Avenue. We were perched at eye level with passengers traveling south to the city. The window was locked because top floors were notorious for a quick robbery and exit up and across adjoining rooftops. Pigeons nested on our fire escape, and we enjoyed their soft coos and family commitment. The contrasting thunderous roar of regularly passing trains soon faded from our consciousness. Our kitchen had a dumbwaiter once used for garbage but now was the preferred means of travel for roaches and water bugs. These were also new creatures in our lives.

"Holy shit, I hate it here," was Steve's daily declarative ritual. "Those ladies pushing wagons all over the place, they're ugly; everything here is ugly, disgusting. I hate it." Although he thrived before the move, at fifteen the transition was a bad time to adapt. He missed his friends, the relative quiet, and anything else he was used to. He made sure my mother knew just how much he hated it. The irony of the move being done for his safety and well-being was not lost to me. The new irony was that I was thriving here. I loved it.

Having left no friends (save Diana) behind, a school where I wasn't even a "token" white girl, and an apartment lacking any aesthetic redemption, I was happy for a fresh start. I was transferred to JHS 80 for my last year in middle school. My class assignment was to a low-functioning group of twelve strange-looking kids. It was hard to know if the placement was based on past performance or classroom census. It would only be a year and actually the teacher and students posed no demands or initiation issues. Little to no expectations enabled me to settle into my new surroundings on my own terms. I was actually smarter and more normal-looking than anyone else in the class. I was a relatively superior student to my cohorts, who slouched or wiggled in their seats or looked off blankly into space.

I checked out other kids in my neighborhood. I explored the wonders of Jerome Avenue. The street was one big exciting bazaar as far as I was concerned. A festival of sounds and sights I explored and savored on my way home from school. It wasn't just all the good food that I found there. Tween-Scene clothing for girls and the Greenwich Village Shop for leather goods, jewelry, and art were just two of my favorites. A gift shop sold Limoges serving pieces and Hummel figurines. How I loved to window shop! It didn't matter at all that I couldn't buy anything. I was content with the process of imagining the day that I would have real purchasing power. I understood that not owning things didn't diminish their value. I made believe these were museums and art galleries. A beautiful painting could be loved without owning it. When I could buy them, it would be evidence of my own discriminating taste, my own worth. For now,

I could afford an occasional treat at the candy store. Tompkins' candy store and soda fountain was on the corner of Jerome and Gun Hill. He was a lecherous old man, who looked like a frog. He made a great vanilla egg cream soda that made his wandering hands worth fielding.

Our new building had two families with girls my age, and up and down the street other young teens all knew each other. There were a few cliques, but everyone fit someplace. It wasn't long before I had a small group of friends. In spite of himself, so did Steve. There were no rich kids or poor kids. No one went to church or synagogue. No one much cared if you had two parents. The new neighborhood offered relaxed urban attitudes. It seemed to be a no-judgement zone. This was adolescence and the important things in life revolved around looking like each other, hanging out, flirting, and current music. At night, when the old people folded their beach chairs and retreated, we owned the sidewalk. We hung out on front stoops, walked around the block, listened to transistor radios. We put lots of energy into flirting and trying out the idea of being couples. First kisses, crushes, heartbreaks. We did homework reluctantly. While Steve continued to focus on grades, PSATs, SATs, Regents Exams, and AP classes, I was having exceptional success in my own way. I affected the current 1960 mod look—teased hair, white lipstick, skintight jeans, and black eyeliner—to perfection. My mother was appalled. "Do me a favor, Barbara, walk ten feet ahead of me or ten feet behind me. I don't want anyone to think I even know you."

"No problem, fine with me." At thirteen, I was officially a teenager, and embraced the distance. Her opinion was less important to me than that of my newfound friends. Her beliefs and her behavior were fodder for my newfound oppositional teenage criticism.

The big Buick might be waiting outside on any given night. Mom still had an occasional weekday evening date with the fat-headed Long Island liar. It was clear to me he hadn't moved his fat ass off the front seat of the car or improved her life in the past two years. Her new life included a full-time job at the phone company, another part-time job, and a new best friend. All of these changes were minimally important to me. I was past the point of being influenced by her new best friend, the neighborhood's biggest *yenta* (gossip). I realized my mother had a pattern of choosing undesirable female friends and unavailable men. I was no longer her neophyte and rejected the role of disciple. I had a different plan. What was primary right now was not family. I had friends, and most importantly, I was like everyone else. For the first time, I tasted the sweetness of belonging, of fitting in. This was life on the inside. It was wonderful to be accepted and included. I managed to retain everything I had observed, been taught, and valued. All the accoutrements of culture were safely and permanently etched in my brain. It was all stored there for future reference. Someday, I would value them again. They'd return to mislead me as they had my mother.

By ninth grade, I had nearly achieved nirvana. I gladly surrendered my past and was enjoying the transformation to finally fitting in. I loved the stores and the people in the neighborhood. The large hospital complex that dominated the area remained a mystery, and I could no longer resist exploring its physical presence. It was in my neighborhood, which emboldened me. I planned to stop by after school. Seeing nurses and doctors in uniform at lunch, in our stores, or sitting on a park bench for a short break intrigued me. My mother had unwittingly planted me right in a scene I may have envisioned in a Cherry Ames nurse novel. Simply watching them in their work uniforms doing things ordinary people did transformed my deities to flesh-and-blood reality that sparked my ambition. Their confidence was evident in every gesture and conversation. The ugly urban backdrop of kosher hot dogs, Yetta's Corset shop, and the noisy rambling, grumble of the number-four train above only served to elevate them to movie-star status. Everything around them receded. They were larger than life. They were celebrities in my own backyard. But they were real people just like me.

Aunt Dorothy was confident; Mrs. Bridgewater was kind. They were regular people but far removed from being the movie-star nurses and doctors working in a hospital. I needed to explore the larger landscape and greater possibilities now a part of my world.

The main entrance to the hospital was on 210th Street. It was almost on my way home. The emergency room entrance was around the corner. I had been there just six months before, when Steve was brought there from Villa Avenue. That night, there was only Steve to think about. Now, it was part of my neighborhood. Like everything else that was new, I wanted to explore the hospital in my backyard. I had graduated from barred owls and residual suburban salt marshes to concrete and steel and the life that existed within that framework.

The hospital, for most people held the same status in a neighborhood as the post office or public school, just part of the landscape. In a state of heightened awareness in my new surroundings, the hospital stood out. Receptive and curious, I thought I would just go in the main entrance and take a look. Here, the doctors and nurses were even more impressive. In their own environment, they moved about with purpose and confidence. This place was theirs. They reigned supreme. This went beyond belonging. They owned this place. I wandered a bit farther, past the main lobby. I noticed a girl my age in a pink-striped pinafore, white shirt, and white nurses' shoes. She was too young to be a nurse, but she seemed to belong here also. I needed to understand how she could be my age and be working here.

"Excuse me, can you tell me where the bathroom is?"

"Sure right over there," she pointed left.

"Do you work here?" I asked.

"No, I just volunteer on Wednesdays after school." That was all I needed to know for now. I filed the information away and didn't wait more than a couple of days to figure out how to start volunteering there myself. I took a first tentative step into my future.

Chapter Nine

HOMEOSTASIS

Homeostasis: Any self-regulatory process by which biological systems tend to maintain stability while adjusting to conditions that are optimal for survival.

—Britannica Dictionary

We achieved a state of homeostasis for the next two years. Steve maintained perfect grades and test scores. He graduated from the Bronx High School of Science and earned a full scholarship to New York University. Books and extra fees were not included, but free tuition and the ability to get to the University Heights campus from the number-four train made it a dream come true. Timing here was also good. Eventually, the University Heights campus near Fordham Road closed. NYU in lower Manhattan remained as an iconic New York City campus. Steve never took a single class there. He was happy in the Bronx where he had a few good friends, learned to drive using my mother's car, and had two summers of work as a busboy under his belt at the Spring House Hotel on

Block Island. There, he fell in love with the island and a year-round resident. Both experiences changed him for the better. He was, for now, completely happy.

My mother continued working full time at the telephone company. She enjoyed a regular salary for the first time in twenty years. Despite the dependable income, it was still never enough. There were many occasions when we scrambled in the basement to find bottles that yielded a five-cent return. This was subway money or lunch money for Steve. I babysat after school every day for an hour or two for a toddler in our building to earn my own lunch or spending money. We were still poorer than everyone I knew. Since no one was really wealthy, it was simply an impracticality. I was bothered occasionally by a clothing shortage. One navy-blue denim wrap skirt, three shirts, and a white cardigan were my entire wardrobe my junior year. That skirt became so familiar that if I close my eyes today I can imagine my hands sitting in the two front patch pockets. I didn't bother to complain; it was comfortable and indistinct. Mom dated less often now since taking a full-time job. She had a few friends at her job as well as the older *yenta* from the third floor who seemed to live in our apartment. The new best friend supplied informative minutiae about neighbors that may have interested my mother, but not me. Compared to Mary or Elaine, she was an educational lightweight. I had the impression that she kept a log of tenant illnesses, deaths, and indiscretions. I was more intrigued by her mostly missing dentures. She had become so comfortable in our apartment that the formality of teeth was abandoned. Her two remaining eye teeth seemed long against her pale-pink gums. Steve and I referred to her only as "Fang."

Mom's occasional date was still marked by a waiting Buick and anonymous, detached large head seen through the window. The Long Island liar hung on. Only the car model changed in those few years. Mom loved his Buick Riviera best. I hated all Buicks, and I hated Sal. Surely Fang had the make and license plate number of his car in her log. I hoped she kept other gory details of that affair to herself. But not much else upset me.

Her stagnant pattern of dating unavailable men tapered off but still included Sal and a man I knew as Dr. Leopold, a doctor who worked on the Upper East Side. Dr. Leopold was different in every way. She loved him, and I know that he loved her. Still, he was unavailable. I think I always knew they were in love. He existed in the shadows of my awareness for as long as I could remember. Awareness of him may even be as old as the memory I have of my father in that chair, which was permanently etched into my heart and mind when I was only three. I'm not sure when he entered her life. Neither of these two men ever thought I knew about them or realized how that knowledge later influenced me. The doctor was never a presence, just a shadowy figure. He was like the faded wallpaper you live with so long it simply recedes without thought to its pattern or color. He never intruded, and she never embarrassed me by speaking about him as if she were a teenager. There was never the last-minute primping or fresh coat of lipstick I observed before her dates with Sal. There were no silly comments about his physical appearance to embarrass me. She never mentioned his hair or eyes or voice. She was never giddy before seeing him. It felt nothing like the frivolous excitement I saw when she waited for that Buick. It was easy to dismiss his existence completely. He was always in her life and ours like an unknown element we breathed in without noticing. She was content with the smallest amounts of his "always." He doled out "always" in stingy portions, because he was unable to give more.

"Barbara, Steve, I'm going to the city to do some extra typing for Dr. Leopold. I'll be home before eleven," she'd casually announce. Monday night typing for Dr. Leopold was a long-standing work ritual, an extra job and extra money, always understood. I never questioned the logic of a trip to the Upper East Side of Manhattan from the Bronx, a two-hour round trip and gas for two hours of typing. His office was in a desirable area to serve his affluent clientele. I believed almost everything my mother told me. I never doubted that she was typing and helping out with extra, needed money. Knowledge gleaned as we grow is metabolized, internalized, and incorporated as fact. I ingested the premise of work as I ingested other facts about Dr. Leopold that were only casually mentioned. I simply grew up and older, knowing he had once been my mother's gynecologist. He had switched to psychiatry for reasons unknown to me. Perhaps it was related to insurance or license or maybe a scandal. I'm not sure. I absorbed information about his other life. He had a wife, two daughters, and a full-time secretary, who never seemed able to complete her typing. He had a large home on the waterfront in Mamaroneck. I knew when the family took European vacations. Postcards from Zurich or Paris were on our kitchen table and typing was cancelled those weeks. I knew when his daughters graduated from Fieldston and which colleges they would attend. I knew he loved her because he told her many times. The postcards and the letters were saved and hidden because she loved him and because bits of "always" were enough for her.

I found these letters one day when I was searching for something in her middle dresser drawer. I was about fifteen at the time, close to sixteen maybe. It may have been a sweater or it may have been more I was looking for. I don't remember. Her drawers were neatly lined with heavy white paper. The edges were crisply folded and fit perfectly into the drawer. That day, one edge in the rear right corner lifted up. I found the letters in a neatly tied stack.

Each one was signed, "I love you, Harold." I was not surprised. I was old and aware enough to have instinctively known. I understood then that they were making love in his office and probably not typing. I imagined a chaise in his office was a suitable substitute for a bed. No bills or patient histories were generated. Some heat may have been generated, but no bills.

He occasionally came by our house because they missed each other, I am sure. He arrived and greeted her formally for our benefit. She made him instant coffee, and he removed some papers from a large leather briefcase. They sat across from each other and spoke quietly and infrequently. She'd set up the typewriter and paper in anticipation of his arrival. My tiny, portable Smith Corona with a broken letter E was a prop that stayed, untouched, in place between them. If Steve or I came into the kitchen, we received a cursory greeting. There was never eye contact. A psychiatrist with no eye contact is a man experiencing avoidance and guilt. I would only recognize this many years later, but knew it intrinsically then.

Before I found the letters, he was unimportant to me. I considered that she was infatuated with his position and wealth, with his European manners. She had lived vicariously before. Before the letters, he was one more man dangling luxuries to blind her from a truth. I resented him more, because she was always sad after being with him. She was sad when she spoke about him. He was a persistent aching presence in her life. I think he shared that pain. He remained unavailable forever. In the final analysis their love left me with the same questions I'd always had about infidelity and men. It left questions too painful to entertain. It forced me to think about my father for the first time. Why had he really left? After the letters, I considered other possibilities and dismissed them quickly. Ultimately, did it matter at all? This man, my father, my mother's dates were all just a collective of men that added nothing good to my life. My mother's culpability or deficits were left for me to consider many years later. Even when love was part of the relationship, it was still imperfect and complicated.

For the time being, I was fifteen and needed to get on with my own dating and love life. These serious thoughts were deeply buried. They were irrelevant to me then. The letters were eventually forgotten. I didn't want to consider my mother's part in this infidelity. I still preferred to assign blame for corruption to men, and to trust my mother. I was distracted by my newfound social life. It was my time to grow and enjoy life. It was a state of twilight. Teenaged boys were not yet men. There was still time to capture lighthearted fun before considering the inevitable transition. The erosion in my ability to trust most men had already happened. The damage was done. The presence of men and the absence of men had served up equal doses of destruction to my psyche. In the early years, men were absent when they were supposed to be there to provide and protect. They were present later to corrupt my mother's sound judgment and normal thought processes. They became a virus that targeted her brain. They made her bat her eyes, speak in tongues (Yiddish), and leave her senses. They were a sexually induced chorea in her life.

If men were a necessary evil in my future, I would inoculate and immunize myself. I would never be vulnerable or influenced. I was too smart to let that happen. I understood the need to be in control. It seemed simple enough—be in control or be vulnerable. Fully immunized at fifteen, I was ready for exposure. The immunity lasted thirty years.

School was not my strength, but friends were. In spite of bad clothes, I was pretty, nice to everyone, and always ready for adventure. Fortunately, academic expectations remained low. My track record for summer school included algebra one, algebra two, and geometry. "You will never be a nurse if you don't improve your grades," my mother told me daily. By now, I had logged two years of being a candy striper at Montefiore. My intentions had been clearly stated. "You can plan on sitting at a desk and typing all day if you don't do better. Maybe selling lipstick at Woolworth's?" These were my mother's words of encouragement.

I had no intention of doing either. I had little to no concern about grades and somehow knew it would work out. I was completely happy just to belong somewhere and fit in. My mother's threats had no impact. Twilight continued to be a magical time. That same magic would enable me to be a nurse.

"Steve, please sit down with her and try to help her with homework. Just half an hour. Please." My brother always obliged her, but the half hour typically lasted ten minutes.

"Mom, she is just stupid, forget it, nothing I can do." I wasn't offended; I loved him and was proud of him. He was a good brother, and I didn't want help any more than he wanted to give it. We were on the same page. Usually, our albino parakeet perched on his shoulder when we sat to study. The parakeet had a better chance at understanding math than I did. Even without his help, I was really good at summer school and generally got an A or A minus the second time around.

I would soon add Spanish to my summer school portfolio. I was hanging in and narrowly passing, but the Regents Exam finally made me worry. New York Regents Exams often resulted in failure for me. Regents Exams required long, disciplined, and organized hours of study. I lacked the discipline or desire to devote those hours.

Do you know how much time it took to write samples of

every noun, verb, adverb, and preposition on the plantar surface of ten fingers and two palms? A great deal of time and concentration went into the plot. I was sure to pass, and I finished the test in record time.

"Niñas, permite revisar la prueba. Algien me puede decir la respuesta correcta a una pregunta?" ("Girls, let's review the test. Who can tell me the correct answer to number one?") Mrs. Vogel looked around the room. She looked directly at me.

My hand shot up. I knew that answer. I knew most of the answers! Incredibly, simply by writing and rewriting in miniature print on my fingers. I actually managed to memorize everything. I didn't have much respect for learning. Learning seemed pointless if it wasn't driven by a curiosity for the subject. Math and Spanish were boring and seemed then to have no relevance to my future. Cheating was a practical way to circumvent these obstacles. Mrs. Vogel thought otherwise. My arrogance was surpassed by my ignorance. How did I not consider the reality of a cumulative academic record? It wouldn't take much longer until I confronted this reality. A few short years later I discovered the importance of basic math in nursing. I am more than a little grateful to Mrs. Vogel for sending me straight to summer school for Spanish. It was humbling even then to be caught blatantly and carelessly cheating.

"Ahhhh haaaaaa, Senorita Barbara. *Venga conmigo, ahora.*"

Shit . . . summer school for Spanish for sure.

School wasn't all bad. I excelled in English, art, and social studies. They were subjects I loved. I was on the yearbook committee and had two pencil sketches appear in the school's literary magazine. Still, the overall picture looked bleak for higher education.

"Forget any nursing school. Your average and math grades will prevent admission," the guidance counselor told me. "You will be best off just going to night school when you graduate and then try applying." She was dismissive and disinterested. Guidance counselors seemed to spend their time talking to the smartest kids and their parents about college applications. Those of us who were underperformers for any reason were on our own. I knew I was really good at being on my own. I would consider her advice when I needed it. For now, I was having a very good time not being alone at all. I was enjoying my new friendships. Living in the present was what mattered more. It was too late to start high school over. The damage was done.

My grade point average was below average. I was probably the only person who understood I just hadn't cared to do better. I didn't care to work hard. My mother had created an arrogant academic sloth. Why waste intellectual energy when I could daydream or doodle my way through geometry? I'd just pass it later in summer school when it was easier and there was less to do. All bets were placed on my brother to excel in school. No one bothered to encourage, discipline, or support an effort until the damage was done. No one expected me to get good grades, so I didn't bother to. I never doubted I could do better. I am reminded of the joke about the five-year-old with delayed speech who utters her first words to her parents' great relief. "The soup is too hot." The parents ask the child why she hadn't spoken in all these years. "Well," she said, "until now everything was always perfect." Until now, it hadn't mattered to me either. Now that it mattered, I'd succeed on my own terms.

My social circle expanded. I had a few new friends from high school. They were friends of friends, both male and female. The original group of eight was now more than a dozen. Life was never dull. We went to several different public high schools,

DeWitt Clinton was for boys, Walton for girls, and Evander Childs was co-ed for less-serious students. In time, couples formed. We were dating, breaking up, and re-forming new couple configurations. When the dust had settled, somehow Steve Davidson and I were a couple. He was perfect for me. He was tall and skinny and had wiry, wild black hair. He'd rather talk about art than sports. He wore black turtleneck sweaters and Frye boots with bell-bottomed jeans in winter. He switched to faded plain cotton tees with Indian leather sandals in summer. He looked like an artist. I loved his mother, Jean. She was the personal secretary to the director of nurses at Montefiore, a position close to being the right hand of God in my mind. He was different than the other boys, but we all loved him. His artistic persona was respected. He had acidic, biting humor. Most of all, he preferred art to sex. Now that was a perfect man! While the other girls debated the ethics of allowing their boyfriends to get to first or second base, I was considering whether I preferred Andrew Wyeth to Edward Hopper. This was perfect. Body contact ended with holding hands. I was enjoying the first benefits of my fully engaged immunity to vulnerability or control by an almost man. I had made the perfect choice.

We cut classes and took the number four to West 4th Street in the Village. We hung out at Washington Square Park and sketched in charcoal or bought cheap canvas and attempted acrylics. We went to the Museum of Modern Art and marveled at Picasso's "Guernica" when it was installed. We enjoyed cryptic jokes and shopping for cheap, weird clothes. Before Fred Leighton became the jeweler to the rich and famous, he had a tiny shop on West 4th Street. That shop sold Mexican arts and crafts and cheap handmade jewelry. It was a destination we never missed. I still own a sterling silver ring that was crafted from the lost wax technique. It may have cost less than five dollars, but it is a Fred Leighton. It was before his fame or fortune, making it more valuable to me now. We timed those special days perfectly. We'd hop back on the number four at West 4th and be back before school dismissal time. No one knew we were not in school.

We both got our working papers and began part-time weekend and summer jobs as ward clerks on different floors of the hospital. Steve wasn't at all interested in a future in medicine. He already knew he would do something more artistic. He talked about graphic art and design in no specific terms. He shared my appreciation for living in the present. This new job offered him the simple pleasure of a small paycheck and, maybe, some added pleasure in wearing a pale-pink version of a doctor's short jacket. It looked great with his black hair and carefully selected neckties to match.

My first exposure to the reality rather than the movie-star version of nurses and doctors took place on an adult surgical unit with a head nurse that was Nurse Ratchett before the movie character had actually been created. Shelley Hopkins was not anything like my movie-star version of a nurse. She was more like one of my middle school tormentors in grown-up form. She was short and built like an English bulldog. She was a very dark-skinned middle-aged black woman with hair dyed an unnatural carrot orange. She had a scowling expression at all times. She chewed gum constantly and seemed to be looking out from under half-closed eyes. She didn't like me. At the time, I thought it was because I was young and asked too many questions. Maybe I did, but now I think the racial overtones I felt in middle school were clearly the same. As soon as I'd finished filing papers or straightening out the desk, she'd bark new orders at me. Often, they were not things in my understanding of my job description. "You," she'd say, "if you have nothing else to do grab a rag and dust off all the shelves in the utility room." She was mean and perpetually annoyed. It made no difference; I was happy with the job and had great practice at being invisible and compliant. I don't remember feeling disappointed in my first working relationship with a nurse. Not even angry, awful Shelley Hopkins could ruin this opportunity.

There was so much to hold my interest. The hospital became my learning lab. I had a small salary and was enrolled in the best program money could buy. I read patient charts as I filed lab reports. I noted abnormal lab values and checked vital sign flow sheets. I did dust the shelves and took that opportunity to become familiar with catheterization trays and drainage tubes and every type of dressing stored and piled on those shelves. This was way beyond homeostasis. This was happiness. I was working in a hospital. This was progress.

At home, we were comfortable with ourselves and each other. Mom, Steve, and I had dinner together every night. We watched TV and put up with Fang, the nosey *yenta* neighbor. We had a series of albino parakeets, all named Bubbie, that never lasted long but always preferred Steve to me. (Who didn't?) Our friends flew in and out of the house but often hung out there as well. Ours was the house kids liked best. Our mother was pretty, irreverently funny, and not too worried about feet on our secondhand furniture. She often held court as if our friends were there to visit her. For sure, we had a popular mother. Every now and then, I had the same twinge of resentment I used to have when she'd begun dating. *Who is the teenager here?* I thought. On the other hand, I was proud of her and happy we were all so liked as a family. It was my first realization that our tiny family was a perfect but tiny solar system. Some special gravitational force pulled and held us together. We each had a purpose. We had each other. There was an unrealistic belief in permanent and prolonged homeostasis.

If I could remain optimistic after working with Shelley Hopkins, everything else I'd hoped for could be mine. Wasn't it logical that having it all was part of some preordained plan that assumed balance as a natural state?

There were all the years of wanting more. I was patient all those lonely, uncertain years. I rarely complained or cried. I tried not to criticize out loud. I kept anger at bay when I could have acted out. I always knew it was just a temporary holding pattern. I never doubted that I was worthy, but just unlucky. I was always deserving of better. I was raised on a diet of intellectual arrogance; I was my mother's daughter in that way. It took adolescence and a second chance to recognize my own resolve and then to separate from my mother. I sustained myself those earlier years, depending on some intuitive optimism when I couldn't depend on anyone but my mother. Independent thought sustained me. Now optimism was not enough. My resilience was about to pay off. I was forced to consider my own strength and intrinsic worth. My luck was about to change. Resilience and resolve never left me, but I wasn't waiting for a man or anyone else to save me. I was just waiting for my luck to change and for time to move forward. Deprivation was the dark side of reward. All along I was just waiting for the planet to balance and tilt so the sun would warm me. That is what I believed.

HUBRIS

Was it hubris that we assumed a sense of well-being and security would not be exceeded by the greater chance of bad luck? I'm sure it was.

I liked the smell of the blistering August sun on city pavement. It was an amalgam of newly rained-on cement, hot tar, and day-old garbage. I liked the way the Bronx smelled in summer. The summer I was sixteen was a good Bronx summer. I repeated Spanish in summer school and got an eighty-two on the Regents Exam. It didn't get dark outside until close to nine o'clock. The old people snapped shut their webbed folding chairs around dusk, and my friends and I claimed the apartment house front stoops for the next two hours. We hung out but I can't remember what we talked about. If I were forced to recall the language of those summer nights, it would be body language. I would have a foggy image of laughter and young bodies in constant motion, sitting, standing, posturing. I would remember being happy. I would remember the lovely, rough warmth of the trapped heat on granite steps against the bare backs of my thighs.

My brother had a different kind of sun-blessed summer.

This was his second summer bussing tables and washing dishes at the Spring House Hotel on Block Island. He loved the constant ocean breeze and rolling green hills. I suspect he loved the time away from us almost as much. He had earned a 3.9 GPA in his freshman year at NYU and couldn't wait to be away.

When he returned the last week of August, he seemed to resent everything that was in contrast to his summer away. He only casually mentioned a girlfriend from Block Island and a nasty cut on his foot. The cut and his demeanor were equally angry. "I forgot how ugly this street was," was his greeting to Mom and me.

"Thanks," I answered. "We missed you also."

Within a week, he fell back into old friendships and routines. He was looking forward to his sophomore year and new courses at school. Labor Day was only days away. The delicate shift between summer and fall was barely perceptible. But evenings were cooler and the planet was shifting. It was wobbling away from the warmth and comfort of summer. Looking back, I believe the delicate balance had fostered a false sense of security. School was around the corner, and life was about to change.

School began, and Steve's schedule was variable. Sometimes we left together in the morning to hop on the number four together. I was sixteen and a junior at Walton High School. We sprinted down Mosholu Parkway, bought a hot bagel or bialy, and continued to run up the clunky iron herringbone-embossed stair treads. We took them two at time, felt for a token in our pockets, squeezed through the turnstile, and made the train. I exited at Kingsbridge Road, offering a casual offhanded goodbye. He continued on to Burnside Avenue to walk to University Heights. We didn't think about each other again until we ended up together for supper. That carefree innocence would soon end for us and for everyone else. A new version of insecurity and pain was about to enter our lives. Two profound events were about to alter our universe. Balance is a precarious state.

November 22, 1963, was the first event. The assassination of JFK stopped the world in its tracks.

Ms. Reiger was at the blackboard for seventh-period geometry. I was ignoring her and the blackboard. I did take note that she was wearing the same shapeless dress for the second time that week. It had a beige background and interlocking purple squares. Even her dress was geometric in spirit, surely her favorite. After analyzing her dress, I focused on the graph paper in front of me. The grid had a large isosceles triangle in its center. I had doodled climbing, twisting vines emerging from each corner. Where flowers might have sprouted, large, soulful eyes stared in full blossom. Not a single straight line on my creation . . . pretty. The graceful curves of my drawing were in sharp contrast to straight lines and angles of the graph paper.

Above Ms. Reiger, the PA speaker suddenly scratched and crackled to life . . . a quick screech. It was an unusual time of day for an announcement. The voice of Mrs. Heffernan, our principal, was next. Her somber tone was even slower and more serious than usual.

"Teachers, students, please be seated and silent for an announcement." Then she paused. "I have received word that President Kennedy has been shot while on a trip to Dallas." She paused again to summon her strength. "We have now been informed that the President has died. . . . President John Fitzgerald Kennedy is dead. . . . Classes will be dismissed at the end of this period." *Scratch, screech,* static, silence.

I am certain of the silence. No one spoke. No one cried. No one screamed. I don't remember hushed whispers, although there probably were. I only remember faces and profound silence. The silence can only be compared to the absolute quiet experienced when submerging your head under water. We left robotically.

The number-four train should have been near empty late afternoon, northbound on a weekday, but instead it was packed. Standing room only. Each seat was occupied. Each hand strap wore a hand connected to a dangling arm and silent human. So many people crowded into the space. They could lean into each other without falling as the train moved forward, rocking left to right. What was also different was the eye contact. It is an unwritten rule of subway etiquette and safety that eye contact is best avoided. But that day, eyes looked at eyes and other faces. They searched as if to acknowledge their shared shock and grief. I thought they resembled my isosceles eyes.

I searched in hopes of finding my brother. If everyone, everywhere had left what they were doing to go home, then maybe he was also on this train. I looked over and around the others. I looked in between when any space appeared. He wasn't there. I wanted him to be there. I needed him to be there. I longed for his presence.

By 5:00 p.m. we and everyone else were gathered with family in front of the television, and we would remain there for the next few days without moving. We were glued as we watched in real time the images that would become iconic for generations to follow. The Kennedys and their Camelot were taken. The air and energy seemed sucked out of everyone. It seemed as if the TV was on all the time, and we were tethered to it. So great was our incomprehension that the solemn voices and surreal images projecting from the small screen became our navigational guides. Incapable of meaningful speech or comforting interactions, we sat passively absorbing information and grieving collectively with millions. Our small apartment was silent when the television was off. We ate, slept, read, cried, and watched without the need to say anything in our own voices. Silence had never been the culture of our family. Silence prevailed for almost a week. In the face of this new silence, we hadn't noticed that Steve's silence was accompanied by fatigue.

Steve was tired. He was less able to stay awake late to study. He, too, lacked energy. "Are you okay?" my mother asked. She was beginning to think it was more than second-year complacency or a continuation of the national "hangover" we all felt. It was now mid-December, and life as we had known it was resuming. Steve conscientiously did his work but seemed to take to bed whenever he could.

"Just tired, and I think I may have caught a cold. I feel warm." His temperature was ninety-nine that first time. Later, it would hover between ninety-nine and one hundred. After a week, she thought it was time to see a doctor. He seemed anxious to rest as soon as he came home from school. His normal routine had been to tackle homework before dinner or spend an hour with friends.

"Probably a cold or virus, just some aspirin and rest, he'll be fine" was the opinion of the first resident who saw him. A week later, a new symptom accompanied the low-grade fever. There were small, pin-prick red spots covering his feet, ankles, and fingertips. On the return trip to the emergency room, he got a different doctor.

"Mother," the self-assured young doctor addressed her, "do you see how the rash is on both feet and stops exactly at the sock line on each? That is called contact dermatitis. Switch detergents and it will go way." My mother felt she was being casually dismissed.

"But doctor, it doesn't itch, and he still has a fever."

"Well, I see you were here last week because he was tired and had a fever of ninety-nine." He looked at his notes, no eye contact. In a singsong light voice now, "So . . . he's a college kid, probably burning the candle at both ends. He has no cough, no big change in temp." Again he urged her to change detergents and stop worrying.

My mother was incensed at his flippant attitude. Within earshot of the young doctor, she began speaking as they left the room. "Arrogant little schmuck. Who does he think he was speaking to? Some moron? What a little asshole. I haven't changed detergent in ten years. We need to get a doctor."

Keening—there is no vocalization quite like it. It is not like crying or whimpering. It is not screaming. It is a sound that starts with suffering of some kind and passes through the soul before it passes the mouth as sound. Sometime in the early-morning hours of a cold January night, that was what we heard.

"What, what is that? Steve? Oh, God, it sounds like Steve." We followed the sound to his room to find him lying on his side clutching his head between his hands.

"Uh, ugh, pain . . . head . . . uh . . . help," was all he could utter.

"Stay with him," my mother ordered. "I am getting the car. When I come back, we will get him into the car together."

She ran out, decisively, calmly, and quickly. "Where are we going?" I asked, now totally awake and totally frightened.

"We are going to New York Hospital. We need a big city hospital, a teaching hospital."

She seemed to have known facts I didn't understand. "If we take the FDR at this hour, it will be fast," and she was right. We made it to the hospital in record time. She parked in the circular, cobblestoned driveway in front of the emergency room and bolted out of the car, leaving us in the back seat. Steve was quiet. I thought he may be dead. I was numb.

I have forgotten most of the details from that particular night and those first few hours of a new saga. The prolonged nightmare that followed would be harder to forget. I would be spending more time than I could ever have imagined in a hospital.

For the next long weeks, New York Hospital would be both home and prison to all of us. We were tethered and unable to escape a horrific reality. I became an extraneous nonparticipant. The awful pain, the fever, the rash, the exhaustion were not symptoms of an allergic reaction to detergent or too much schoolwork. It was obvious from those first minutes in the emergency room that he was critically ill. His symptoms and his neurological exam were suggestive of an eighteen year old having a cerebral vascular accident. The grinding wheels of diagnosing, treating, and monitoring his condition and future had been set in motion. Again, we were speechless and powerless in the face of an event that seemed to steal the ground from under us. We were left to balance the daily rituals, which required nothing more than simple movement forward.

The number-four train became my welcomed sanctuary. The daily trip after school was a relief from the burden of school and a respite from the awaiting nightmare of the hospital. I was a homing pigeon. Mindlessly riding between Kingsbridge Road and 68th Street and York Avenue. I disliked Manhattan. I disliked it with the same energy my brother disliked the Bronx. I disliked the absence of shopping-cart ladies and candy stores. I missed the ugly, stooped, grizzled old people on their folding chairs. The Upper East Side was sleek and slick and self-important.

New York Hospital was nestled on the banks of the East River, just a bit north of Sutton Place and easy walking distance to Madison, Park, and Fifth Avenues. This was, and still is, the epicenter of New York affluence. Some streets had lovely brownstones with elaborate wrought iron bannisters and five-foot-long windows shielded by warm wood shutters. Other streets had elegant postwar apartment buildings with terraces and corner casement windows. The pigeons were discouraged from settling on any horizontal surface by metal spikes, which capped rooftops and garden gates. The rock dove, or pigeon as it is more commonly known, is part of New York's living landscape. But they are discouraged from getting too comfortable on the Upper East Side. People here looked down on pigeons, and I thought they looked down on me. People looked better here, more polished and purposeful. They dared you to look like them and to fit in. I did not. Once again, I was an outsider. I didn't belong here. I wasn't as good. I hated this part of the city.

The joy of being sixteen is in having the beginning of insight, which told me that I preferred not to fit in here. I remembered that I hated wealthy, perfectly dressed women. On autopilot, I exited at Lexington and 68th, walked past Park and Madison. I walked past Second and Third to York. Finally, the Gothic gray buildings faced me. Through the elegant cobblestone circular driveway of the main entrance. First elevator, corridor, second corridor, elevator, corridor, corridor. The neurological unit. I had arrived. But why was I here anyway? I remained invisible.

There was no pleasure in being in this hospital for this reason. I felt none of the excited anticipation that I had whenever I walked into the main lobby of Montefiore as an insider, as someone with a position and purpose. I didn't want to look at all the details that fascinated me before. Now, they were those things to do with illness and pain and maybe death. They were things that had no business in my brother's life or in mine. These were details I wanted to reject. As a child, I learned to observe and even ruminate on the details available to me when I felt alone. They brought me a measure of comfort and an activity. That loneliness was gone. I didn't need to fill that void. I came to this place every day because there was a void in the place my little family lived. No one was at the apartment after school. The little white parakeet waited on the kitchen window sill, and the neighbor waited upstairs for news, but our apartment was empty and quiet. I didn't want to be with friends, because I simply couldn't be happy or think of much beside what might be happening at any moment in the hospital. And so, that is where I robotically headed every day.

I often felt that existence here was like being in a sinister snow globe. Doctors and nurses were no more than white flecks of particulate. They circled and swirled around Steve. They lit upon him and then fell away. The movement was constant but unpredictable. I watched this dance of the white flecks with boredom and fear. It seemed like hours of sitting on uncomfortable leatherette chairs at his bedside or in a visitor lounge. Hours just watching and thinking. Hours of boredom laced with fear.

In the very same year I spent traveling to New York Hospital, New York City was hosting the 1964 World's Fair in Flushing Meadows Corona Park. The crown jewel of the event was the temporary installation of Michelangelo's sculptural masterpiece "Pietà," which translates to "Pity." It was on view at the Vatican Pavilion. Viewed through bulletproof, floor-to-ceiling Plexiglas, it was surrounded by vertical strips of votive candles and set against a deep-blue celestial drape. The statue and backdrop demanded piety and respect. The seminal work, depicting Mary as she held the newly dead Jesus, was breathtaking. Thousands of onlookers viewed the *objet d'art* daily. They waited in line for hours to finally step onto a mobile walkway that faced the statue. They moved at two miles an hour, a rate which afforded them perhaps thirty seconds to behold and commit to memory the treasure. This was not a snow globe. This seemed to be universally relatable. Regardless of religion, the tragedy was compelling. I visited the Fair when it opened in April. Like all the others, I moved on a conveyor belt looking forward and moving sideways. I thought of death. Everyone seemed so reverent. I knew that their reverence would last as long as the lighting in the room dictated it to last. My sadness didn't lift as easily.

Medical students and neurological interns and residents gazed at Steve as if he were an insensate statue, unaware of their gaze. They came in groups of five or six or more. They discussed him as he lay there listening and understanding. He was objectified, but not perhaps relatable. Many of them were not much older than their patient. The young male interns were the lucky ones. They were the smart ones, the rich ones, the healthy ones. I believed they had wealthy parents and grew up in split-level homes in the suburbs. They went to rich kids' camps or fat kids' camps in the summer. They were privileged and spoiled. They had a semester abroad and ate in restaurants. Maybe they weren't spoiled, but it didn't matter to Steve or to me. They were lucky, and he was not. Maybe they weren't really spoiled, but it didn't matter. It wasn't their fault that he was sick. They were just strangers. But they were strangers that reminded us of our bad luck. I hated them for being lucky. It was easy to displace my anger onto these smug-looking young men dressed up as the doctors they would become.

The white jackets had bullseye targets over the breast pockets that held their nametags. I shot poison darts at their healthy young hearts. *Get away from my brother,* I thought. *Leave him alone, or I'll shoot you in your heart.* I had perfected the art of soothing imagery and silent voice way back in fourth grade when I imagined the faint sound of a cracking skull as the heavy, hated wall clock fell and landed on Mrs. Wilson's head. Now I was a wild Indian with poison darts, a fully engaged taut bow, and the power to annihilate the interns. I knew he was as smart, handsome, and ambitious as any of them. They could not have known my anger or his resentment as they approached his bed. They were on their own observers' conveyor belt.

They stood over and around him. He looked up at them and spoke. Steve's anger and coping mechanisms were unlike mine. He may not have thought about good or bad luck. He probably understood that these strangers were there to take something from him and give nothing in return. He understood these strangers were there to learn. He presented an interesting lesson, much better than any textbook. They offered nothing in return for what he gave them. All they could give him was a reminder of his miserable plight. I believe he was outraged at the inequity. I sat right next to him as he let loose.

"Get . . . the . . . fuck . . . away . . . from . . . me. I do not want company, but thanks for asking! Show's over, get lost." He hated the constant teaching and gawking. Sometimes, he would simply turn on his side and pretend to be asleep. When they left, he would quietly weep.

My mother's patience was wearing thin. Days and days of IVs, antibiotics, blood work, and x-rays had not relieved his suffering. He endured two agonizing and nauseating carotid angiograms, which proved more traumatic and painful than expected. She was aware of grave expressions, of heightened interest around him. She noted the way grand rounds culminated with Steve as if he were the main attraction. She was smart enough to understand an unusual situation. Her fears were not unfounded and growing. Like Steve, she grew emboldened, becoming more a participant than witness. She found her voice.

"I need to speak with the chief resident today," she told the nurse in charge. It was now February, and Steve had been in the hospital for two weeks while they analyzed, stabilized, and considered a plan for him. She had signed permission forms and waited for results. She had used up all her sick time and vacation time at work. She had been patient and trusting, but now she needed answers. "I will be waiting and expecting to speak with him today." She was commanding in her request for answers. She no longer worried about being out of line. The doctor arrived later that day and escorted her to a small conference room.

"Mrs. Payne, let me explain exactly what we think has happened here and what the next steps might be. Please stop me at any time if there are questions or for any reason." He spoke in a measured mix of medical and lay terminology. He continuously confirmed her ability to understand. Her understanding was key to her ability and willingness to consent to what he was about to propose.

He continued patiently and laboriously to explain. He watched her face to determine how much detail to include. I sat with my mother and listened to his explanation. She rose respectfully to her full five-foot-eight-inch height. She wasn't much shorter than he was. I knew how anxious she was because she quietly fiddled with the flexible metal Speidel watchband on her left wrist. I'd seen her do this before. Usually it was when she was angry and formulating an acerbic response. This time, she wasn't searching for her own words but digesting his. As he spoke, she snapped it against her wrist, twisted it, and even turned it inside out. The band was not as gently manipulated as

Greek worry beads or a rosary. She needed more than reflective comfort. He continued to speak.

"I need to begin with what we know and understand. The excruciating headache was a symptom of blood leaking into his brain causing pressure. The angiograms revealed two large aneurysms in separate blood vessels on either side of his brain. They are, unfortunately, both deep and not near each other. One is near his left temple and the other on the opposite side of his head, a little farther back. The area is called the parietal area. This is an important area of the brain because it controls speech and language." She twisted the band and worked it rapidly as she slowly, very slowly, stepped back. Her eyes never left his face. I watched as she seemed to float back and lower herself into the navy-blue vinyl love seat she usually slept in. I never doubted she would reach it safely. She and that love seat seemed bonded to me. The placement of furniture and room dimensions here were as familiar now as our own home. As she sat, he spoke. I remained seated in my own matching vinyl chair, in my own matching fear. "Aneurysms are like little bulges or bubbles along the walls of a blood vessel. If they are very big, the wall is thinned out and may leak or rupture."

We knew something had happened in his brain. We knew the headaches had to do with bleeding. We knew what a stroke was because everyone had heard of that. Neither of us had ever known about aneurysms. We assumed he had a stroke, which was getting better. We assumed he was being watched this long because of his age.

Now, we were becoming aneurysm experts. We learned the dangers of untreated strep infections and were experiencing the worst-case scenarios and outcomes when the bacteria went unchecked. Strep liked to settle in the heart valves and wreak havoc. We had new words, not Scrabble words, but medical jargon that we incorporated into our vocabulary. We understood endocarditis and myocarditis and mitral and bicuspid heart valves and petechiae and clubbing of nails. We listened intently and with a degree of disbelief. I had trouble imagining fulminating microorganisms, larvae-like creatures in my brother's heart, and more problems, envisioning weakly flapping heart valves that should be crisply and urgently pumping blood. It was repulsive and unfair. I was angry at the bacteria.

My mother's anger was directed inward. Without being told how this may have happened, she held two possible explanations. She believed the bacteria had entered his body through the uncleaned and deep cut he returned home with in August. She was therefore angry at herself for allowing him to be away and then for dismissing the wound as it healed over. Although the doctors never speculated about or discussed the origins of the strep, she was fixated on its causes. She believed that for almost three months the bacteria had multiplied. Every day, she thought, they divided and multiplied and mercilessly took up occupancy in his previously healthy eighteen-year-old body. Incensed at the damage, she needed a responsible person to blame for what she understood could have been prevented. She was angry at the emergency room doctors, who had seen her son twice in December and dismissed what she now clearly understood were signs and symptoms of an untreated strep infection. The persistent low-grade fever, the pinprick red dots on his ankles and fingers were textbook warning signs. But they'd dismissed her; they dismissed the signs. They'd neglected Steve, and they allowed the bacteria to settle in his heart and chew away at his valves and cluster and clump and form a blood bullet called an embolism that shot up to the blood vessels in his brain and stretched them to a breaking point so they exploded. Perhaps they'd dismissed her because she was poor and single and had no personal doctor that knew or cared.

In my own struggle to understand the causes, I believed that if my brother had both a mother and father things may have been different. Maybe the emergency room doctor would not have so readily dismissed a worried father and mother. Maybe we would even have had a real family doctor to go to instead of an emergency room. We didn't have a regular doctor or a regular father. These men were not there to protect Steve. I could add my brother's illness to the list of reasons not to depend on men. I dismissed that anger to concentrate instead on the man who was explaining what could be done.

"If the strep is treated," the doctor said, "further damage will be halted. Arteries are elastic, and he is young, but the priority is to repair the aneurysms. Later, we will consider the damage to his heart. But time is not on our side. If there is a rupture, he could have a fatal stroke. The depth of one is a particular surgical challenge. It is a high-risk procedure. We have spent the last weeks discussing the risks and benefits of surgery and best surgical approaches. Unfortunately, the only option is surgery to repair the damage. Tomorrow, you will meet Dr. Russell Patterson. He is a fellow here and a specialist in this surgery. He is willing to take on the challenge and is the best person to do it. You are very lucky that he is available and able to do the surgery. Dr. Patterson has been studying Stephen's situation and recently cleared his calendar and assembled a team to proceed.

"Tomorrow he will explain his plan and exactly what needs to be done to get Stephen well again." The resident's words were comforting. Mom welcomed the first suggestion of hope. He nodded and left us sitting side by side and speechless. My mother was still. She hadn't touched her watchband or spoken a single word. He had her undivided attention.

Lucky? Isn't that a relative concept? I thought when the doctor told my mother we were lucky. I didn't think any of us were particularly lucky people. I hated the concept of luck completely. It wasn't doled out fairly. It was given out randomly and sometimes to undeserving people. And now, just as I was feeling lucky because I had a neighborhood I liked, because I belonged and had nice friends and a boyfriend and passed Spanish with an eighty-two and was grateful for my little family and the great plan I had for my future, my luck had changed. My good luck was tarnished. Instead of joy each time I entered a hospital, I had fear. Each hospital visit reminded me of what I might lose rather than what I had hoped to gain. Now, the hospital was a place I didn't want to belong in. This reversal of fate handed me a reversal of roles to consider. My brother's life was at risk, yet I felt as vulnerable as he was. I couldn't imagine life without my brother or life with a handicapped brother. It occurred to me that we were helplessly dependent on everyone here.

Two classes of people lived and worked in this building. Their roles and status were clearly defined. I realized that patients and their families were compromised and dependent. Their lives and identity were on hold. Illness had stolen their autonomy. The doctors, nurses, and other staff held complete power. Their lives and identities were bound to this building in a positive and empowered way. I longed to change places. I longed for their power. For now, we were in a holding pattern I couldn't escape. For now, I had no option but to accept second-class status in this building. I now wanted to be a nurse more than ever. I had to believe Steve would recover and my own future would go as planned.

In time, of course, we would appreciate that luck was in fact on our side this time. It seemed that Dr. Patterson was at a critical point in the development of the technique he would use to repair the aneurysms.

Chapter Eleven

LUCKY

Dr. Patterson had pioneered the use of deep hypothermia for use in neurosurgery. To remove and repair the aneurysms he would use the technique not once, but twice, in procedures weeks apart if all went well. He would cool the body temperature to 5 degrees Celsius and the brain to 12 degrees Celsius. At that point he would drain the blood from the body. The heart would slow and stop. Surgery would be performed on an almost-dead person. These were the details the resident had promised Dr. Patterson could explain. My mother asked questions he couldn't answer. "In your experience," she asked, "do patients suffer less brain damage than with traditional surgery?" There were no previous patients to refer to. "What if he can't be warmed and his heart re-started?" she asked. He reassured her that he was confident it would. Finally, she asked her last two questions. "Will he be aware, awake, or in pain during surgery?"

The simple answer was a comforting, "No."

"When will you know if it is successful?" That question could only be answered in time. The next six weeks were measured not by hours or days but by constant monitoring for signs of recovery. We had no idea when he explained how unknown it all was for everyone.

Dr. Patterson was compassionate and honest. "This is in no way routine surgery. There are risks of damage to his brain as in any brain surgery. There is a risk of death in any surgery. This is unchartered territory, but it has been meticulously researched and planned. I believe," he said, "it's his best chance for returning to normal."

Mother understood completely and trusted him as well. I remember how she loved his sparkling blue eyes and confidence. She signed the consent form. Surgery was scheduled in two days.

"Barbara," my mother said, only hours after speaking to the doctor. We sat on our matching vinyl chairs in our hospital home. At last I was included, considered, though not really. "Your brother is scheduled for surgery in two days. It is very risky, and he may not survive. I think we need to call your father. Any parent needs to know this kind of thing. He doesn't deserve to, but I am calling him tonight. I am sure he will want to see both of you."

This news was almost as unsettling to me as the surgical risk. I had not seen or spoken to my father in more than six years. He left when I was three and then was absent in my life until I was ten. In those seven years, my awareness of him had only to do with an occasional long-winded letter and a check for sixty-five dollars that arrived every month or two or three. She read his letters to me. She was always disdainful of his whining about money and what she called "affected, phony, flatulent language." She read his words aloud with her own sarcastic intonations. He had beautiful handwriting. I loved his perfect cursive penmanship. Every first letter of a new sentence began with an oversized, curling font. The writing made me feel he was special in some way I didn't understand.

He visited once when I was ten. I remember my mother explaining he had a short visit to New York and wanted to take us to dinner. My brother refused to go. She refused to go. She encouraged me to go. Obediently, I sat next to the stranger, who held my hand across the gear-shift panel in a rented car. The stranger's hand unsettled me, and I was speechless. Odd that my two most vivid memories of my father are of his swinging foot as he sat in the French chair when I was three and then of his warm, large, and unfamiliar hand when I was ten. I don't remember words but do remember his voice. Now I was being asked again to entertain the stranger. I wasn't ten years old anymore, but I was obedient.

Holy shit! I thought. That is what my mother, in her own words, would define as "insult to injury." I was terrified for my brother. I was terrified for myself and the prospect of living without him. I was angry for all of it. I was angry for becoming invisible as this drama went forward. I ate alone, traveled alone, sometimes did homework alone, and no one cared. Now I had to face seeing my father alone. I remembered his last visit when Mom and Steve bailed out on being with him. There was no question in my mind about this visit. Steve would never want to see him and my mother would be too preoccupied to bother with him. How was I supposed to handle this? I no longer knew which was greatest. Fear or anger? Would simple obedience get me through this again?

They shaved Steve's head the night before the first surgery. Oddly, they only shaved half his head. It looked as if a madman had drawn a perfectly straight line down the center and shaved from forehead to nape of neck. Half his head had a ridiculous long ridge of thick brown hair against the stark baldness of the other half. It was ugly and disgusting and humiliating. It was beyond belief. I doubt he had any idea of how freakish he looked. He was, I was sure, paralyzed with fear. A half-shaved head was just one more thing out of his control.

This sight, more than anything I had seen or heard or imagined in the past two weeks of his hospitalization, was the first thing that brought me to tears. *What had happened to my perfect brother? Tomorrow at this time,* I thought, *would he even be alive?* I deliberately sat myself on the side of the bed that faced the unshaven hair. It was easier to hold back the tears on that side.

The night before surgery proved to be unpleasant in other ways. There were visitors. My father was on his way to New York. I had no idea when he was arriving. I knew my aunt and uncle would visit also. Having to entertain unwanted guests was challenging. It was unbearable to speak and act normally. There was no energy left to be sociable. It was ludicrous to entertain guests. These were unwanted guests for sure. It ended badly.

Aunt Dorothy and Uncle Walter came to the hospital that evening and brought flowers. Something any eighteen-year-old boy would surely appreciate. Aunt Dorothy went immediately into nurse mode. She straightened sheets, checked his IV. She looked over the flow sheets on a clipboard at the foot of his bed. Uncle Walter made one or two corny jokes about Steve's new haircut. She continued to assess the equipment around him. She ran her hand across the bed rail, now in the up position and looking like a crib. She lifted it slightly to make sure it was engaged and locked. *How dare she?* I thought. *How dare she escape to align with the privileged class of nurses and doctors?* She had chosen power and control over compassion. She hadn't once touched him or spoken to him. Maybe she would have if she'd had the chance. Maybe she was afraid and inept when illness threatened to come too close. Perhaps she needed to ease into the miserable sight of him in a clinical way before she could be his aunt. But she had missed the opportunity to comfort him. It was too late to redeem herself.

Steve leaned over the bed rail. He stretched across and over the railings. He was trying to locate an object he needed. He grasped the nearly full stainless silver urinal. He gripped the handle over the flat depression of its side. It seemed as if he was considering if it would be a vase for the flowers she brought. He lifted it as if in offering. Slowly at first and then with great force, his arm arched above his half-shaven head. With great force, he threw it directly at Aunt Dorothy.

"Leave . . . now . . . please."

Just those three words were enough. Those words and a coat saturated with urine that smelled strongly of penicillin sealed the deal. Wordlessly, they left. *Hooray, Steve!* My mother was seated against a far wall of the two-bedded room. The other bed was unoccupied, and we were grateful for the extra chair. After initially greeting them she sat there to allow them to visit. Now, she remained seated and seemed silently shocked. It was time for her to decide which side to choose. Power and control were not her issues. Compassion was at the heart of her decision. She stood and went directly to Steve. I heard the elevator bell ding and was sure they rode indignantly down to the main level in shocked silence.

Next was my turn. Since the business of meeting and greeting my father had been relegated to me, I had not given it much more thought. But now, I was ready. My anger was fueled by my brother's outburst. I took my cue from him. We didn't need to be polite or respectful. This was war. Our army of three was armed for battle.

Steve, in his hospital gown and half-shaved head, was exceptionally quiet. There was little any of us could say. We sat in silence and waited, each of us locked in private thought.

Dr. Patterson had been to see Steve earlier. He explained the pre-op stuff and reassured him he would be asleep and unaware of the surgery. He told him he would be there when he woke up to greet him. He spared him the details of aneurysm clips, bone saws, and chilled blood. We all understood the risk. Silence seemed most appropriate. We were sitting in the room quietly when we became aware of voices and evening visitors arriving. My mother and I stood and ventured out as Steve seemed to be asleep or feigning sleep.

The elevator doors opened and several people emerged. One was my father, wearing light-colored slacks and a linen shirt. I knew this stranger immediately. His features matched mine exactly. He walked toward us. He simply said hello to us and put a hand on my shoulder to signal it would be my turn to speak after he talked to Mom. I understood the urgency of sharing medical information first. I went into Steve's room and waited. My parents spoke outside the room for a few minutes. Muted voices and serious expressions were all I could glean as I left to rejoin them in the hallway. He turned toward me and gave me a loose hug and weird head nuzzle.

"Barbara, how about you have dinner with us?"

Us? Who was "us"? My mother was not leaving the bedside for a minute tonight. He turned to expose a silent young woman standing timidly behind him.

"Oh, sorry, this is Liz," he said, a big sheepish smile on his face. *Who the hell is Liz?* I thought. Was she a stepdaughter, his secretary, a girlfriend? My father, a stranger to me, had brought another stranger.

"Let's go to the cafeteria and eat and then come upstairs."

Okay, I thought, *this is my chore.* I understood this was a non-negotiable task.

Liz wore Florida clothes also. This furthered the strangeness of their presence. They and their clothes were misplaced, out of season, out of place. She was petite and had shiny long black hair. I could only get that kind of hair by weighing it down with empty soup cans. Blunt cut, stick-straight hair that moved in wavelike slow motion with the slightest head tilt was the beauty standard for anyone under thirty. For those of us with natural curls or hated frizz, the answer was either store-bought jumbo plastic rollers or empty soup cans. Removing both ends of an empty soup can produces a superior heat-conducting jumbo-sized metal roller. When rolled onto wet or damp hair and dried, it yielded almost straight hair, as long as the enemy humidity didn't counteract the effort. My collection included Campbell's Cream of Tomato or Mushroom soup.

I just knew her hair had never seen a soup can. My trained eye recognized the genetic gift of naturally occurring straight hair. Each strand of hair as obedient in its duty as I was now. That was reason enough to hate her on sight. She looked ridiculous in her sleeveless minidress and even more outrageous with my father. I guessed she was around twenty or twenty-one. I felt fat and frizzy and ugly in her presence. I was aware of rising anger toward her. *Who are you?* I thought. *Why are you here?* I had before me a natural enemy. It was so natural for an insecure and ordinary-looking sixteen-year-old to instantly hate this perfect specimen for no good reason at all. But I had solid reasons to justify my mounting anger. Certainly, the real enemy was my father at this moment. But there was nothing natural about hating a father you didn't even know. There were so many questions to ask and accusations to hurl at the man I looked too much like. Those questions were on my mind, but now was not the time for complex questions or conflicted loyalty. Now, my brother's life hung in the balance, and I was disgusted by these strangers in stupid clothes, who distracted me from the business of giving all my energy to thoughts of my brother. I was barely able to breathe because I was now enraged. Robotically, I walked through the now-familiar labyrinth of corridors. I took the lead because I knew the path so well. They followed me obediently, I thought. I imagined they were holding hands now. I picked up my pace to challenge them a bit. *Let's go, guys. Pick up your pace because I feel a power surge coming on.* By the time we got there, I thought I'd be ready to do more than eat. I'd be ready for battle.

We went to the basement in another building to get to the cafeteria. You could smell its steamy, overcooked medley of food scent immediately. We took our plastic trays and began to slide them along the counter. We surveyed gelatinous Salisbury steak, smoothed-over mashed potatoes, and a large tray of yellow pudding.

My father took a bowl of chicken soup. I chose the pudding (of course), and little Liz pushed an empty tray along the rails. She looked like a deer in headlights for sure. I thought she looked frozen. It was as if she knew the slightest movement of her head would activate a smooth swing of her perfect hair and send me even deeper into my hate hole for her. Perhaps she had a primitive survival instinct. I wondered later if the hunter takes a last look at the lovely deep, warm, brown eyes of a deer before he pulls the trigger. She was as still as the deer hoping to blend into the background to confuse the hunter. I was not confused.

It was busy. Doctors, nurses, and visiting family were all trying to squeeze in a quick meal. They all queued up in a very slow line. The line didn't seem to be moving.

"So, Dad, who is Liz?" I asked casually, with a big phony smile. Liz looked down at her tray and hung back a little. She may have sensed some primal female rage emanating from me. She may even have felt warm in her silly sleeveless dress. We were too close in age. She got the vibe. They may have even expected some discomforting questions. They were, however, caught off guard. After all, they had to have hoped I'd be distracted by the greater issue at hand. My father may also have remembered my previous silence and obedience from a visit six years earlier. But this was sixteen-year-old me. I was better at expressing myself and good at channeling anger to its proper place. The ten year old he may have remembered was nowhere to be found.

"Liz is my friend," he replied, giving my shoulder a paternal pat.

"Dad, is Liz your friend or your girlfriend?"

"Both," he said, too quickly now. His eyes on mine, testing the waters.

The headlights of my eyes were now shining directly at the deer, or should I say, the doe. I was neatly poised to spring the fatal arrow.

"Liz, what high school do you go to?" I asked, coyly waiting for response.

Liz was stunned silent. She was definitely going to need my daddy to help her out here. I left no time for either of them to reply. Now my anger was rocket fuel. These two were about to be launched as far away from me as possible. I wanted to be sure I'd never have to see either of them again. I may even have wanted them dead, but outer space would suffice. "So, Dad, you're basically fucking someone a couple of years older than me. Do you think you could have managed to leave her home and made the trip alone?" The clanking of dishes and cutlery, the background voices were eclipsed by expectant silence. Wow, I had an audience. Better yet!

"So, why don't you guys enjoy dinner and while you're in New York catch a show. I have to get back upstairs, good-bye." This time, they didn't follow me obediently. I imagine they found their way out of the hospital and hailed a cab.

He wasn't there the next day or the next or the next or actually, ever again.

Hooray, Barbara! My outburst was cathartic. The new anger at Steve's illness and any remnants of old rage at past slights I'd endured created a verbal attack that may have, years before, been only silent comforting thoughts. Now they were real life bullets that inflicted a beautiful, fatal wound. Now, I was empowered and ready for the real battle. The next day, we needed to be warriors.

The first repair took forty-three minutes. Two weeks later, the second procedure was successfully completed in just twenty-nine minutes. These two procedures were the genesis of all modern neurosurgical techniques. They are considered landmarks, and Dr. Patterson an iconic pioneer. Steve's reward was not fame but continued life. For the next six weeks, we tracked progress rather than time. At first we waited for him to wake up, then to move fingers and hands and feet. Next, we asked him to blink or shake his head yes or no to simple questions. His speech returned slowly. At first the chosen words made no sense and his articulation was sloppy. He was aphasic. He sounded like an old person who'd had a stroke. My mother worried about it being permanent. She remembered Dr. Patterson's explanation of the parietal lobe.

But each day he improved. He had therapists and nurses, and now he even had a roommate. The next bed was occupied by another eighteen year old needing heart surgery. They became friends. Kenny and his parents spent their days and evenings contained with us in the two-bedded room, shared by young men whose lives were on hold. The only nod to privacy was a pale-yellow curtain on a shower rod that was pulled when doctors consulted, or if either of them needed a urinal or bed pan. There was an intimacy only possible in the face of illness or death. We witnessed each other's greatest fears. There could be no facade—other than shared fear and shattered plans, we had little in common. They lived in Short Hills, New Jersey, an affluent community. They owned a house and took vacations to the Hamptons in summer. They were a family with a father and a mother. Just for now, illness had leveled the playing field, and we were equals, friends even. We had something most important in common, and our families formed an elite inner circle of shared experience uniquely ours. But then the roommate left the hospital and the bond was broken. Kenny recovered quickly, and their family reclaimed their lives. We all understood the common ground was temporary. We all wanted the ground we shared to be a fading memory. There was no reluctance in letting go.

In just a few months, the crisis resolved. Steve's hair grew back, and he regained the speech he had lost after the second surgery. He had spent almost two months in the hospital and the next four recuperating at home. He had missed one semester at NYU, but had not lost his scholarship. The aphasia was temporary but really frustrating for him. He occasionally flung objects when the words were not retrievable. At home, he existed in a suspended state between illness and health and between purpose and boredom. His anger fulminated. The anger was understandable. Gradually, he recovered his physical health, but his deepest scar would be a distillate of anger that would reside in him for good. This was to be a challenging facet of his adult personality. Anger had never been a part of his personality.

Steve was courteous, engaging, and absorbed with doing well in school. Before the surgery, he seemed to have a commanding ability to sail gracefully from day to day. He had long-term goals and daily rituals that supported them. He had traveled to school, took courses he chose, and got good grades. He had old high school friends and new friends he'd met at NYU. He spent time with them when he wanted to hang out or go to a movie. He had it all under control. Now, at home, those rituals were replaced with endless and boring time in bed and the challenge of retrieving words that often escaped his reach. It was probably his first taste of absolute frustration.

I understood his indignity and anger at suddenly losing this state of grace. I'd spent enough time wanting the same easy success in school and friendships that he enjoyed. I could appreciate how profound a loss it had to be for him better than anyone could have known. I was sorry for him, but thought I'd be better at coping than he was. After all, while he was living in his state of grace, I was learning excellent coping skills. He was admitted to his first-choice college on a full scholarship, while I had to repeat work I'd failed in summer school year after year. He missed the lesson I learned about the dangers of lazy habits, and the importance of perseverance and patience. He never had a teacher or family member that failed to praise his intellect or good looks. He missed another lesson I learned about digging deep to find what I valued in myself that could be cultivated in that social drought. Of course he was unable to manage his rage. He never learned the art of unrestrained, silent, angry word balloons or paying attention to minutiae that floats around as invisibly but importantly as any of us. He never had to learn these coping skills.

I would have acquiesced to his compromised state more graciously and gracefully. Maybe, I thought, when I couldn't retrieve a word I wanted, I would have enjoyed thinking of an opposite or meaningless word or outrageously vile word instead to amuse myself. Instead of "Can I please have a cold soda?" I'd say, "Can I please speak to the president?" or "Can I please have a jelly donut?" I'd take that aphasia and turn it into an ally. I would have accepted those long thoughtless hours just passively watching television. I was an old hand at mindless television shows. They were always a good alternative to homework. I'd think of the time as license to escape responsibility that can always be retrieved at a later date, unlike those now elusive words. Somehow, I managed to have greater faith in a better future than my brother. It was just a matter of waiting out the bad time. Finally, I understood there was something that I was better at than my brother.

The prolonged hospitalization affected me differently. The fragile stability we had begun to enjoy before this crisis was a memory. During my own long hours spent at the hospital as a marginal participant, I had retreated to observation. My limited experience as a hospital volunteer and ward clerk had fostered my confidence and self-esteem. A hospital environment was familiar to me. But there, I was an insider. This time, I had no clearly defined purpose or structure. The most natural response was to retreat to invisibility and learn as much as possible in the environment. I focused on absorbing as many details as I could about medicine, nursing, and activities of interest. This exercise enabled me not to think about our family nightmare. Without benefit of a formal classroom or curriculum, I completed a fractured, asynchronous Nursing 101 experience. Vital signs, flow sheets, IV maintenance, diagnostic tests, pain management, and dressing changes were just some of my lessons. Most importantly, I observed the nurses and doctors. I could distinguish between caregiving and caring. All of this would fortify me in the future. I was determined to go to nursing school. I wanted to help and to care. I had witnessed the importance of compassion. There were still the homework and reading assignments I lugged from school to the hospital every afternoon. Math, English, and Spanish were junior-year requisites. I did the bare minimum of homework and resorted to CliffsNotes for English. There were long evenings of enforced captivity. I picked at my homework the way one would graze on pumpkin seeds while watching a good TV show. Mindlessly processing as my full attention was given to the real drama and to more interesting subjects.

Meanwhile, my mother was grappling with finances. It always came back to money. My mother's favorite saying was: "Rich or poor, it's good to have money." Woody Allen put it differently, "Money is better than poverty, if only for financial reasons."

In either case, my mother's leave of absence and subsequent part-time return to work were essential. As a single parent, she had to be there. Now, collecting bottles for deposit refunds and eating pasta most nights was a way of life. This was the year in high school I have trouble remembering. My friends were less important, and schoolwork as unimportant as ever. I went to school and came home to watch TV with Steve. I was happy to have him back home. I felt a continued need to be with him and my mother. I was extending the hospital ritual beyond its walls. It was probably as much a factor of insecurity as it was adherence to the prolonged routine. It was a year marked by unimportant rituals as we all recovered. The denim wrap skirt with patch pockets was a daily uniform. Now, I recall clenched, angry, frightened fists in those pockets.

Dorothy and Walter visited the first week home. They sat with Steve while my mother made coffee in her Corningware percolator.

The smell of fresh coffee always seemed part of their visit. That and stale cake and poorly timed pep talks.

"Steve, we are so happy you are home and better. Before you know it, you'll be back at school. Don't you think it would also be a good idea for your mom to get back to work? She really needs the money, and we simply can't help any more than we have. Mark starts Cornell next year, and that is going to squeeze us. Please tell your mother she must go back next week."

"Sure will, I'll tell her." When they left, he did just that. He had no idea how this would humiliate and infuriate her. They had breached her cardinal rule. Protecting Steve from stress was her primary concern. Her plan was to return in two weeks anyway.

We saw less and less of them. Our childhood lives and Uncle Walter's "wooden nickels" for the Whitestone Bridge were squarely behind us. This was a new era. In young adulthood, I was as angry as I was determined—determined to become a nurse. I had a new resolve, a plan. I hated being at the mercy of ungracious charity and dependent on anyone.

There was, I suppose, always a plan and logical goal. Its foundation first poured like cement as I sat at my father's swinging foot. That was the last time we were a family, when I was three. The French chair that he sat in has stayed with me forever. His absence from it, and from me, cast the first die of difference in my life. From that point forward, we were different. We were less than other people. An unconscious plan was informally and painfully born the day I stood beside a blue blow-up pool no bigger than a kitchen table and gave physical life to my anger. That first taste of thoughtless reaction to hurt only served to further isolate me from the friends I wanted. I would never again reflexively strike another person. I learned the futility of thoughtless response. After the pool incident, there was a reserve about my friendships with the other girls. Even now, however, I can recall that savory mixture of satisfaction and shame that accompany anger. Even now, I will admit to feeling pleasure at the memory of my own power, just for those few minutes, as I flung another child to the ground. Later, when there were no friends, the plan evolved and became a silent thought. When there were no friends, I enjoyed the companionship of the inert and observed the complex behavior of people.

There was an empty hollow space where people should have been. That deep hollow became the center around which a strong scaffolding of thoughts and words, information and opinions connected and framed a durable alternative to friendship. My own valued thoughts and opinions of everything allowed me to be in control. The empty space lacked defined boundaries, but I found security in building around it and adding to it. I learned to be an independent thinker. That space gave me room to grow in a unique way I may otherwise never have known. I learned the power and pleasure of collected information and insignificant details that I owned and guarded. It was empowering and enjoyable to know about art and language and anything else I could file away and recall at my own will. These details were my companions. I was distracted and entertained while I ingested knowledge I might otherwise have dismissed. I held on to information and opinions because they framed my identity and moved me into some future I believed would reward me for both, a future I could control. Now, the plan was a trajectory. There was logical forward propulsion that took shape as I listened to the confident and controlling voice of Aunt Dorothy. I understood that nursing was at the core of that confidence. I admired her ability to control others even as she offended me. The plan had other older forces that factored into the course.

I stored that fuel even as I sat with Mrs. Bridgewater, the school nurse who was almost as invisible as I was in fourth grade and the person who saved me with simple, nonjudgmental, quiet kindness I associated with nursing. I understood her support and understanding as an intrinsic part of her job. She seemed to exist there only to offer respite and comfort, and she became a part of the matrix.

The plan was irrevocably determined when we moved just blocks from the hospital that would ground my self-confidence. It was there I was first successful in tasks, first as volunteer and later at my first formal employment. It was there I was happiest and observed how illness was a great equalizer and the importance of kindness. It was my brother's illness that taught me compassion. The plan was preordained in part by living in an era where career choices for women were also limited. Is it wrong to admit I am grateful for being narrowly channeled to nursing?

Finally, there was my brother's nightmare. His helplessness and pain were the final galvanizing ingredients. I completely understood both the impotence of poverty and the impotence of illness. I understood how either could rob you of power and pride. I understood that I didn't want to be poor and that, unlike my mother, I wanted to work and be independent. I never wanted to feel invisible, as I often felt when I walked on 68th and York, because my wardrobe was deemed inferior. I never wanted to be in a position of needing mercy or handouts from reluctant relatives. I never would let a man take advantage of me because his money gave him some power. I had seen my mother's beauty and poverty abused by men who saw her need for recognition and love of luxuries she would never have. I was, by now, completely aware of my need to have control and authority in my future. I knew that nursing was where I would leave my anger and find my self. The plan had taken years to form and finalize. Now it was time to put it into action.

But there was the anger that might have impeded me and didn't. That part of anger I chose to hold on to. Somehow, anger had brewed in both Steve and me, but fermented differently. For Steve, there might have been more early anger. He was slightly older and more aware when our father left. I believe my mother's outrage fueled his own internalized anger at being abandoned. He was able to ignore it as he grew older and was distracted by success and security. He was handsome, smart, charming. There were always friends. There was always an acknowledged understanding by everyone in our lives that he was special. He never felt unlucky or lonely as I often did.

He was almost unscathed. But then there was the illness. I believe he was more outraged and insulted than I might have been by such an experience. He expected things to go his way. He worked and was rewarded. He smiled and everyone smiled back. How could that dynamic so suddenly change? I believe that outrage, coupled with the long buried internalized anger, overwhelmed him. The lasting anger left a greater scar than anything surgery might have. I know his anger often overshadows his still-amazing gifts.

Anger was part of the seasoning that flavored our lives. For Steve, the anger was added in clumsy, large doses. It overwhelmed him. I think of it in culinary terms. It was infused too early and then a heavy-handed dose at a critical point melded with the residual and created a "cured" and permanent result.

My own anger is more like a delicate marinade. It enhances the flavor. My first awareness of anger was only a little later in life, but late enough for reflection. I understood it as an entity I needed to control. I understood the satisfaction and the shame of uncontrolled anger. After that early lesson, I learned that a little anger can be a good thing. If laced with humor and kept inside, it helped me survive bad teachers and selfish men. If mixed with four-syllable words and a confident voice, it commanded respect. Wasn't I therefore fortunate to be less fortunate? In the absence of friends and positive feedback and that easy path, other important skills and ingredients were thriving in negative space. Now, with just a little thought and planning mixed with that angry seasoning, I might serve up success. I understood the need for balance. I had learned the importance of compassion and also how precarious life can be. I would never discount those things. I believed in kindness and hope. But I can't underestimate the value of anger. It can be a wonderful fuel source, an important ingredient.

I am married to my anger. It is a part of me I meter out and self-administer as needed. I simply couldn't unlearn the pleasure of its crude justice, albeit mostly only in my thoughts. Now, I have affectionately renamed it. It is my honesty, my Bronx, my bravado, my irreverence, my edge, my "salt" if you prefer. Call it what you want. When mixed with ambition and compassion, it blends well.

In the absence of anger, I might have succumbed to simple obedience. I may have believed my mother was right in suggesting a career in Woolworth's as a clerk or the guidance counselor who thought night school might be my highest level of education. Fortunately, the addition of anger to negative space enabled me to become a nurse. The chemistry was perfect.

Chapter Twelve

SWINGING DOOR

There were more than three hundred graduates from my all-girl high school that June of 1965. Senior year is the crystallization of work, grades, and plans. My yearbook reflects those hopes. Under black-and-white photos, which now seem comically dated, were short lists of clubs, awards, and career choices. Tilted headshots with enormously teased, piled, curled, and flipped hairdos can distract the reader from the also dated and limited careers most chose. More than half were happy to declare being a secretary or executive secretary as their lofty choice. Only four expected to become doctors, none of them lawyers, but many hoped to become teachers and nurses. A few listed hairdresser or model or airline hostess as their choice. The feminist movement had not yet happened. Some of my friends were off to City College or Hunter College. A few were accepted at SUNY campuses. They were the ones that studied and did well on SAT exams.

Now it was my turn to receive the underachiever award I deserved. I hadn't tried hard enough to do better. I never believed I was as smart as my brother. I assumed the banner of family intellect was already bestowed upon him. No one ever told me it could be shared or surpassed. It was easy to become complacent and lazy. The bar wasn't just set lower for me; it had never been put in place to begin with. Left to my own devices, I was free to ignore subjects that didn't interest me and put only a feeble effort into more interesting subjects that still seemed irrelevant. For as long as I can remember, everyone we knew talked about Stephen becoming a doctor. I was spared the trite but important question, "What do you want to do when you grow up?" If no one else cared, why should I? But that changed once I decided to become a nurse, and with that goal in my sights, it was time to get serious.

Under the photo of my tilted head—large eyes lined in black and bangs swept dramatically across my forehead—were two simple words: Registered Nurse. No two words ever held more conviction. I'd failed to take school seriously before. Now, the reality of a connection between school, studying, and the desire to become a nurse meshed. I was off to night school. I realize now that high school graduation was marked by a subtle and more significant milestone in my life. It marked the beginning of an enduring understanding that I needed and wanted to take control. For years, I had practiced soothing but self-limited inward thoughtfulness. It was a masturbatory mindfulness that helped me control anger or boredom or loneliness. I could always turn inward to make things better. When I left high school, I understood that both action and interaction were the tools I'd need to control my life. It was a transition I welcomed. I was about to take control. Being in control was empowering. There was no award at graduation for most wisdom gained. I deserved that award.

I loved night school. I could still volunteer a couple of days a week in the hospital and otherwise enjoyed watching episodes of *General Hospital*. I had classes with non-English–speaking adults and the secretaries and hairdressers that realized too late there had to be more and returned to night school to find answers. It was easy. It wasn't easy like summer school math that required reluctant regurgitation of meaningless facts. Perfect grades came easily once I was studying something of relevance. These grades would admit me to nursing school the following September. Step one of the plan could be checked off.

There was lots of time to spend with my now-steady boyfriend, Steve Davidson, who'd weathered my temporary absence from his life well. I resumed a more normal social life when my brother returned to school, and my boyfriend had waited. He was enrolled at CCNY and had exotic new friends, classes, and interests. His college friends were different from our neighborhood friends from the Bronx. They had mostly grown up in Manhattan and Brooklyn. Any New Yorker can attest to the cultural differences that exist between the five boroughs of New York City. Bronx kids were like the poor relatives of suburbia. We had one foot in the city and one foot out the door to greener pastures. We could navigate and comfortably straddle either side, but most of us saw success as a move to suburbia. His friends had both feet firmly planted in a more diverse place. His new friends grew up going to off-Broadway shows and art galleries and roaming Central Park. They seemed worldly. They were more liberated and vocal about their clothes, opinions, and choices. They impressed me with what I thought was sophistication lacking in the Bronx. They were from Park Slope or Central Park West and aspired to life on West End Avenue or Central Park South. The suburbs were sorely lacking culture in their view. Looking back, I understand the intrinsic, bold honesty that defines the Bronx; the simplicity of language and purpose and absence of affectation that I prefer. But at that time, I loved being a part of all the social aspects of his college life and sharing friends that were different. I lived vicariously, and had no shortage of rich experiences in that year.

If the months in the hospital solidified my career plans, the year of auditing Steve's campus life in 1965–1966 awakened my passion for social activism. Who needed to be angry at a few people in my own life when there was so much more out there to be incensed about? They were in a sustained state of outrage at the world. I loved sharing being indignant with them.

There was Vietnam and Watts and MLK and Bloody Sunday and who could resist hating LBJ? We sang songs from the play *Hair*, "LBJ took the IRT down to 4th Street USA, ayaaaayyy. When he got there what did he see? The youth of America on LSD." Yes indeed, that's my IRT number four to West 4th, my very own train that I could see right from the fire escape outside my bedroom window, immortalized in a Broadway show tune. I'd arrived!

None of us actually did drugs, not weed or LSD. Mentholated Newport cigarettes and Tab diet soda were as dangerous as it got. We liked to dress and talk the image anyway. Woodstock was a few years away, but we were the seeds that would germinate and grow that iconic event. I wore peasant shirts and long Indian print, gauzy skirts. I wore my hair in two long braids. We listened to Bob Dylan, Paul Simon, the Stones, and Hendrix. We thought we were so cool. Image was everything. It was a year pulsating with music and color and righteous indignation. I was good at righteous indignation and loved tie-dyed anything. We took the number four to West 4th. We sat around the fountain and talked about war and race relations and political candidates. I'm not sure now if we really understood or cared as much about the issues as we did about our image. We wanted to be intellectuals and free spirits.

Six of us went to Provincetown, Massachusetts, for a few days that spring. The other two couples copulated enthusiastically to a background of Jefferson Airplane. Steve and I played Scrabble and sketched sand dunes. Steve delighted in identifying gay men strolling at the dock.

He was so good at that. He had gaydar before that term ever existed. We were all impressed with his insight. I'm not sure where my libido was hiding. Perhaps my energy was diverted by my newly assumed deep "intellectualism" and reflection on plans for September when, finally, I would be a student nurse. I was relieved not to consider sex as a necessary or normal activity. My feelings about men were already so conflicted that I couldn't have been happier with any other man. We held hands and talked art and movies and politics. He was my best friend. We were in love and relieved to be off the market. Each of us was hiding from deeply conflicted issues about sexuality. Together, we presented a credible facade of normalcy.

Deeper love came in the form of nursing school that September. I went to Bronx Community College, where I would earn an associate's degree in nursing. That would enable me to take the nursing boards and to obtain a license as a registered professional nurse (an R.N.). From there, my plan was to work at Montefiore and eventually earn advanced degrees. The very same hospital where I had been a junior volunteer (candy striper) and summer clerk would see me return as a registered nurse.

I lived on campus. There were dorms for the nursing students only. The dorms were conveniently located within walking distance of three major hospitals. At age nineteen, I finally had my own room, a six-by-four-foot cubicle that fit only a bed and a desk. It was heaven. There were classes and labs, and after a few months I was assigned hospital days. I studied and read constantly. I went home every weekend but also studied there. I became an exemplary student with perfect grades. Sometimes, when I was tired I would think of my dismissive high school guidance counselor and her vision of my future. That was usually enough to get me back on track. *Hello anger, can you help me out here tonight?* I was restored. I could even imagine a scenario in the future where she might find herself at the mercy of my nursing skills.

I saw my boyfriend, Steve, occasionally, and we still enjoyed our time together. He seemed equally immersed in school and his theatre group and became less of a presence. My grades were solid. I never had less than a B plus on anything. Suddenly, math made sense. Why hadn't someone converted all those numbers into grams and milligrams and medication doses before? Division made perfect sense when I was calculating saline drips and CCs per minute or hour.

We were unleashed on real patients after only a few months. After weeks and weeks of making beds with drawer sheets and make-believe dead-weight patients, beds were "army standard" perfect. We did vital signs on any willing live person in our paths. We learned procedures and treatments for everything from catheterization to enemas. We learned equipment and memorized the steps and protocols for any possible intervention we might do or assist with. We studied systems and diseases as if our lives depended on conquering these facts. In truth, they did. The omnipresent Boards loomed over every task. We were purpose driven. I am sure now, and I was then, that no one was as purpose driven as I was. Failure was not an option. Success was not only a career guarantee, but it was also vindication from anonymity and passivity. Every libidinous cell in my body was diverted to this goal. Sometimes, however, the path was obstructed by events beyond my control. Even the best-laid plans could meet with failure.

Mrs. Connelly was the first real patient assigned to my care. The instructor furnished me with her history a day before our actual hospital day. She was eighty-four, with a history of type 2 diabetes, COPD (chronic obstructive pulmonary disease), and congestive heart failure. Her admission was for treatment of viral pneumonia. I arrived on the unit the next morning armed with an ironclad care plan and understanding of both medical and nursing interventions that might apply to my patient. I was ready for Mrs. Connelly. Wearing my gray-green striped student nurse uniform, I walked to Jacobi Hospital with several other nervous students. We all wore white stockings and sturdy white lace-up oxfords. Our below-the-knee plain shirtwaist uniforms were as drab and utilitarian as possible. I felt beautiful in it. I had worked hard for the right to wear it. The uniform proclaimed my special status. We arrived a little after the start of the 7:00 a.m. day shift.

Without discussion, I left the other students and ventured into the small, brightly lit nursing office. The other students hovered behind, near the elevator, waiting for our instructor. I wanted a head start. There were six nurses sitting in gray plastic chairs informally set around the room. It was shift change from night to day. One nurse seemed to be the spokesman and rolled off a steady stream of information, accounting for the data of the last eight hours of each patient's life. I felt like a trespasser, but I was no more visible to them than the custodian emptying trash or a fly buzzing around a ceiling light. I went unnoticed to the chart rack at the far side of the room. I found my patient's name and pulled the metal jacketed chart out. I quickly reviewed her chart and recent entries. I was anxious to get started and had artfully bypassed greeting the nurses quietly talking. They hadn't noticed me or any of the arriving students. I hadn't listened to or registered a single word spoken by the reporting nurse. That was my first mistake of the day. I headed to my patient's room. I still had almost ten minutes until I needed to meet up with my group. Enough time, I thought, to get a jump start.

Her bed was one of four in the room. It was the one near the window. I could see the faded yellow privacy curtain pulled to near the foot of her bed. My patient sat up in an oversized orange vinyl hospital lounge chair and faced the view of a service entrance to a two-story brick building. Sad view, I thought, but better than looking at the other three open-mouthed, shriveled, and sleeping roommates.

I became aware of a dull, rhythmic whooshing sound: *whoosh-click, whoosh-click, whoosh-click. Oh shit,* I thought, *she's connected to a ventilator; she's intubated.* The sound continued and created fear and anxiety in me. I wasn't expecting a very sick patient. I was expected to know how to read, maintain, and operate any medical equipment that was presented. All I'd been given the day before was a name and laundry list of medical diagnosis. I had not concentrated enough on what nursing care and skills might be required. I couldn't imagine being assigned a critically ill patient on a first experience. I had spent hours reviewing disease processes and lab data. I knew about ventilators and IV's and trach tubes, but I never expected to need those skills my first day. My mind raced, I reviewed vent care, suctioning, settings on machines. An IV was hanging. *Damn it,* I thought, *she is really, really sick.* What did her chart say about the IV? Maybe just a "keep-open" line for meds I hope. *Do your best,* I thought. *One step at a time, you know how to do this on a dummy. Just make believe she's another dummy.*

"Hi, Mrs. Connelly," I said, approaching her. "How are you?" My name is Miss Payne."

She didn't look at me and didn't even move. The sound of the ventilator continued, *whoosh-click, whoosh-click, whoosh-click,* a relentless rhythm. She didn't move, didn't blink, didn't respond. *Good, act like the dummy, and we will both be fine,* I thought. I wondered if she might be deaf. I thought maybe the sound of the machine made it hard to hear. I moved closer and gently touched her pigeon claw of a hand . . . *Cool, no, cold,* I thought. Her circulation was probably impaired. I spoke in a louder voice above the *whoosh-click, whoosh-click.* "So, I am going to just take your blood pressure, okay?" I asked. *Whoosh-click* was the only response.

I took my prized, personal cobalt-blue stethoscope out. I aligned the marker on the blood pressure cuff with her brachial artery. I pumped the bulb and listened carefully for the first pulse of the systolic pressure . . . listening, listening. *Whoosh-click, whoosh-click* was all I heard. *Fucking ventilator,* I thought. I couldn't hear anything else. I palpated the crêpey skin near the edge of the cuff. *This sucks,* I thought, *her veins are not even palpable, she's so cold.* I decided to check her pulse instead. Radial, nothing; carotid, nothing. I only heard that damned double *whoosh-click, whoosh-click* sound. I rubbed the still new and shiny circular diaphragm of my stethoscope. I admired the engraved initials that were my own. I thought that rubbing its surface would activate some sound. I imagined some simple malfunction I'd missed. I placed it over her thin chest wall. *I will get an apical pulse,* I thought. There was no way I wouldn't hear that. But in fact, I could only hear the pounding of my own, anxious heart. I considered just putting my ear to her chest. I was getting desperate, but kept the stethoscope to her chest. *Whoosh-click. Lub-dub*? Had I heard a *lub-dub* under the *whoosh-click*? No, I heard nothing in those little gray ear buds feeding information to my brain. NOTHING! NOTHING. Did she arrest? Was there a DNR? I listened once more, but there was still only the *whoosh-click*. Shit! She continued to stare out the window with unseeing eyes. I ran out the door in seconds and to the nurses' station. The same six nurses were quietly looking over something. I managed to speak, to blurt out "MRS. CONELLY, NO PULSE, ARREST? DNR?" I couldn't form complete sentences. I breathlessly bleated senseless words, "Help, quick, pulse!" I moved around the small room and waved my useless stethoscope up and down to get their attention.

The other nurses finally noticed me. They seemed expressionless and annoyed, and all I could think was *Why are they so slow?* I looked at them and felt like time was also too slow. Everything was off-kilter. It was a frozen frame and not the urgent reaction I'd expected.

"Mrs. Connelly expired at 6:47 a.m.," one of them said. Had I listened to them speaking at 7:00 a.m., I would have been spared the experience of ministering to a corpse. "We are doing the paperwork now. Just leave everything in place. You better ask for another patient."

She had died less than an hour before I'd so eagerly entered the front door of the hospital. My instructor was unaware of this change in plans, and I was unprepared for death as my first nursing challenge. I believed I was in control, beginning with the hours I read and the careful plans I framed on paper, and the thoughtful consideration of associated health issues that might present themselves.. I believed getting a head start on the unit gave me more control, an edge against anxiety and unforeseen changes in her status. I had confidence in my ability to control outcomes. I had no control over death.

I was ready, really I was, for Mrs. Connelly. I believed this very first patient would be the beneficiary of all my good intention. I planned on following a care plan executed after hours of studying diseases and systems and therapies and symptoms. I planned on knowing her and helping her. I planned on giving her comfort and companionship for a short time. But she'd never know that. She has eternal life in my memory, as my very first real patient and as a good reminder of best-laid plans and lofty omnipotence. I was humbled but still convinced that being in control could have changed things. I reflected on how that worked in the face of death.

For some convoluted reason, I remember some other patients that have died forever. There are a handful of patients whose deaths remain indelibly etched in my mind. I think of them to this day. Maybe it is how I control the sadness of defeat. My first patient as a student nurse and the first deaths encountered as a graduate nurse are benchmarks as important as any personal milestone. Maybe it's my way of giving dignity to the brief but intimate contact we shared. Mrs. Connelly held the status of first patient. The others died in my first year of working and were only a few years younger than I was. Perhaps my brother's narrow escape from death distinguished them. Maybe it is my way of continuing lives too short and coping with the sadness I feel. They remind me that my ability to control is limited. These memories are only slightly offset by the small group of unusual, humorous, or miraculous success stories of other patients that lived.

I recovered from my brief encounter with Mrs. Connelly. My confidence actually grew with each day and each patient. I was humbled by that embarrassing experience, and although I made no mistakes, I replayed my own anxiety and mounting insecurity as I confronted all the equipment and responsibility that first confronted me when I saw her. I was reminded of my inexperience. I understood that gaining confidence in my newly learned skills would be a long process. Compassion without confident skills was simply not enough, and confidence without compassion, I learned with my brother's illness, is also inferior care. I was eager to find that balance.

The two years passed quickly. Graduation and a capping ceremony were special and surreal. *I am a nurse,* I said to myself over and over. I don't care how dated that photo of me in that nurse's cap seems today. The starched white cap with a thin black velvet band is an iconic symbol I still love. The Boards followed graduation and were a three-day challenge of number-two pencils, endless bubble grids to fill, and a constant insecurity about skipping an answer and throwing off the remaining entries. Hundreds of us sat in a huge convention room in the New York Coliseum, a seat apart and a row in between. Cheating was not possible. This was, of course, before the existence of cell phones or sophisticated technology. The second-year Spanish Regents Exam had cured me forever of a desire to write on my hands or anything else. I didn't need to cheat now. I was confident. I passed easily and was ready to begin my career as a licensed professional registered nurse. I would soon come to know my license number as well as I know my birth date.

Finally, I was a nurse. The plan was successful. What more could I want? Now it was time to put the plan to practical use. I never considered working anywhere but Montefiore, the hospital in my backyard. This hospital had allowed me to peek timidly inside when I was only thirteen. I was a homing pigeon, returning to a most logical home.

The newly opened Adolescent Unit (NW-6) at Montefiore Hospital was my first nursing placement. It was new and exciting and offered a treasure trove of medical experiences. Patients between the ages of twelve and eighteen were admitted for medical, surgical, or psychiatric diagnosis. Some patients were just a year or two younger than I. The exposure to this wide variety of conditions and interventions was the richest opportunity a new nurse could hope for. It was also a continued opportunity for me to confront the reality and fragility of untoward outcomes. The impotence of poverty might be conquered, but illness and death were still beyond my control. At the tender age of almost twenty-one, I was not emotionally ready to accept all facets of this reality, and there were those other early deaths that I cannot forget.

Had they lived, three patients lost in my first year on the unit would now be my contemporaries. I have never dismissed them from my memory. I need to see and say their names every so often. I am never sure what prompts these memories, perhaps a milestone birthday or a similar diagnosis in someone today. Their names are like well-worn prayers that bring comfort without further question.

Mitchell Berger: Crohn's disease. Multiple admissions, surgical resections, and failed medical strategies. Dead at eighteen; I attended his funeral. His entire senior class attended. His siblings and parents were inconsolable. I thought about my brother's fortunate outcome at the same age.

Carmen Martinez: type 1 diabetic. Multiple admissions, blindness in both eyes and renal failure, secondary ailments. She smiled easily and was surrounded by relatives and music constantly. Carmen died on a night shift when only nurses were with her.

Sandra Della Donna: leukemia. Died after multiple admissions and chemotherapy. She was only twelve. Her grandmother made crochet-edged hankies as thank-you gifts for the nurses.

I have three of these pastel hankies in my underwear drawer to this day. They've had a long life. Sandra did not.

Is this my grown-up child-self magically thinking them back to life? Sometimes, I think it may be residual processing of the close call in my brother's life, or a prolonged case of survivor's guilt, or gratitude for good luck. More likely, it is not residual processing but residual anger. I've kept that safely tucked in a pocket of my mind, ready to pull it out at a moment's notice. During my formative years, I often felt dismissed. I was often angry. I respected everything around me in defiance of being ignored myself. I staked my claim to existence by ingesting that world, piece by piece, detail by detail, until I felt satiated with this fusion of facts and sometimes people. Internalizing enabled me to belong when I was rejected. I changed the paradigm of rejection. I manipulated the reality to change the truth. That same smoldering anger later energized me and changed the passive course I may have followed.

But what is more irrevocable than death? Death dismisses and disregards all effort to change its will. It has ultimate power to control. It is the "dismisser-in-chief," and my response to its power and total control is that measured, defiant anger that has always helped me cope. *FUCK YOU, death, I will keep them alive. I will hold onto them in the safety of my thoughts. I'll hold them tight so you can't win.* The memories of these lives are part of an elite group that continue to live because I don't let them die. They are alive in my thoughts of them. For those of us who doubt an afterlife exists, this is an afterlife I can give them. I held no skills or power to change their outcomes. I hold only the power to remember them, and to say their names so they live. I remember them because it empowers me.

They remind me that I can be compassionate instead of angry. I can "pray" their names instead of reaching for the anger.

I can recall that compassion gives me peace and anger does not. Oh God, does this count as religion? I can be grateful for being a nurse where my compassion is called upon and my anger is inappropriate. I have only finite moments to enter others' lives and help. When the outcome is not aligned with my intentions, anger fails to help. I need reminding!

The hospital and my job became all-encompassing. Few things rivaled my passion for work. I lost interest in my friends. Even my boyfriend became less important. I didn't mind evening and night rotations, and there were no complaints from him. We were enjoying parallel but separate lives and the safety of couple status. Our passions lay elsewhere.

Both Steve Davidson and I were aware of passing time and the expectations associated with a four-going-on-five-year relationship. We were launched into career paths and aware there should be a logical progression to a formal commitment. The maturity of our relationship was in the context of time rather than growth, however. In reality, we spent less time together than ever. I worked full-time and had shift rotations. He had an entry-level job in marketing and was taking a few grad courses at Hunter College. We often didn't see each other on evenings or weekends, but when we were together, we still enjoyed each other's company.

We went to the Paris Theatre across from The Plaza Hotel in the city to take in foreign films, which we'd spend hours dissecting afterward over coffee. We went to Serendipity Cafe on cold nights. There we ordered hot chocolate, Fatatita's French Toast, and enjoyed the energy of all the tourists or occasional celebrity we noticed. We kept up with his theatre friends and went to a few awful performances. We read the same books and discussed protagonists and plots. We spent some days at each other's houses. We both had strong, opinionated mothers, who enjoyed our company. There was always something to laugh about, and an event or place to enjoy as a couple.

There was not so much a formal proposal as there was a consensus. We should get engaged and married, and that's what we decided to do. I had no template or model for the qualities important to marriage. Longevity, comfort, and a good discussion about protagonists in movies and books seemed sufficient.

"You are friends, nothing more than that," was my mother's reaction to the news. "I see no passion or affection. To be perfectly honest, I've never even come home early and seen you jump off the couch. I think he's gay."

"Mom, you really have a dirty mind," I countered. "Just because we aren't jumping all over each other all the time doesn't mean he's gay."

"But you should be jumping all over each other at your age," she said. "That's normal." She chuckled a bit and continued. "But what's the rush? For God's sake, you're beautiful, young, and working with smart young doctors every day."

"Got it, Mom," I said. "The Jewish mother's dream—a doctor for a son-in-law. No thank you."

She remained silent as I spoke. "Did you ever consider that Steve is sensitive and smart and also simply respectful?" I asked. I didn't believe my mother much valued respectful men. Her own standards for sexual behavior had long disturbed and confused me. What did she know about companionship and marriage? Nothing I'd witnessed.

The truth was, the doctors were interested in me, and that was frightening. I could talk about patients with them, but was rendered mute otherwise. The old demons of status, money, and class catapulted me back to childhood. I was less than they were, but I was aware of the subtle sexuality in their conversation and eye contact. That created more fear. I simply could not reconcile the sexuality with the intellectual and social qualities I prized. I couldn't overcome my sense of inferiority and fear. It seemed an either-or choice to me, and I chose either. I believed the other option rendered me vulnerable and powerless. I had come this far and was not going to compromise. I wanted safety, status, and security, and to be distanced from having to interact with other men. I could control the relationship with Steve. There was no sexual tension, just parity. It was easier to control or reason with a man who presented no social or sexual challenges. The decision was clear.

The ring was a two-carat pear-shaped solitaire. A respectable ring. There were announcements and gifts and a party. There was a deposit at a Reform synagogue neither of us attended. It had a nice catering hall with three obligatory ornate, oversized crystal chandeliers and palladium windows that we liked enough. We resumed our normal lives and routines of occasional Saturday nights together and shopping for clothes or registry items. We set a wedding date six months out and rarely discussed it. We were safely shielded in a protective bubble of propriety. Almost everyone was married before the age of twenty-five in those years, and we were satisfying the rules of societal norms for the decade. We were safe.

For my twenty-first birthday, my mother shocked me with an unexpected gift: tickets for two to Aruba. Also included was a voucher for a weeklong stay in a moderate beachfront hotel. The gift was well beyond her financial ability, and I knew she was saving some money for the wedding. But twenty-one is also a special birthday. I was overwhelmed with gratitude. "I want you to buy the sexiest nightgown and the sexiest underwear you can find," she added when presenting her gift. "I want you to have your honeymoon now. While you are away, I want you to think about what should happen and how it should be. I want you to do a lot of thinking."

I understood her message. Her generosity forced me to consider her wisdom. I never doubted that we'd be able to consummate our engagement, however dispassionately. Sex was a necessary evil I secretly hoped I might learn to enjoy.

I bought a lacey black teddy that made me feel like a hooker. I imagined it would be okay to pretend and hopefully embrace my inner, unknown vixen. Liberal doses of wine and sun and humor would bolster my new image. I had to be able to reconcile the real me with the seductress me, and I hoped we would laugh and drink, and hold hands and drink more, and kiss and consummate our engagement. Finally, it would be behind us. It was a rite of passage and task we had to check off before marriage, no more exciting to either of us than the marriage license we'd applied for at the Bronx County Courthouse. Maybe we could laugh at our achievement and move on. In the deepest recesses of my mind, I hoped it would bring us closer and more in love.

On our first day in Aruba, he lathered his lean, long, olive-skinned body with a baby oil and iodine mixture. The black hair on his chest glistened in the sun. He rubbed his thighs and calves in long, careful strokes. I began to think that he was really quite sexy. He timed his exposure on each surface and rotated as if he were a chicken on a rotisserie spit. I hid under a plastic, thatched beach umbrella and read a local guidebook. He seemed to be sleeping or concentrating on the task of achieving an even tan. I ordered a Mai Tai and relaxed as the rum began to circulate.

Soon we had both lost track of time. It was late afternoon and time to get ready for our first dinner. I decided I would save the seductress costume for later that night. There was a fantastic orange-gold sunset. I had never seen the sun so large and deeply colored. Was this the same sun that set over our buildings in the Bronx? The steel drums played island music and there were two more Mai Tais each. This was paradise. It was difficult to not have a sense of well-being and optimism.

By the time we returned to our room after dinner, we were completely relaxed. I took great pains to dress. Drunk enough, the black lace was more exotic than comical. Looking in the long mirror, I could admit to liking my sexy reflection. Halloween was several weeks past, but costumes could always be fun. Now I just needed to reach inside to find the persona that matched the willing seductress in black lace. I slowly opened the door after shutting the bathroom light. The darkness helped my courage. There he was, flat on his back, snoring loudly. I spoke his name. He grunted even louder and turned on his side, away from my voice. *There's always tomorrow,* I thought.

The next day, the baby oil and iodine mixture had fried his knees and face to a pulpy, swollen state. It was painful. He lay in bed with face and knees packed in ice-filled towels. He no longer seemed attractive. On the third and fourth nights, the burns became weeping blisters. They were fragile, and he was immobilized. Fixed in place, he lay perfectly still all night, afraid to move.

On our sixth and final night, he felt better. I dug the black lace out of the drawer. "This is so contrived, don't you think?" was his reaction to my sexy little teddy. I felt silly. My mother's voice was echoing as well. I needed to know what the problem was. Clearly, there was a problem.

"Steve, could you be honest with me? Is there something wrong with us?"

"Yeah, probably," was his nonchalant response.

"Is it something about me? Am I unattractive to you sexually?"

"Probably," he said.

I let it go. In my mind, there was the likelihood that I was simply that unattractive. There also was a creeping admission in my mind that my mother was a genius. This gift had more significance than a simple birthday or wedding gift. This generous gift was intended to open my eyes.

"So, how was the trip?" she asked, my first day back. I was not quite ready to admit to the reality of her victorious insight.

"The hotel was great. The food was amazing," I babbled rapidly. "The island has these trees called divi-divis that are permanently bowed against the trade winds." I was racing through my mind to recall details that might distract her.

"No, how *was* the trip?" she demanded. I knew exactly what the inference was.

"Mom, leave me alone. We will work it out. Stop worrying." That was my plan, to work it out. I was unwilling to face instability and change in my life. Comfortable and safe was good enough.

But it was not good enough for Steve.

I was working the evening shift the week we returned. It was almost 10:00 p.m. the Saturday he called to ask if we could meet after work, which was an unusual request. Working Saturdays for me never included going out after work. Clearly he knew the timing might alert me to a problem. I met him at the front entrance of the hospital, walked past the white plaster life-sized statue of a surgeon with his sterile, gloved hands raised and ready. I'd always thought it a foreboding piece for the main lobby that seemed to state, "Hello, folks, no going back, you're in for some serious shit now, but welcome to my world."

Wouldn't it have been better to have a tacky reproduction of an impressionistic pastoral landscape to escape to?

Steve's white Toyota Corolla was waiting. I got in and said only, "Hey, what's up?" We drove in silence just two blocks, and he parked along the edge of the park.

He spoke first. "I've given this a lot of thought," he began, "and I don't want to get married. I can't get married." There was silence while I digested what he'd said. It was shocking, but not surprising. We'd seen and spoken to each other less and less since returning home. Without discussion, we each had been ruminating over the events of that week away.

"So, obviously, we have a sex problem," I began. "We can just wait it out, work on it. Do you think I'm too fat?" I asked. There was always that extra ten or fifteen pounds that plagued my self-confidence. I thought about how that sexy black lace probably showcased my chubby thighs. As I thought back, I imagined how aggressive and repulsive I may have seemed. Tears were welling up in my eyes.

He watched me and put a hand on my shoulder as he spoke. "It's not you. Not you at all. It's me. I am in love with someone else. I'm in love with a man." I was speechless. I sat quietly as he elaborated. The details became painful. "I'm gay. I've known that since I was fourteen. I knew it when we met, but we were so happy, and I thought that was enough." He looked right at me and went on. "I'm in love with an older man. We've been together for two years, and now I am going to live with him. I'm going to tell my parents about him this week. It's what I want, I'm so sorry."

My mind raced. I could not and would not accept this. I could change this. I could convince him that it would work. "You need therapy," I offered. "I'll pay for it. You're just confused. Let's take a break for a month and postpone the wedding a few months." I was desperate to salvage the relationship, desperate to keep him in my life and to continue living behind the safety of our attractive facade. I could live without sex, why couldn't he?

But he was not willing to compromise. My offer of therapy and time was flatly rejected. His betrayal at least freed me from thinking I was repulsive. I was not angry at him, just confused and afraid of what the future might hold for me. But I loved him enough to want his happiness.

I returned the ring and the gifts. I reluctantly carted the beautiful Dansk Blue Mist dinnerware service for twelve back to Bloomingdale's. The cobalt-blue fondue pot that promised cozy evenings of melted Gruyère and bits of baguette went back to Macy's.

Immediately and without fanfare, Steve was no longer part of my life. Our future had come to an abrupt end. He was free to live and love the way he wanted. A familiar sense of insecurity and imbalance settled in. *What now?* I wondered. *Whom could I trust?* For now, what I could trust was the security of my job. I was a nurse. That was what I knew and loved and trusted. I'd figure out the rest of my life later on.

My mother was uncharacteristically restrained when I told her the engagement was broken. She knew when to rein in her opinions. She assumed the role of skilled mother of a challenging teenager, being supportive rather than triumphant in her victory. "Hey, how about we go to Jade Garden for dinner tonight?" was her response to the news. My mother knew me well. Nothing like a greasy egg roll and some subgum chow mein to heal my broken heart. We were off to the neighborhood Chinese restaurant to drown my sorrow.

Chapter Thirteen

KEYSTONE

The hospital and my job had become keystones, the supportive centerpieces that held all the less predictable pieces of my life firmly in place. Here everything changed minute by minute and day by day, but my fundamental role and importance were solid and consistent. I had grown more confident in my nursing skills. Aruba and marriage and sex were put out of my thoughts, and I returned to NW-6, a twenty-four bed adolescent unit with a plethora of distractions. We were a staff of attractive young nurses on a newly opened and exciting unit.

Even in this safe haven, the air was sexually charged. There was no escaping that reality of men and sex. My unsuccessful attempt at plying my talents with sex and seduction on a homosexual man only reinforced my lack of confidence. I believed my deficient libido could surely be detected by men. No matter what I looked like on the outside, I felt like a female eunuch. It was difficult for me to dissociate sex from memories of my mother's boyfriends or my father's too-young girlfriend. Surely, there was an aura about me men could sense. They might avoid me if they knew how disinterested and afraid I was of sex. Would I feel safe or sorry because of this? I wanted it both ways. I hoped they'd notice me, approve, and then leave me alone. All I wanted was to look as if I belonged there, with the other nurses. I wanted affirmation that on the surface I fit in. My failure to make eye contact or engage in conversation soon conveyed my apathy. Most of the time, they moved on to greener pastures.

New interns and residents floated through each month, some stayed longer. There was hard work, sad events, and a social life that mirrored the intellectual and sexual energy inherent in the culture of hospitals. The 1960s pre-dated the era of male nurses. It predated today's educational standards for bachelor's or master's degrees in nursing. Nurses typically had less education and received lower salaries than doctors; nurses consequently held lower social status in the rigid, male-dominated hierarchy of the day. There was an acceptable subservience to the nurse-doctor relationship. Nurses' "inferior" workplace status was not questioned. Upward mobility in that and previous decades meant marrying a doctor, not becoming one.

The stark reality of illness, pain, and death seemed to create a sexual candor that was uniquely acceptable in this workplace. I've never worked in the corporate world. In the pre-feminist decade of the sixties, I imagine there were workplaces with sexual similarities. I can imagine high-heeled, big-bosomed, doting secretaries vying for the boss's attention. There were trim and flirtatious airline stewardesses in their version of "the hunt." But the hospital offered an enhanced version of sexuality in the workplace. Women were not objectified so much as they were willing participants. Here, there were equal numbers of hunters, or "sportsmen" if you prefer, and prey. The playing field was larger. The sport took place against a backdrop that shimmered with drama and a nod to perceived heroism. And perhaps it was the constant reminder of life's ability to be frail and fleeting that emboldened the players even more. There seemed to be a sexuality to white uniforms and scrubs and stethoscopes that trumped any lingerie or high heels. It seemed as if, by sharing the intimate misery of other people's lives, we were entitled to extend the boundaries of intimacy to each other. I had all the confidence, maturity, and experience of a fourteen-year-old in this social setting.

At twenty-one, I had never dated anyone other than Steve Davidson. I was more seasoned nurse than grown woman. I only felt safely removed from that social scene when working nights. Doctors were day-shift inhabitants. At night, I was free to work, struggle to stay awake, and not think about my aura or appearance. By choosing this less-desirable shift, I was spared the flirting, dating, and sexual energy rampant with the full company of nursing and medical staff on daytime duty. But there was a problem—night rotations were usually just one weekend a month. The three eight-hour shifts that made up each twenty-four-hour hospital day were permanent assignments. Day-shift nurses were usually required to do evening or night rotations for days to weeks to cover the deficit in permanently assigned nurses on those shifts. This meant I was more often faced with the daily challenge of my arrested development. The one-hour transition from night to day was my safety zone on either shift. Whether leaving or arriving at 7:00 a.m., there were rarely doctors present. That first or last hour of either shift was a safe cocoon I loved. It was a transitional time when I'd take a deep breath, before facing the arrival of men dressed up as doctors. While the night nurses used this time to freshen up their appearance and the newly arriving day shift arrived with freshly charged sexual energy, I wrapped myself in the comfort of knowing it was a male-free, time-out, safety zone.

Infrequent night rotations were welcomed respite from working closely with doctors. I especially loved the transition as night softened to dusty gray or pink and heralded freedom from the stage about to be set by the staff beginning their day. The curtain would rise on a new day of challenges without me. Last-minute chores at 5:00 a.m. included IVs, vital signs, dressings, pain medication, and, of course, handwritten notes to document the care. How strange today's paperless, electronic world seems when juxtaposed against the more personal effort of well-chosen words and subjective data thoughtfully added to clinical, objective data.

All that written data, which was and still is part of the morning report, serves as the backdrop for each new day. It was the very same morning report I had so unceremoniously intruded on only a year before as a student. Now, first light reminded me of the weighty responsibility of transferring information and escalated my anxiety about the encroaching medical staff.

The morning shift began at 7:00 a.m., but I was always there by 6:30 a.m. when I had a day shift. I liked to get a feel for the unit before the workday started. I liked to take the figurative temperature and vital signs of the unit before the others arrived and chaos began. Another lesson I'd learned in that student-nurse experience was to simply observe and feel the mood on the unit as the day began. Patients in crisis or unexpected admissions translated to tension in the nurses. I'd make fresh coffee and check out my hair and uniform. I wanted to look good and be ready. I observed the mood of the departing staff. I needed that half hour to gather my confidence and prepare to face both the inner battle and outside challenge of my position.

Like any adolescent, I cared about my looks. There was some basic need for positive feedback and acceptance. Beginning the day in quiet met my need to have control. In many ways, I was both similar and different from my student-nurse days. I had grown exponentially in my profession, and yet I was still struggling for control. I could settle for nothing less than perfection in my professional performance or my outer persona. I held tight to anything I was able to control. Couched in all the science and theory and practical lessons of nursing school was the most empowering life lesson to date, the ability to control. Yet the need to control could become more handicap than asset going forward.

It would not be long before the rest of the staff arrived in bright fluorescent light, and I'd be surrounded by an assault of people and noise. I needed to gather up my armor and resolve. The other nurses would arrive soon after me and soon after that, the doctors, one by one, or in small groups. They brought with them that sexual energy and powerful purpose inherent in their field. I would be armored up and have had two coffees in me by then. Caffeine and Very Berry lip-gloss readied me for battle.

There were four other registered nurses on the day shift. It was a colorful cast of characters. Roberta Mackey was in her early forties. A tall, heavy-boned, bleached-blonde, she was the outrageous, bawdy linchpin who set the tone from her vantage point of safety. Unhappily married to a cop and saddled with four school-aged children, she lived vicariously. Work was her playground and escape from home. The three other nurses were in their mid-twenties and very single. Roberta was a skilled nurse but would have made an even better madame. She was fond of setting the stage with shocking statements that provoked naughty reactions that heightened the already sexually charged atmosphere. Her behavior often reminded me of my mother and her off-color jokes to Jack the fabric man. Meant to tease, provoke, and gain favor as a form of banter was something they both excelled at. Looking back, it seems to me that it must have been Roberta's pathetic way of fitting in. She'd missed her own opportunity, but was still able to manipulate libidinous doctors and hopeful young nurses.

By 7:00 a.m., Pat Bishop had made her grand entrance. Our head nurse was a hospital legend. Wearing a mid-thigh, skintight, simple white uniform a size too small, she sauntered out of the locker room with her perfectly combed, straight, glossy, chin-length, chestnut-brown hair swinging under her tiny organdy cupcake of a cap. I've since seen naughty nurse Halloween costumes that attempt to duplicate this look, albeit poorly. She undulated to the nursing desk, awaited the remaining nurses, and efficiently took report from the night nurse. The official start to the day's games would begin at this point.

Donna and Colleen, the remainder of our nursing cadre, arrived next. They seemed to do everything in tandem. They'd graduated from the same New Jersey college nursing program where they'd been roommates. Now, they worked the same shift on the same unit and were roommates in hospital housing a block away. Their shared lives extended to a common goal. They were hell-bent on meeting and marrying doctors, I was surprised to learn that these two, fresh scrubbed WASPs, complete with freckles, straight noses, and long legs, had latched onto the Jewish mother's idea of nirvana. It was unbelievable to me that Christians shared this obsession, too. It was obvious that they eagerly entertained dating Jewish doctors, which were in greater supply. They smiled often, engaged all doctors in friendly conversation, and looked pathetically hungry to me. In any case, Pat stole the show from other contenders. There simply was no competition.

I can remember a morning in the fall of 1970. An hour into the day with several more cups of coffee fueling me, I sat reviewing six charts, histories of my patients for the day. Pat sat next to me at the desk. She continuously crossed and uncrossed her thin shapely legs, revealing some thigh above her garter-belted stockings. The advent of pantyhose had been joyfully embraced by women for several years, but Pat preferred stockings. She wound and unwound her legs, hooking a foot behind the opposite calf each time with an ease I envied. I studied the agility of the move, knowing my own plump thighs would foil any attempt to emulate her. As I pondered that inequity, Doctor Bob Gold arrived and sat next to me. He had a long torso, too-short legs, slick black hair, and would be described by my grandmother as a "*shayne boychik,*" a cute guy. I didn't think so. He looked thick and inelegant to me. He was not as esthetically appealing as Steve Davidson, not as tall or lean. His eyes were not as large and deep and his gait was clumsy compared to Steve's more graceful stride. He was, however, considered a catch. He was bright, single, completing his residency, and quietly confident, and he was Jewish. I should have been honing my hunting skills, not hiding or pondering the art of tightly bound crossed legs.

He'd noticed me before and said hello. "Hey, great coffee, thanks," he said, and turned to face me. "Who do you have today?" He was looking at the stack of charts I had balanced on my lap.

I answered quickly, "Oh, I have rooms 622 through 627." Those were my six patients. I avoided a more detailed discussion of names, diagnoses, or problems.

He didn't give up. "Any of those rooms have my patients?" He was trying to help me out, to establish common ground for a conversation, but I wasn't biting. I retreated to my old habit of inner thought and cryptic but unspoken conversation. My inner voice was having a field day judging me: *You maybe close to thirty, but I amreally a thirteen-year-old. You are probably rich, and I am not. You probably have a great studio apartment overlooking the Hudson River in Riverdale, and I live in this very shabby neighborhood near the hospital with my mother and brother. You are a man of the world, and I am still a virgin. You are smarter, I am sure. No, no, no. We have nothing to share.* My sense of inferiority was as deeply etched as my resentment of those I believed to be cavalier in their entitlement. I resented their presence in my life, their inherent control.

I stood up abruptly, abandoning the desk and the conversation. I was missing the comfortable couple status I had with Steve Davidson. I longed for the companionship and conversation, but I wasn't ready. Inherently, I knew I'd have to venture out into the world of dating, but I hated the thought of what that might mean. I just needed some remediation, which was not part of a mentoring program or any hospital in-service education program. I knew I'd have to take the plunge into those icy waters and hope to adjust, but I'd hold out for as long as I could.

Eventually, I accepted a date with a timid, short, heavily accented Indian pediatric cardiologist. I thought the cultural differences, and his possible humble beginnings, would deflect his judgment of my living situation. I imagined he'd be less blatantly sexual because he was East Asian. I imagined chaste, sari-wearing virgins in his past. He seemed a safe bet. This was a safe starting point. We had just one date. He had bad breath and talked incessantly about heart defects and surgical techniques. I enjoyed my moo shu vegetables in a Chinese restaurant, and was only somewhat disgusted when he described surgical rib splitters as he chewed on a boneless rib. Some thick orange sauce dripped on his chin. The kiss good night was the final nail in his coffin. He had to rise up on his toes a bit to reach my face. His breath was overwhelming as he thrust his tongue into my mouth. A residual sesame seed that transferred from his teeth to my own tongue would be a lingering memory. I hoped his surgical skills were more refined. I went back into hiding for a while.

Chapter Fourteen

SAFETY IN PRISON

There were no in-service programs for proficiency in dating, but the hospital did offer a wonderful opportunity to escape a year later. I could escape *to* prison. This opportunity was better than hiding in medication closets. In 1970, the hospital signed a contract with the New York City Department of Corrections. They assumed responsibility for all facets of medical care at a juvenile detention center in the Bronx. The hospital agreed to establish out-patient and pharmaceutical services for incarcerated adolescents, ages eleven to eighteen at two sites. The plan initially was to rotate staff from the hospital as systems and regulations were established and refined. Previously, the "inmates" had infrequent visits from Department of Health physicians and costly transport to clinics and emergency rooms as needed. The new model hoped to establish a permanent onsite ambulatory care program. Staff were asked to consider rotations for three-month periods to both Spofford (boys) and Manida (girls) Centers in one of the most dangerous neighborhoods in the South Bronx.

This was not juvenile court, it was a real prison. The inmates had been arrested and arraigned. They were held for short periods until they were old enough for real jail (the famous Rikers Island) or high-security residential placements. Sometimes, they were released with parole and oversight after serving some time. These were young people familiar with knives and guns and violence. Many of the inmates would learn the ropes here first, before moving on and up through the revolving door of the prison system. I was the first (and only) nurse to volunteer. As I said, Hunts Point in the Bronx was notoriously dangerous. Jail, however, seemed a logical distraction from my own fears. If nothing else, it was a short respite and gave me time to think. I was a hero to the other nurses, who were horrified at the prospect of forced rotations to the South Bronx and a prison setting.

Two weeks before I was scheduled to leave, the first volunteering pharmacist was sent to our unit to become familiar with the population and medication delivery systems. It was an opportunity to meet as a team. There would be the pharmacist, a medical resident, and me. The pharmacist, whose name happened to be Steve, shadowed me on our floor and shared the medication room with me up until the point we were scheduled to leave. It was close quarters, but we managed to keep a professional distance from one another. He seemed as tense and insecure as I was. He was, ironically, the third important male named Steve in my life. There was some inherent comfort in this detail.

Pharmacists were typically not present on patient units. He was out of place in a clinical setting. Our conversations were perfunctory and technical. He asked about patient histories and staffing structure. I found out that he lived in New Jersey, and we spent the last hour of his last day on the unit discussing travel time and the issue of parking safety. The prison was less than five miles away, but a different universe as a neighborhood. Before I left, Roberta told me that the pharmacist had asked her if she knew my religion. *Bingo*—I was Jewish; he was Jewish, too. I realized the very timid, quiet, and insecure young man was interested in more than just medication doses. He was as socially awkward as I was.

The three of us were a minority in the prison system as the only Caucasian, non-prison personnel, and our bond was immediate. The existing staff were prison-smart, tough, and resented the influx of rotating white staff from the outside world. They barely spoke to us. The nurse in charge made no eye contact with any of us and answered exclusively in monosyllables.

The low white brick building in Hunts Point was surrounded by chain-link fences and gates. Barbed wire was coiled at the top of the chain link. Every door and corridor was guarded and locked. The holding cells had either one or two subjects. Sick call was twice a day, and a similar schedule existed for medications. We were as intimidated by the staff as we were by the prisoners. I had a comically cynical awareness of how ludicrous it was for three timid, unprepared Jews to find themselves in this alternative universe. Twice daily, the three of us, accompanied by armed guards, were shepherded to an almost-empty room painted in high-gloss lime green. Windows covered with heavy grates offered bits of daylight. The only furniture was a folding table and six chairs. The room had all the appeal of a rec room from an asylum for the criminally insane.

I dreaded the sick-call line. Ten to twelve allegedly sick boys and girls accompanied by one or two guards presented to the nurse alone or to the nurse and doctor with complaints. Some of them went straight to the pharmacist, who dispensed single-unit doses of antibiotics, asthma meds, or pain relievers. They all hoped for some medication to use as barter. They were verbally out of control, in spite of the guards constantly telling them to shut up. Mostly, they hoped for time out of their restricted environment or for any medication they might trade later.

Jail was a place of hard sounds. Sliding heavy gates, clanking, self-locking doors, jangling keys—all forms of metal against metal. All of it echoed in empty, large spaces. Voices also came in sharp isolated bursts of echoing sound.

"Hey, nurse. Hey. Can I fuck you?" This from a random sixteen-year-old with a sore throat. The guard shoved his arm and told him to shut up. "My dick hurts . . . can you fix it?"

Amazing how quickly you can learn to focus on a single task. Oddly, their sexually offensive words were less frightening than the subtle gazes of the doctors I'd left behind on the adolescent unit of Montefiore Hospital.

One afternoon, at the girls' center, the resident and I were taking sick-call visits in the upper floor of the old three-story house that was an annex building. The girls and the counselors lined up along a narrow winding staircase. We were in a windowless room on a hot summer day, and the space seemed airless. It was poorly lit and a ridiculous substitute for a waiting area. It may have once been a small bedroom when the wood-framed house was built in the early twentieth century. The girls became bored, angry, and uncomfortable with the wait in an even hotter, cramped stairwell.

The first two girls behind the closed door were being examined for upper respiratory complaints. We heard yelling and the sound of bodies being pushed against walls. Everyone was screaming. The counselors screamed up at us to lock ourselves in. We resorted to chairs and our body weight to hold the door closed against the angry group. One of the girls with us pushed the doctor. She was either panicked or simply wanted to be part of the event.

"Move asshole, I'm gettin' out of here," she shouted at the ghostly white, immobilized doctor. We cracked the door a few inches, and she ran out. Then we re-barricaded and waited for rescue. It took an hour to restore order. Extra counselors were called in. We eventually saw all the girls. No mention was made of the incident. It was simply an outburst, a normal event in jail.

Traces of my altruistic, socially conscious self remained. A young woman of the sixties, I was able to consider the disadvantages that accounted for some behaviors. Sometimes that altruism was tested. It was a challenge.

Altruism was a reflexive behavior. I was raised in a home where we cheered for any losing sports team (unless the Yankees were winning). We cried at the sight of a three-legged dog and brought home doomed fledglings that fell from their nests, feeding them sugar water with eye droppers and giving them formal funerals. We honored any picket line by never crossing one and put coins in any collection can on a counter. My mother, a child of the Great Depression embraced the liberal social programs of the New Deal, which guaranteed Social Security and established the National Labor Relations Board. These programs were as sacred as a religion to her and others raised in the poverty of that generation. I grew up hearing her tales of outgrown shoes lined with cardboard when the soles wore through and sharing two chicken legs for dinner with her sister and brother. Work and the unions that protected workers mattered to her almost as much as they had to her parents.

I am as fiercely proud and moored to my socially altruistic roots as the royals are to the crown. I was raised on the legends and folklore of my Jewish, immigrant, maternal grandparents, who fled the pogroms of Russia and Poland at the turn of the century to find religious freedom and financial security in the ghettos of New York's Lower East Side. They lived on Elizabeth Street and worked in the sweatshops of the garment district. My grandmother made ladies' blouses (shirtwaists as they were then named), and my grandfather made coats in another factory.

They were newlyweds in March of 1911, when the famous Triangle Shirtwaist Factory claimed the lives of 146 mostly young Italian and Jewish immigrants. They were witnesses to that great industrial tragedy, which predated workplace safety. My grandfather belonged to the Socialist Democratic political party, which was largely supported by the trade unions. He embraced the underdog status, being a Jew and factory worker. Jews have enjoyed the longest run of scapegoat status, which may explain their soulful response to other victims. It may, by now, be a recessive genetic trait that I've hopefully passed on as well. I love that my grandpa Philip was a socialist in a time when it meant he was an idealist and not an anarchist.

As for me, I was born with the other seventy-six million postwar Baby Boomers, who were less impoverished, better educated, and made more secure by past generations. We were newly connected by the presence of television and unafraid to be outspoken. Collectively, we questioned the moral and spiritual authority of the world in the 1960s. Empowered by our numbers we could be outraged by civil rights issues, the Vietnam War, and women's rights. We had the luxury of being righteously and indirectly indignant about the wrongs we witnessed. We embraced our altruism by wearing it, rather than by living it. Still, it was and will always be as intrinsic as my need to eat, sleep, and breathe. I just needed to hone the art of exercising that reflex judiciously.

I grew fond of a small, curly haired, brown-skinned boy. He visited almost daily, complaining of stomach pain. There were never significant findings. One day, I asked him how he came to be in this place. He had a shy smile and interesting hazel eyes. He told me his mother moved and left him with his grandmother.

The grandmother didn't have money to feed and clothe him. He didn't know his father. He said he was picked up because he stole a bag of potato chips from a grocery store.

"Poor, Michael, I can't believe an eleven year old ended up here because he stole a bag of chips," I told one of the older male guards after one of Michael's frequent visits.

He laughed loudly. "Girl, you gotta be kidding me. Little sweet-faced Michael raped a nine-year-old girl and threw her off a roof. She's lucky to be alive. Shit, no damned potato chips. Attempted murder." I was aware of my reflexive need to scratch the altruistic itch, but instead, I considered the entirety of the issue. It was less gratifying.

That was a wake-up call. I pondered my own gullibility and judgment. This was a whole new kind of nursing. And it was an enriching three months. There were pregnant teenagers, drug selling and using teens. Sometimes there were kids who just made poor decisions and got arrested because they were part of a bad crowd. I learned to be neither cynical nor gullible. The revolving door of the juvenile court system turned rapidly. There was little time to do more than daily tasks.

The three of us plodded along and did what we were asked. The doctor, charged with documenting outcomes of new systems, spent any free time alone, entering data. He brought a sandwich from home and ate in solitude. By day three, the timid pharmacist and I were fleeing the hard sounds and foreign world to enjoy an hour respite each day at lunch in a local deli. We clung to each other like lab monkeys behind bars. We were part of an ambitious experiment. There was never a shortage of stories to share about work. We were aware of our unique window into an alternative world. That thin sliver of shared experience fostered an unspoken trust that perhaps we could venture beyond the self-imposed barbed wire of paralyzing fear of dating also.

After all, if we were surviving the violence of this environment, we could survive the risk of a date. We were a team now. Perhaps the last two twenty-one-year-old virgins in the world, certainly the only two in Hunts Point.

At lunch one day he asked me to dinner on a Saturday night. I had passed the first requirement of being Jewish. He had passed my first requirement of having no need for the usual small talk. How I hated the predictable feigned interest of first encounters with doctors. It was especially difficult when the questions included where I lived and had gone to school. I could imagine the conversation. "Yes, I live two blocks from the hospital in this very congested, noisy, less-than-middle-class neighborhood with my mom and big brother. I attended Bronx Community College and had to go to night school to get in. Are you impressed yet, doctor?"

No, I knew they would not be impressed at all. The residents, who grew up in wealthy suburbs of Long Island or Westchester or Connecticut and went to Cornell or Columbia, couldn't possibly relate to my life in the Bronx. We didn't do Disney vacations or semesters abroad. I still didn't have my own car. I had only recently gotten my own room and only because my mother slept on the couch. Light conversation would be difficult with these foreigners.

It was different with Steve. He didn't engage in casual conversation. He was sincere and direct. We shared stories about broken engagements and living at home. By the time we had been having lunch daily for two weeks, we had expanded the conversation beyond the daily drama in jail to stories about our families. We were comfortable friends carrying similar baggage into adulthood. His own engagement to a female pharmacist he'd dated throughout school ended at graduation. She told him she was bored and wanted more. We shared shredded and frail egos, and only tentative trust in the opposite sex. I was looking forward to learning more about him. Our brief lunch breaks allowed only enough time for a shared work anecdote and a basic, superficial glimpse of our dating histories.

"Is the Rainbow Room okay with you for dinner?" he asked. I'd heard of the Rainbow Room. It was an iconic New York restaurant sitting sixty-five floors high in Rockefeller Plaza, known for its unique circular, window-walled room and revolving dance floor. By 1970 it had become a relic of the glamorous 1940s, mostly popular with tourists and old folks. I realized it was an offer meant to impress, but the stodgy atmosphere I associated with my mother's generation held no appeal to my inner flower child self-image. I knew it was a relic of the big-band era. I envisioned old movies I'd seen with Ginger Rogers and Fred Astaire swirling around in dated clothing.

Until then, I had only been to one real restaurant, for my graduations from high school and nursing school. The Red Coach in Yonkers was fancy enough to require jackets for men. On both occasions, I enjoyed the dinner and hated the stuffy atmosphere. It seemed to me that being dressed up and fitting into this formality had little to do with enjoying dinner.

"Of course the Rainbow Room is good. We could just go someplace less expensive," I offered. "I am fine with something local." But he insisted on this venue for an impressive first date. He was seriously anxious to please me. I appreciated his ambition. Did it really matter that a good slice of pizza or bologna on a Kaiser roll were where my culinary preferences would stay for life? It has taken a lifetime to learn to feign believable delight at a thin slice of Dover sole or a crisp, juicy apple. I've never met a piece of fresh fruit that can compete with an Oreo. Learning to pretend, I was beginning to understand, was another grown-up skill I had to master. I was now confident I could, but arrested development of the palate was easier to overcome than sexual backwardness.

On Saturday night, he found a parking place at the end of our busy and cavernous street. My mother draped herself on folded arms across the sill of the only window facing the street and watched from the vantage point of sixth-floor anonymity. He was over six feet tall and easy to spot as a visitor. His thin brown hair was slicked down and side-parted. He looked intellectual in horn-rimmed glasses. He was dressed up. Wearing gray slacks and a navy sport jacket that had an unfortunately bold windowpane white ticking, he looked self-aware even from six flights up.

"He sure looks like a pharmacist," Mother said with a hint of disdain. Knowing my mother's preference for car salesmen and big-time businessmen, I took no offense. Being in the same social strata as accountants, librarians, pharmacists, or teachers may be dull but seemed to include a level of integrity missing in her choices.

"Wow," she continued, "look at that jacket. . . . Harold Teen for sure." Harold Teen was a character in a 1934 comic strip. Because I had always listened to and ingested my mother's words, I knew Harold was a lovelorn teenager fond of flashy clothes and foiled dreams. Although it was her era, I got the negative innuendo. He wasn't smooth or confident-looking enough. As she was considering other snide remarks, he was entering the food-scented lobby of our building. I could hear the hum and rattle of the elevator. I wondered what he thought of the unnatural, fleshy-coral-colored chipped paint in this moving cubicle. I wondered if the old crones in the beach chairs had also scrutinized him. The doorbell of apartment 6E buzzed.

He was timid, quiet, and formal with my mother. She made small talk, and he answered without much elaboration. It was too soon for her easy conversation and cryptic humor to have any impact. It was obvious he couldn't take his eyes off of me, and I was anxious to be alone with him. We drove to the city in his dark-green Chevy Impala. "Is this your first car?" I asked. I was still sharing my mother's old Buick and was years away from owning my own car.

"Yes, it is," he responded. I wondered if it was a graduation gift or if he had saved to buy it. I guessed his efficient answer was because he was more nervous than he was at work. Still, I was hoping to find out more about him.

"If you don't mind driving in the city, maybe we could take in a museum one day. Do you have a favorite?" I asked.

"Anyone you pick is good," he said. He offered little information about his own interests. I imagined I'd know them in time.

Dinner was expensive and formal, and the room was crowded with awestruck tourists twenty years our senior. There were a few women wearing mink stoles. My nostrils and brain collaborated, causing me to recall mothballs, which overtook the smell of rosemary chicken. A few couples shared a lazy foxtrot on the dance floor. "How's your chicken?" he asked.

I smiled sweetly, not sharing my thoughts of mothballs. I wore an off-white classic and simple knit sheath with soutache-type ribbon embroidery in black and cream around the scoop neck. It was a great $39.00 purchase at Loehmann's flagship store on Fordham Road in the Bronx. In my grown-up dress, I watched the old folks and feigned delight. "Beautiful chandelier," I said.

"You are beautiful," he answered.

We took note of the slowly revolving view of New York City

at night. An inner dizziness had set in, having nothing to do with the revolving room. *Who are these people and what is so strange and false about this place?* I thought. *Why am I here?* I wondered. I continued to smile and show gratitude. I was indeed grateful for the safety and security of this spinning new universe. In the elevator on the return home, he asked if he could see me again and if he could kiss me good night. I said yes to both. Why not? We had both survived the first class of Dating 101 for remedial students. For now, we were on solid ground and moving forward on a straight path. I assumed the spinning was just a temporary sensation.

"He's not for you, I can tell," my mother said as soon as I walked in the door. She was waiting up for me. "He acts like he could be your father. What exactly is the attraction?" My response cut her off before she could offer more.

"I don't care what you think." For now, I enjoyed the idea of being able to date at all and be comfortable with a man. I didn't need to be clever or able to share stories from college or travel plans. There was no need for a marketing campaign. He liked the packaging and was interested in the product. There was no need to waste energy on false facades and feigned interest in topics we didn't care about. At twenty-one, I was already weary and didn't feel like either competing or marketing. I was happy to skip over dating other men. I had no interest in the field of possibilities. If I was interested in politics or art, he would surely enjoy sharing these interests, I reasoned. He was happy to be with me. In time, I thought, we would find common ground in our interests. After all, he was well educated and intelligent. He offered little information about his own interests. I had no idea what he enjoyed, besides my company. I thought all he needed was exposure, and we could share all the interests I'd had with Steve Davidson.

His willingness to please me gave me confidence in eventual success. We had easily overcome the first hurdle we faced. My mother should have been proud of how fast we jumped out of bed or off the couch when we heard her key in the door. We had overcome virginity with flying colors. It had taken only a few months before we were comfortable enough with each other to consider that next step. He was protective and sweetly affectionate. His hugs and kisses were welcome affection. I could see the relationship between love and sex. I trusted him.

He was secure, in a respected profession, Jewish, and wanting commitment. We spent more time together. We were relieved to have regained the security and status of a committed relationship. By the time our rotation ended, we were engaged. I had a lovely and large pear-shaped diamond. We endured family dinners, and our previously practiced engagement rituals. My mother reluctantly rented dishes and table linens, which were set up on two folding tables in our living room. His mother, aunts and uncles, and a sister were invited for dinner. Mother ordered food from the kosher delicatessen and pretended to enjoy her company and hosting the gathering. His mother checked out the apartment for evidence of Judaic artifacts and was probably disappointed to find only one mezuzah on the entry door to our apartment. I was sure they recognized the rental status of our dinnerware. After they left, she abandoned her role of gracious Jewish hostess and mother of the bride to give her synopsis of the evening. "Nice people, I guess. So that's really how you plan to be happy the rest of your life?" I didn't bother to answer her. They were nice people. Why did she want to ruin my happiness? I thought she might even have been jealous of them. They were financially secure and had at least two sets of Lenox china for twelve in addition to everyday dishes and a closet full of hand-embroidered table linens. I hoped they didn't know our dishes were rented.

On August 31, 1970, we had a wedding with an Orthodox rabbi who disliked my maiden name, broken family, and refusal to commit to a kosher home. He wore a large felt wide-brimmed hat instead of a less religious yarmulke. I asked him to remove it before the one hundred and fifty guests arrived. He did not. Instead, he managed to spill some ritual wine down the front of my ridiculously expensive Henri Bendel Alençon lace gown. I told my mother I did not consider this wedding to be a spiritual bond. Out of character, she offered no response. Months later, she asked if I missed the museums, political debates, and book discussions I'd had before. This time I offered no response. I knew he loved me. I loved his sweet and loving concern. I loved his self-effacing humor and desire to please others. I loved his work ethic and dedication to his job. He shared my habit of arriving early to work and talking about the job when home. He was a devoted son to his widowed mother and embraced his large extended family with a loyalty that I respected. His aunts, uncles, and cousins shared birthdays and holidays and truly cared about each other. What a contrast from my small extended family that begrudged us help and comfort.

His mother was the opposite of my mother: overweight, unattractive, homespun, and perpetually happy; she was as simple and narrow in her interests as anyone I'd ever met. She made great chicken and matzah ball soup but was completely disinterested in anything besides family and religion. My mother called her Edith Bunker, the simple, benign wife of Archie Bunker of the iconic seventies TV series. That was a perfect description. His mother's four married siblings (the aunts and uncles) lived in the same neighborhood of Jersey City, New Jersey, some in brownstones they'd been born in. All their children (his ten cousins and a few spouses) stayed within a short drive. There was a special security in being a part of that large clan. I finally belonged to a larger group, and I loved the safety of my new life.

It was 1970, and standards for a happy marriage were evolving. We were happy with the status quo. There were other new details to savor. Our first apartment was a blank canvas, and I had free reign to create the home I'd dreamed of for many years. I had never been so indulged. While I savored these new details, the larger mural of my life was being shaped and formed without thoughtful insight. It would be many years before I stood back to consider the larger picture. It seemed at first so perfect until I knew it wasn't. I thought this was everything I'd wanted—the status and security of marriage, and a doting loving man who wanted my happiness more than anything else. It seemed more than anything I'd ever hoped for. The apartment was filled with the things I wanted to own, while the intangible collection of opinions, deeper thoughts, and interests I also owned and valued were kept exclusively to myself. They were not part of the marriage bargain.

I had shared my body and my dreams, but my soul was mine. I selfishly held on to that ingrained habit of retreating to inner thought that entertained or comforted me. There was enough to share without giving over that part of myself. I kept the part of me that had helped me survive my first twenty years carefully guarded. I was easily distracted by the seductive details that filled my days, and eventually, my years. We were different species. He was hardwired to work hard, give generously, and glide on the warm air mass of that effort. My own circuitry was of never-ending synapses and sparks that reacted to and considered every detail I confronted, perhaps hyper-reacting. Even if I'd wanted to share my thoughts, he was floating above, unable or unwilling to hear. He was often silent and uncommunicative, and I became content to continue my old, comfortable habit of inner thought. Early in our marriage, I abandoned the "we" for the selfish "me."

We originated from distinctly different stock. I grew in the quiet vacuum of negative space where sharing with others was limited. I learned to actively participate inwardly and thoughtfully. Like an only child, I became reluctant to share. I was selfish and protective of my loneness. I brought that self-indulgence to my marriage.

He grew up in the noise and activity of ten cousins, two siblings, and the associated sharing and sparring needed to survive. He told me that as a child he stuttered and learned that assertiveness was never easy. There were vestiges of hesitant starts in speech remaining. The timid, somewhere-in-the-middle-of-the-group, stuttering child learned that passive, silent participation was a safe strategy. We retreated to the safety of learned defenses.

We became quite comfortable with the silence of my inner thought and his respite from teasing thoughts and words from the unwilling grip of his mind. We began and stayed in that complacent place that was our marriage.

Occasionally an attempt to reach out only ended in that errant spark igniting a fire. In the earliest years of our marriage, I'd sometimes attempt to engage him in a discussion about a movie we watched together (he showed no interest in or time for books). I remember the drama and raw emotion I felt when we saw *Deliverance*. The scenes of survival and abandoned morality surely would open the door for debate and analysis of the characters. I needed this post-script exercise to complete the experience of what we'd seen on screen. As usual, he had little to offer in opinion or deeper thought. He was a minimalist in the arena of conversation or circuitous thought. We were a few short years into marriage, and I was still hopeful he would change and broaden his interests. I still tried to engage him and lead the way at every opportunity.

"Do you think there was a clear turning point in the movie when the old rules were abandoned?" I asked, hoping he'd reflect on the characters.

"They all sucked," was his succinct, efficient response.

Who could fault him for his simple and forthright opinion? Could I have subliminally chosen him for this very quality? I had run from men who might control me or demand more than I cared to share. I had worked so hard to be in control. It would be easier to ride and control a dray horse than a high-strung race horse. Why was I now so irritated at his failure to elaborate and ruminate, and maybe overthink the obvious? But I was. I wanted to dissect the plot and characters. I wanted to make it all layered and complex. I needed to process what I'd seen differently. I needed to own it by intellectually ingesting, then chewing it into digestible bits and pieces. I'd long practiced all that ruminating that entertained me when I was younger. In the years with Steve Davidson, I'd learned the pleasure of intellectual banter and shared thoughts. Now, I believed it could be an acquired skill. He simply needed to experience it, understand it, and practice it. I'm not sure which one of us was more flawed. We seemed to ingest and process our worlds like different species. It was wrong and unkind of me to believe I could whip this dependable and hard-working horse into a gallop.

The pleasure of furnishing that two-bedroom apartment that viewed the Whitestone Bridge and of watching passing barges was intense. We also shared a passion for buying antiques and fine furniture. The passion was, most accurately, mine alone. Perhaps his greater pleasure was in indulging my passions, in indulging me. I was set free to shop. Now, I stoked my memory to recreate a home as rich in detail as those of Mary's or Elaine's.

We had two salaries, and I had no shortage of ideas. We shared the pride in our lovely new home. I immersed myself completely in searching for and possessing a myriad of luxury items I'd quietly savored since as far back as I could remember. I considered myself fulfilled. I was satiated with all that shopping. I barely noticed the silence that filled the space that was our home.

Chapter Fifteen

GLUTTONY 101

I was drunk with purchasing power, inebriated with ideas and plans for perfection. The poor girl from the ugly house and crowded apartment now shopped in the Decorators & Design Building as if she were an interior decorator. The realtor who had first showed us the apartment was a fine resource for acquiring the accoutrements of gracious living. Her borrowed decorator's card gave me entrance to the Baker and Vanleigh showrooms among others. The basics were selected on these field trips. I haunted the antique shops on Third Avenue as if on a life-or-death mission for lamps and accessories.

The first apartment soon held a black lacquered Baker Chinese Chippendale dining room set that had six chairs upholstered in polished chintz, with orange tiger lilies on white backgrounds. Above the table, a simple but elegant art deco chandelier of brass and etched patterned, tiered, geometric, frosted-glass globes hung as planned contrast. I thought the angles and geometry of the fixture complemented the fretwork of the chairs.

There was a simple Lawson sofa, which sat on a fine Tabriz patterned orange-and-brown rug. The rug, which reminded me of Mary's Bokhara rug, grounded the lovely sofa and Baker flame mahogany rolltop desk in the corner. A small Daum Nancy vase was poised on top. The bedroom set was Vanleigh bombe and hand-carved dresser and chests. Antique bronze lamps with cream-colored silk string shades were functional and fabulous.

I shopped and savored each addition as if ingesting fine wine. There was an intimacy with my new possessions I lacked with my husband. I knew every turned spoke and knob in the fretwork of those lacquered chair backs. A fallen moth in the globe of the chandelier drew my immediate attention. I scheduled the time needed to polish the burnished flames of the mahogany desk. I rarely passed the living room without untangling the fringe on the rug edges. I had a special comb for the fringe. All these details had high priority for maintenance. They were the tangible proof of my success. Yes, our combined incomes as working professionals paid for our new treasures, but it was my vision, my plan, my commitment to overcoming memories of Salvation Army secondhand furniture and faded landscape prints in cheap frames that drove me. I loved each and every object passionately. I was docent and guardian to my collected treasures.

We rode to and from work daily, too often in silence. At 6:00 a.m. we were sleepy and uncommunicative, on the way home, tired from a busy day. The quiet became a normal pattern. There were occasional departures in the face of a crisis or pending decision. We were newly married when my patient Mitchell Berger died. "Mitchell is having another resection today. There's not enough left of his colon to work with. The medical team thinks he may die if they attempt it." Mitchell was a patient I spoke about often.

"That's sad," was Steven's reflexive response.

Defeated, I agreed. "Sad, yes, sad."

I was resigned to solitary thoughts in the absence of his willingness to engage in a dialogue. He was generous with everything but words. Rarely was there discussion about a shared movie or current event, or for that matter a new acquisition. There were enough distractions to fill any perceived void. Our days were filled with work, commuting, household chores, and a few new friends we'd made. Our extended families were a major presence and filled any time gaps on weekends. We continued a close connection and daily communication with our mothers. I believe we were both guilty of continued "apron string" ties, which strangled and smothered growth.

Hours became days and weeks, then months. Elusively, years passed in this pattern of superficial routines that erased time while we passively settled into ourselves. There may be internal sensors that detect the need for change. I believe they are as intrinsic as the body's ability to respond to a hand trapped under a hip or neck bent at an odd angle even in sleep. It was time to consider change. We felt a change was due.

By 1975, we had comfortably arrived as members in good standing into America's top 15 percent, upper-middle-class income bracket. After those first few years, the appeal of the high-rise view of water and barges under the Whitestone Bridge had become a little less exciting.

The highly recognizable 1930 painting, "American Gothic" by Grant Wood, depicts a somber couple standing in front of a pristine white Gothic cottage complete with front porch. The image is synonymous with Americana and with the dream of home ownership. We were ready to grab our version of pitchfork, apron, and a mortgage for a similar dream in suburbia. Images of a green lawn, picket fence, and a two-car garage were now beckoning. We bought a three-bedroom split-level home with green lawn, two-car garage, and a picturesque stream in front, almost identical to fifty other mid-century split-level homes in a planned community inhabited by young Jewish families. We wrapped it in new vinyl siding and lined the interior with a warm russet-colored wool carpet and Scalamandré foiled wall-paper. Satisfied with the home, we wished to fill it with a family of our own.

Two years later, in 1977, we completed the tableau with the arrival of our much-wanted and well-loved first son, Mark. Two years after that, we welcomed his beautiful baby brother Scott. The other two, previously empty bedrooms seemed filled with new treasures, our baby boys. These years were a blur of first smiles, teeth, steps, and other milestones. My need to accrue new possessions was blunted by abject happiness and the extremely busy life of being a working mother. I was melancholy at the thought of a future when the boys would both be in school full time.

Mark was a timid and big boy with straight blond hair I kept trimmed into a perfect bowl cut. He was content to play with Matchbox cars and hummed his own musical tunes when bored. Shy as he was, he was slow to make friends but found companionship in his younger brother. Scott had huge hazel-green eyes and curly brown hair. He was happy and sweet and outgoing. The boys kept me busy, but happy, and I knew a third child would be manageable. We planned on that last child and were delighted when Sara was born in 1984. A little girl after two boys would be a novelty.

We were now also enjoying new jobs that dovetailed with family life. I began work in home-care nursing, able to create a schedule that complemented school schedules with some help from my mother. I loved visiting patients in their homes and the unique challenges that they presented. Steve left the hospital and began working in a large and prestigious pharmacy, blocks from our new home. It seemed like a neatly tied and ribboned package.

He had found professional nirvana in this role. Steve loved the interaction with customers, who were neighbors as well. He was following in the footsteps of his own father, who also enjoyed the life of trusted and respected neighborhood pharmacist in Jackson Heights, Queens. There is some sad irony in knowing his father's legacy was that of a man who died at age fifty-seven after "slaving" in that store for twelve-hour days, six days a week. "He was never home," is what Steve often told me. And yet, like him, Steve was a beloved and respected member of our local business community, and this fulfilled him. He was validated with each bit of helpful advice or prescription filled. He seemed more animated and confident while working. He was more talkative with his customers than he was at home. At home he discussed inventory and terms and medication innovations and the ever-present fear of the big-box pharmacies that were still in the future. He was ensconced in a world he loved, but in which I was decidedly less interested. He became a partner in the business. Being an owner of the store gave him confidence, and made him more dedicated and committed. I was settled into my own job and perhaps as self-congratulatory about my now-complete life. But for the first time, our dreams were taking strides down divergent paths. We continued to share the happiness our children brought, but those moments were limited in the face of so much responsibility. We were completely myopic about the larger picture.

I hadn't given much thought to insidious change. When Sara

was born on an Easter Sunday, I wasn't annoyed by his need to spend most of the day at the store, dressed as the Easter Bunny and giving out chocolate eggs to neighborhood kids. I knew how he had planned and looked forward to the day. But somewhere I was collecting bits of resentment that would surface when it was too late. I began to resent the endless hours of single-handed parenthood on weekends and his enthusiasm for work. Once in a while, it would bubble to the surface and I'd confront him. "I feel like the store is a mistress I can't compete with," I remember once saying. He was contrite. He was guilt-ridden. He was even more indulgent of anything I wanted as a result. But he was unable to change. He loved us dearly, but the store was a seductive mistress he couldn't say no to. Our marriage was like the proverbial tale of the frog that is happily swimming in a pot of warm water, unaware of increasing heat and impending doom until it's too late to jump.

Like most treasures, children come with the burden of maintenance. That maintenance kept us busy. We had transitioned from being a partnership to becoming an LLC. He worked harder, and underwrote the major costs of the operation. I was the operations manager and made most decisions about where and how to spend our money. I was a talented spender, having no shortage of lofty ideas about designer children's clothes or household trinkets. I juggled work and home and felt justified in rewarding my hard work with spending. I was drowning in responsibility: bathing, feeding, shopping, homework, and car pools. I was immersed in preschool and after school and Hebrew school. The kids had ballet and girl scouts and cub scouts and softball. There were birthday parties and playdates. There was PTA and camp. Steve put in twelve-hour days, and I adapted to the responsibility and accepted it too graciously.

Looking back, I understand that I embraced the control I was given to run the show. After all, wasn't having control a position that had previously benefited me? I liked making decisions and following through on what I wanted to accomplish or own. But a family with three young children, a house, and full-time employment is the antithesis of a controlled environment. Often unable to maintain order or control, I grew frustrated and angry. By the time Sara was six and Mark almost thirteen, other problems had evolved. Both Sara and Mark were struggling in school. Mark was bright but lazy and needed constant encouragement and support with schoolwork. He had auditory-processing problems, which made him want to tune-out, odd for the child that loved music and always hummed. Sara had a learning disability and expressive language problems. She struggled academically and socially. Her frustration often manifested in outrage. She became oppositional and enraged. Her tantrums drove the boys to seek shelter in their bedrooms, and I was inept at managing her alone.

I was not completely alone, however. My mother's increasing presence in my home was another insidious change. Her companionship and help were welcome but just another force undermining the bonds of my marriage and at times my self-confidence. Soon after my marriage, she moved from the Bronx to Yonkers. She retired from her job at the telephone company and redirected both her ambition and libido from the pursuit of men to total devotion to her teacup poodle, Collette. Her dating days over, she became a vocal participant and critic of the daily management of the children, my spending, and my husband's devotion to the store. I was raised on her strong opinions and was conditioned to consider them as fact. I was raised to be compassionate. Now that compassion included concern for her loneliness and her health as she grew older.

She was clearly diminished in her physical beauty and at times her stamina. The vestigial little girl in me was terrified at these losses. I would always be the child who had just one parent to keep me safe in the world. Now the traditional roles of mother-child and husband-wife were blurred. I worried excessively for her well-being. She became another child I needed to care for. We played tough Scrabble games. She mostly won because she was that much smarter and more competitive. She also became the replacement for a husband whose company I wanted at the end of the day.

My Scrabble handicap was at least partly due to the distraction of needing to attend to the children. Sometimes Sara would demand my attention during a game. "Mom, I want to make chocolate chip cookies"—a request any working mom would refuse at 8:00 p.m. on a weeknight.

"We can do that on Saturday. I don't even have all the ingredients," I'd say distractedly. The next sound would be that of a door slammed so hard it shook the walls.

"Give me that kid for a week, and I'll straighten her out," my mother said, rolling her eyes dramatically. "She knows you're afraid of her, you know." The final jab. But she was right. I was terrified at her outbursts and often indulged her to avoid one. The thought of Mark and Scott's retreat or the sheer force of her physical rage had me cowed. But my mother had me cowed as well. She criticized my weak parenting but remained a passive critic, offering nothing more than snide remarks about Sara's fresh mouth and my ineptitude.

Occasionally, my mother would address her directly. "You little snot, good thing you're not living with me, you'd be sorry." The insult would serve to stop the tantrum, but then I worried it would damage Sara's self-esteem and was silently annoyed at my mother's insensitivity. I'd lost control. I depended on school and professionals to confront her problems and do the tough parenting I couldn't do. There were therapists and tutors and resource-room help. We paid large sums of money for professionals to guide us and then undermined any plan by being permissive and indulgent. We were too tired to discipline, too sad to say no as we watched her suffer.

As parenting axioms go, my core belief was that abundant doses of patience and love trumped the adherence to didactic theories or consistent rules. Even our pediatrician noticed my hesitation to discipline. By the time Sara was school age, he had witnessed or been asked for advice by me on handling outbursts. "Well," he slowly offered, "it looks like you guys are a mismatch. She is definitely a stronger, more determined personality, and you are just too easy for her."

Now I added guilt to my frustration. I felt like the fundamental differences he had articulated were as insurmountable as mismatched blood types in an operating room. A typical evening in our house included after-school activities, followed by dinner and homework, which prompted a tantrum from Sara complete with slammed and broken cabinet doors and me screaming, "Wait until your father gets home!" as the boys retreated. After screaming back at me, she'd fling a book at the wall and stomp upstairs, again slamming her door with violent force. For a few short moments, there'd be an unnatural but welcome silence. It was as if the air had been sucked out of the room. I'd eventually give in to her abandoning homework.

At 9:00 p.m., Steve would arrive home, already spent from having given all his reserve to the store. He'd be greeted with a directive: "You need to speak with her. Tell her to get down here now." He launched into an all-too-familiar nighttime litany. "I'm counting to ten and then you'll be sorry. One. Two. Three. Four. Do you hear me? Five . . . six. I'm not kidding, I mean it. Seven, eight, nine . . . last chance . . . *ten!*" Counting didn't work. Empty threats didn't work. She stayed in her room until she was ready to leave it. Her terms prevailed.

There would be a moment or two of silence in the house. Then she'd resume doing as she pleased and normal bedtime routines continued around her. We shared an unspoken guilt for our parental ineptitude. Love had its way as well. Though our children may have experienced the ill-intended wrongs of our parenting, I am sure they never doubted our love, and for that reason, gratefully, they eventually went on to become happy, well-adjusted people.

My quietly fulminating anger was tempered by abundant love for the children. The residual anger was channeled into eating and shopping for comfort. Limited time for myself made me gluttonous for a stolen slice of pizza or the purchase of household items and expensive clothing for the children. I had become the galloping gourmet and the connoisseur in the car of roadside food trucks while driving from patient to patient. My favorite dirty-water hot dogs were on Central Avenue in Yonkers. I could leave the diabetic blind patient I'd just drawn up insulin syringes for on Midland Avenue and circle around the underpass to be in back of it. I had an Italian deli in New Rochelle that had the freshest Italian seeded bread that went with salami, provolone, and fried eggplant.

There was also a regular meal on infrequent trips to an old woman who'd had a stroke. I was there to supervise the health aide who seemed to enjoy soap operas more than the truthful drama of her helpless patient. Mount Vernon, for me, meant bologna and mustard on a Kaiser roll and a bag of chips. I became a closet eater. In the private sanctuary of my car, I lapsed into a coma-like calm as I ate. I was no different than the alcoholic mother who hides her bottle of vodka in the bottom of the dirty clothes hamper. Now some twenty pounds overweight, I could add self-loathing of my body to the hate hole I was starting to dig. It was passive-aggressive behavior.

My mother, ever outspoken, was quick to comment. "Are your panties starting to roll down at the waist? That's how you know when you're really gaining weight, you know."

Yes, my panties were rolling down from the waist as my slacks and other pants seemed to magically be getting a bit short at the bottom. She meant well, I'm sure. Defiantly buying things we couldn't afford as our higher bills began to roll in and eating foods that fed loneliness rather than emptiness accelerated the deterioration of our marriage. My mother picked at the emerging signs of growing distance by being openly critical of his long hours and even, unfairly, of those little things exclusively the territory of a wife. "Oh my God, he's walking around the house in his tighty-whities. I hate the sight of men in briefs. Men should wear boxer shorts," she'd offer up sometimes within hearing distance of the children.

Mom had a hilarious habit of holding her flattened open hand an inch or two from her mouth as if to shield her voice, and then in normal speaking volume saying anything she had on her mind. When the hand went up toward her mouth we all knew we were in for a treat. When that hand went up in a restaurant or at a family gathering, we were prepared to cringe. Of course, she was out of line at my house too late and too often, her uncorrected behavior one more manifestation of my weakness. Just as I was unable to confront Sara, I avoided my mother's inappropriate comments for years.

Poor Steve. For the second time in his life, the matriarchs had conspired to undermine him. He was, in fact, a model son-in-law. He never complained about her presence. He brought her gifts and loved to share jokes with her. He quietly smoked a cigar in his briefs upstairs as Mother and I shared a game of Scrabble. But over time, the tiny fissures began to expand. He was at her service for any request, anything from shoveling snow off her car to bringing her medications or inviting her on every family vacation. He was generous to a fault, and I felt conflicted in my loyalties. Sometimes, everyone seemed to be speaking to me at the same time. I couldn't keep up with the demands on my time, patience, or loyalties. My home life was a place of conflicting and competing interests.

Still, the facade was intact, each of us tightly gripping the corners of a pretty curtain that hid the backstage chaos.

As our incomes grew proportionally larger, we considered the need for a larger home as a necessity rather than a luxury. After all, why should the children share a room? Didn't my kids deserve more than I had?

We would just look.

The gluttonous beast was growing. The more I ate, the hungrier I became. If you grab that last slice of pizza before going to bed, you wake up with a grumbling empty feeling in your stomach. Lusting for food or possessions beyond real need had more to do with my emotional need. Shopping and eating in excess was my escape. We already had a lovely home, a gardener, cleaning woman, and two new cars. The Volvo and Toyota morphed into two new Mercedes Benz sedans. We kept a Plymouth Voyager for practical reasons. Transporting camp trunks or new antiques required a good cargo area. I had no interest in seeing the bills that piled up in a closet. Money was his responsibility.

Those bills were the first casualty of our newly divergent paths. They were the orphans of the communication void. Neither of us claimed responsibility for their upkeep. He was as preoccupied with store finances as I was with shopping. I looked forward to the many catalogs that came in the mail. This was before the days of Internet shopping or Amazon. Snail mail and glossy catalogues were actually more gratifying. I dog-eared and bookmarked pages of possible purchases. The marked catalogues sat in a neat pile on my bedside table, the stuff of promised dreams and potential gratification. It was almost a religious experience. My responsibility was to order something inexpensive on a regular basis to avoid seeing the dreaded words: "This is your last catalog from. . ." That was a rejection I was unwilling to accept. I already perceived rejection from some of the wealthier, thinner, more religious parents of more perfect children who, I thought, felt superior to me. They were a competitive group with prescribed standards for success. Perhaps they didn't feel superior, but it didn't matter. That old feeling of not belonging and not fitting in still lived in my psyche.

No matter what I had, it didn't help. I think the phrase goes, wherever you go, there you are. I hated skinny moms in spandex and kids in AP classes and all those people in synagogue who were fluent in Hebrew. I belonged nowhere and fit in awkwardly. I did know what I believed in, though. I believed in what I loved. I loved my children and, in a less perfect way, my mother and husband. I don't believe I loved myself, but I loved my home and art and books and everything beautiful in nature. A foggy morning brought me instant peace. A thunderstorm made me feel safe rather than frightened. As a child, I found solace at the sight of a barred owl outside my window or in the microenvironment of weeds pushing through broken concrete. I understood that the other side of loneliness is the gift of openness to beautiful alternatives. And now, I still found comfort in embracing what was there. I was often most content on a quiet walk with our dachshund, Ernie, exploring a footpath in the open woods near our home, or simply taking stock of a favorite painting or watching a sunset from our bedroom window, which faced west. Still, I craved validation even from people I felt were in some ways inferior. It was impossible to stop striving. The remembered lessons of childhood persisted. It wasn't loneliness I fought, it was rejection.

Many years later, in 1998, the social science–themed movie *The Truman Show* would come long after my life began to change, but it's pertinent here because it chronicles the life of a man who is unaware he is living in a constructed reality for a TV series. His daily routines never vary. The dog barks and neighbors wave at exactly the same time each day. Traveling the same roads to and from work can feel exactly like this. We see the same red station wagon with the MY SON IS AN HONOR STUDENT sticker in the rear window at the same place in the road. It may be the woman driving with a coffee in one hand and bagel in the other, her palms barely touching the steering wheel. For me, it was the heavy-set, dark-haired, forty-something guy in a large black SUV at the light at Weaver Street and Quaker Ridge Road. These are our commuter cohorts. He habitually draped his left arm out of the open driver's side window. The hand was out in winter or summer, rain or shine. He kept his splayed-fingered, fat left hand pressed possessively against the door. It annoyed me for no good reason at all. I thought how good it would be to see him get stuck on a narrow one-way road lined with thorny rose bushes. Ouch! Men who possessively drape their left arm out of the car window onto the car door still irritate me. That is a male-only habit that suggests a casual dominance over the car and the road and, by extension, over me. Yes, I know that's silly, but at least I've reflected on the quirk.

When I drove the dark-blue Mercedes 500SEL, he looked into my eyes and maintained as much eye contact as the traffic light permitted. The hated left hand would lift slowly and deliberately in greeting. It was not so much a wave as a hand erection. Occasionally, I drove the Plymouth to work. Then I was invisible to him. No eye contact, no hard-on of the hand, nothing. *Hey,* I thought, *it's me, remember me?*

This experience made me ponder the meaning of luxury. Did I need luxuries to validate myself, or because I loved beautiful things, or both? I thought of a quote by a well-known financial expert that stuck in my mind. "We buy things we don't need with money we don't have to impress people we don't like." I thought about how easily the man in that other car could dismiss me in the Plymouth. It amused me, and it angered me. I hated him most when he validated me in the Mercedes. I hated him and myself for engaging in the facade. He didn't know who I really was either way, did he? More importantly, was I more if I owned more? Did I know myself?

I didn't dwell on this very often, or perhaps not often enough. I understood the details and finer points of luxury. I appreciated those finer points. I believed they alone legitimized my well-deserved need to own them. They didn't define me as much as dominate me. I understood them and therefore was entitled to their ownership. In owning them I controlled and confirmed my social status.

The home we ended up buying in 1987 looked like a castle. The 1924 English Tudor house was in the estate area of New Rochelle. No need to change schools, just status. The three-thousand-square-foot house was set back on two rolling knolls. Edward Hopper, my favorite artist, could not have chosen a better day for the play of sunlight and shadow. Off-white stucco sat above reclaimed brick. A steeply gabled slate roof sunk the house nicely into its place. The slates were graduated, smallest at top to give the impression of vanishing space and ascension. Set within the stucco were sweeping timber arcs that also suggested a nod toward the heavens. A single, perfectly formed, aged hemlock flanked one edge of the house. It may have predated the house but had graciously bowed to a side as if in reverence.

The agent invited us into an entry foyer of classic gray-and-white Carrara marble. Marjorie, our agent, led the way. She already understood my love of classic architecture and charming detail. She knew I had no interest in seeing a contemporary home or any traditional home that had been "bastardized" by the removal of walls, beams, original windows, or beautiful floors. I stayed closely behind her, and Steve was last in tow for the tour. He was now excited to be inside a home in the estate area where his wealthiest customers lived. He had stepped into the very elite world he served with reverence. He had "arrived" at a coveted destination.

He followed silently as I registered the details. Sometimes I was silent in taking note of outstanding details, though more often I gave voice to what I loved. My reverence was reserved for the architectural body of the house while his was a more soulful connection to its elite address on Lyncroft Road. The only voice that could be heard was my occasional whisper, denoting something of interest. All I needed were headphones and a microphone to complete the impression of my being a tour guide in a museum. Beyond the foyer, a slightly curved staircase sat squarely in the center. I loved the symmetry of the home. I find symmetry comforting. The twisted oak spindles begged to be touched. I would enjoy using a soft cloth to remove any dust that dared to land on a spiral. The expansive living room featured a huge fireplace with a mantle of Verde Antique marble. The casement windows were leaded and had several understated irregular corner cuts of jewel-toned glass. I remembered the broken glass jewels I loved in the vacant lot of my childhood.

My breathing seemed to slow. It seemed to be happening in slow motion. Steve and Marjorie now stood behind me and waited for me to give some cue that the tour would proceed. I turned to consider the right side of the house and went into the dining room. All the main rooms had pale oak ceiling beams. A quaint butler's pantry had not been dismantled to enlarge an already-large-enough work kitchen. It was lined in solid shelving. Once upon a time, servants stored cutlery and platters here before presenting the meal. The present owner had a collection of Quimper Faience pottery. I could envision my large collection of canary Depression glass sitting here, catching morning sun.

I may have been able to control these thoughts and remain objective had I not noticed the floor buzzer in the center of the dining room. A three-inch circumference, brass rimmed object almost flush with the hardwood floor got my attention. "What's that under the table?" I asked Marjorie. Grateful to resume her role as agent, she elaborated.

"Oh, that is a charming artifact. When luxury homes were built before the Depression, owners had maids, cooks, and other staff. If they wanted something brought to or from the kitchen, they simply slid their toe forward and pressed the button on the floor. A light and bell corresponding to the room would alert the staff. Let's see if it is still connected."

I went to the wall panel in the kitchen that held a grid of lights and wires. The agent stepped on the bell. A dull, nasal bell rang and a small red light appeared next to the letters DR, for dining room. I noticed that there were similar tags for each bedroom. They were all operational. There was no longer any chance of remaining objective. Just looking was no longer a viable option. The working bells were heralding. This house was my rightful destiny. Clearly no one would love it as much or deserved it more. "Oh my God, it's perfect," I finally said in a louder-than-normal voice. It was an emphatic statement and left no room for dissent.

The castle meant a mortgage of $275,000 at an interest rate of 10.8 percent. We were leaving behind an 8 percent interest rate on a $40,000 mortgage. The math and finances were daunting, but manageable, on our combined incomes. Suffering from dyscalculia, I avoided thinking about those unpleasant details. They were left-brain items, and I am a right-brain-dominant person. Math aside, the wheels were set in motion. Marjorie was pleased with the fast sale, and Steve was characteristically quiet. He smiled approvingly. Surely he agreed we belonged here. We were soaring to new heights.

Chapter Sixteen

EMERGENCY BRAKES

The first year in that beautiful house was a whirlwind rush of decorating. This time, I adjusted my choices and spending to pay homage to the fine bones of the home. This was a home with provenance deserving of new dining room furniture. A distressed cherry refractory table for ten and wheat-back chairs upholstered in polished chintz came first. A marble-topped server, next. Drapes and new lighting fixtures perfectly complemented the timeless interior. And then the buying slowed, and the phone rang often with unwanted callers. My most frequent caller was Rosemary McDonnell. I had asked her name once after an especially heated conversation. The mortgage was three weeks late again. So were the car payment, the gardener's and dentist's bills, and the check to the synagogue. We managed to pay the utilities on time.

"Don't answer it. It's that bitch from Chase Bank!" I would shout if it was dinnertime.

"Mom, I'm expecting a call from Amanda about a playdate

at her house," my daughter whined. Sara had managed to make a first real friend in first grade. She hung on every opportunity to be with her after school.

"So call her back, what's the big deal? Just say we were eating dinner when she called."

She rolled her eyes dramatically. This was before the days of caller ID, and the likelihood was that it was a bill collector. We had come to understand this as a vulnerable time when creditors had the best chance of a live respondent answering the phone.

I hated Rosemary McDonnell. She loved her job too much. If she was recorded, she had a way of erasing any evidence of her verbal torture. I had become an expert in the scripted language of collectors. Often, once you had confirmed your identity, you were rapidly read a legal disclaimer about the call being recorded. Not all collectors followed this ritual, but I had become accustomed to hearing it.

"Hello, this is Chase Home Mortgage. I am obligated to inform you this call may be recorded." *Blah, blah, blah.*

"Yes, I know it's overdue. I would like to make arrangements to pay half today and the other half . . ." I would offer hopefully.

I explained our cash-flow problem. Not only had the mortgage tripled, but the bills from Master Card and Visa were arriving regularly to remind me that the furnishings came at a real cost—a cost that included interest rates of 15 percent. To make matters worse, the economy and stock market had taken a turn by our second year in the house. Never one to care about the market or national economy, I soon learned that 1988 and 1989 would be devastating years. We were sitting on an unprecedented bubble about to break. I had little interest in the terminology of business finances. "Net ten, thirty" held the same foreign sound as a football score to me. I would eventually understand that the 10 percent discount on purchases only applied to bills paid within thirty days. I also knew there was never extra cash on hand for things I previously took for granted, like spontaneous spending in Lord & Taylor or on gel manicures. It also meant that the family checkbook was, in fact, not a self- replenishing reservoir. These were concepts that were new and discomforting to me. I found it easier to simplify my excuses to Rosemary McDonnell. After the fact, I also learned that creditors are hired and trained to be heartless automatons. They are the money police, and when you are guilty in their eyes, their job is to arrest not understand.

I added family illness when there was none. I told her I was about to change jobs for a better salary (which was true). Having the freedom in scheduling home-care nurses enjoy, I had registered as a substitute nurse for the White Plains School District and was enjoying a few days each month of extra income and a distinctive change of pace. Of course, there was no guarantee of full-time employment when I told Ms. McDonnell that lie. But that was my intention, and so I told her that I was about to become a full-time school nurse now that all three children were in school all day. The salary was a bit more, and the hours perfect. But Rosemary McDonnell was the human version of a military drone. She had a mission and target, and could not be diverted once launched. She wasn't interested in my future plans.

There was one phone call I will never forget. It started out intimately. "So, Barbara, do you like your house? I hope you do, because it won't be yours too much longer. The bank is considering foreclosure options."

Wordlessly, I hung up. I stopped taking calls altogether.

The snowball was rolling downhill and picking up force and size. We borrowed from my frugal yet generous mother. She initially kept a record of what was owed and a payback plan. But at some point, she stopped expecting to be repaid. She became more cautious but still supportive. She once gave us $500 needed to apply for a loan. We were responding to the ad appearing in the back pages of our local paper. BAD CREDIT? NEED CASH? That was us. I called the number. A loan officer, so much nicer than Rosemary McDonnell, took all the information needed to begin the loan application. He was sympathetic and efficient. He was happy to complete the application by phone, because he understood our need to process quickly and have the check for $5,000 mailed out as soon as possible. We simply needed to forward a money order to the company post office address in the amount of $500. It was mailed the next day. It took less than two weeks to realize that the unanswered and eventually disconnected phones were our official notice that we had been scammed. The indignities mounted.

Mail was my enemy. Store catalogs continued to be welcomed. I separated those from the mounting bills I chose to ignore and studied them as if there were a test on the contents at the end. I could no longer order from them but was duty-bound to at least consider a small purchase. I still worried about being removed from the mailing lists of the more unique stores. The other mail was left for *him*. Those long white, rectangular envelopes with our name appearing through a window were the real enemy. Since I had officially withdrawn from all matters concerning math, however, I was absolved. The store had long ago become Steve's world and responsibility. As the result of my underlying resentment, I abused my relationship with him and the store, insensitive to the vulnerabilities of either of them. I ignored the limitations that should have been imposed. Surely, he was anxious and perhaps panicked. But in his guilt-ridden need to please me, he enabled my insensitivity and absolved me of responsibility. And so, the charade continued. Those balances due and dates due and percentage rates and late charges were not my concern or responsibility. It was just more math, and I didn't do math. We did our worrying as separate entities, but our divergent paths were leading to a shared failure.

Drowning in red ink and pursued by hungry vendors at the store, Steve stayed awake nights and worried. The long white envelopes arriving at home collected on a pantry shelf in the kitchen, behind closed doors. Soon there were several shelves of unopened bills. At some point, it was hard to close the door unless you shoved your hand inside and churned them into an obedient pile. It was easier to ignore them behind closed doors. The facade of normal life was maintained. Neighbors and "friends" and the children detected no sign of the crumbling infrastructure. Our children certainly heard the promises and excuses to the phone collectors. They knew that a request for a special gadget or toy was met now with "we'll see" rather than a "yes." But because we worried silently and separately, life seemed the same. There was barely an admission to ourselves that it was a crisis. The kids couldn't perceive what we denied. If nothing else, we were skilled actors. We went to synagogue, PTA meetings, and dinner with a few neighbors. We helped with homework, went to work. We made small talk at the supermarket and bagel shop. We smiled at people we knew at the coffee shop. We went through the motions of normal life until we were exhausted with the deceit.

A single event saved us from ourselves. The defining moment was not actually a moment but a night filled with events more often associated with TV crime shows.

A pounding on the front door and loud male voices woke us at 4:00 a.m. on a June morning in 1989. We were asleep in our bedroom, under its barrel ceiling and the airy wallpaper of climbing vines and morning glories. It was the time of day—or night—that even insomniacs or the troubled finally succumb to sleep. The only sound usually heard at that time would have been the first forceful spurts of water as the underground pop-up sprinklers began their synchronized function. I heard the loud fists first and woke up, startled. What was it? A robbery? An emergency? Was it the police? Now we were all awake. The pounding got louder. "Open the door now!" one of them commanded.

We told the kids to stay in their rooms and keep the doors closed. Without ever stopping to consider a call to the police, we opened the door. I guess we assumed it might be an emergency. Malevolence was not part of life in an area with estates. Crime happened in bad neighborhoods. What criminal would have the audacity to make this much noise and assault our mammoth oak door with the heavy wrought-iron hinges?

The door was pushed open. Two beefy, ugly young white thugs were suddenly standing on my Carrara marble. One wore a bandana tied in a tight knot at the base of his too-small head. He had acne scars. The other wore a long-sleeved cotton shirt emblazoned with some beer logo. It dawned on me that they were both ugly and, of course, criminals.

"Where's the car?" shouted the pinheaded one. *The car?* They were asking me to locate the Mercedes so they could steal it?

"Where the fuck is the Blue Plymouth van?" His voice was louder, angrier.

I was totally confused, scared into silence. I was still trying to rationalize the potential value of a three-year-old family van. Would it be for an easy escape? Did he want to use it to store stolen goods? The van was in the driveway that curved behind the house, not visible from the street. Better to hide it there in this neighborhood of impressive facades. Easier to load and unload from the back door as well.

"Give us the keys, we're taking it now! Stand in the other room." I was regaining composure now.

"You can't take that car. I need it tomorrow for car pool. There are five kids. They won't fit in the Mercedes."

The thugs looked at each other and laughed. "How is that, lady? You have a Mercedes, too. Do you pay that bill on time?" The light bulb finally went off. They were here to repossess the van.

Sure that I could find a solution, I offered up my plan. "I think we just missed two payments. I will give you a check now for last month and catch up next week with the rest."

"Not the way it works, lady. Pay up in bank check or cash right now, and we leave. If you can't do that, give me the keys." That was when I told them I was calling the police. I was done speaking to imbeciles or criminals.

I moved toward the wall phone. One of them actually grabbed my arm and told me that this was all quite legal. He flashed some paperwork at me. It was in triplicate and wrinkled and had lots of numbers. Numbers again. It was like garlic to a vampire. I retreated.

Steve offered another alternative. At work, in the store safe, there might be enough cash to cover it. They weren't happy but must have had their own best-case scenario, which was money not a Plymouth Voyager.

"Okay, both of you get in the car. One of us is going with you and the other stays here till you get back." It was happening in a flash, but I felt as if I was hearing and understanding his words and instructions through a thick slurry of altered sound. It took what felt like a long time for me to register his intent to stay in the house alone with my children. My perception was that the children were his ransom and insurance. If we were separated from them and together, we'd be less likely to call the police, and we'd want to rush home.

"No, absolutely not happening," I said. "You think I am leaving either one of you alone with my kids? Take the God-damned car then."

Now it was their turn to reason. It was clear they preferred the money to the car, so I suggested another plan. "I will stay here with one of you guys, but you can't be alone with my kids." Now Steve's wheels were also turning over the bleak possibilities. His quiet demeanor hid his fiercely protective nature. No self-respecting man could possibly stand the thought of leaving his wife and children with this unsavory character. He was no exception. He had seen the guy with the bandana's swift grab of my arm only minutes before.

"No", he said, "the kids will be alone for fifteen minutes. Let's go." A decisive Steve was a welcome change.

Perhaps this was all illegal, and the police would have intervened if called. In retrospect, their unwillingness to chance my calling the police may have had more to do with their probable cocaine-induced agitation, which seemed obvious to me and would also be to police. Steve sat up front with one. I sat in back with another. Before we left, one of the kids yelled down the beautiful spiral staircase.

"Mom, Dad, are you okay?" I couldn't see them but knew, from the sound of Mark's voice, that he was sitting on the top step of the second small landing leading to the bedrooms. I had no doubt that the three of them were closely huddled together for support. In spite of their age and personality differences, they were allied in fear and concern for us.

"We are fine. Be back in fifteen minutes. Stay in your room.

Don't open the door for anyone!" I shouted. Of course, the present situation seemed to negate the likelihood of any other bad guys stopping by for a visit.

There was a God that night. There was enough cash in the safe. Our captors drove us home in our own van and dropped us at our front door. For some absurd reason, I felt as if I was in a car pool, a simple drop-off at the curb. The side door slid open and the two men fled to their tow truck. We told the kids there was some bank error that led to the bank wanting the car. They were old enough, scared enough, I believe sensitive enough not to ask any follow-up questions. Yes, the bank had made a mistake. In just a few hours we would be carpooling in the van. It was the loudest wake-up call imaginable. The irony of the drama being over my least-valued possession was not lost to me.

It wasn't my fault. I was my own victim. I am a right-brain-dominant person. I love visual images, have a vivid imagination and good spatial relations. My left brain, which controls functions like logic and math, is undoubtedly underdeveloped, maybe even atrophied. It is often bullied by the right. It is submissive at best. I am an avid reader and lover of history, politics, and social issues. I knew, from Greek literature, that hubris or overconfident pride is punished by the gods. Surely, I now reflected, I was guilty of overconfident pride. Pushing my back against the overstuffed pantry door to keep the bills contained was tempting those punishing gods. Why hadn't I practiced a more moderate ascent into the social stratosphere of nouveau riche life?

I was no smarter than Icarus, that classic example of hubris in Greek mythology. Wishing to escape Crete, Icarus's father, Daedalus, fashions a pair of feather and wax wings to help his son fly away. He warns Icarus to avoid the heat of the sun that will melt the wax, or the spray of the sea that will clog the feathers.

He warns him to be moderate. Icarus soars with pride and power toward the sun. The wax soon melts, and he falls to his death into the sea. Had my mother given me flawed wings as well? She helped me to both love and lust for those finer things that others had and we did not. I placed my confidence in the trappings of success and hoped to ascend to a self-confident place in heaven by owning them. I failed to confront my own limitations and misguided path. And now I had fallen from grace.

Disoriented and confused, I had plummeted from the lofty perch of the grand Tudor to confront my reversal of fortune. I was dizzy with the need to right myself in the spinning world of available choices. And so, in falling, I reluctantly embraced the previously overlooked thin limb of moderation, which now broke the fall, but which would still support me at a station slightly above the simple split level we'd left less than three years before. I could salvage some pride if we moved to a lesser house in a lesser but still-affluent neighborhood. Perhaps it would be seen as a need for change. After all, the new house was in a gated community of large homes constructed in 1978.

I remembered being impressed with the concept of contemporary homes meant to emulate classic colonials and Tudors, when I was still grateful to own any home. They were ersatz facades that offered open-concept floor plans, central air conditioning, and golf-course views. And now I was settling for a house I disdained for its pretension because of my own pretension. We lost $75,000 on the real Tudor and moved to its costume jewelry copy, which was still above our means if saving for the future was ever a consideration. But for now, I was more concerned with saving face. This was a salvage operation. I needed to salvage my wounded pride and damaged ego. I needed to belong and be accepted by the community our family was so entrenched in by now. I told myself this was best for all of us.

The children liked the new thin-walled house with big-windowed bedrooms and a golf course view. They loved the double-sided fireplace that I hated most of all. Its arched brick facade reminded me of a pizza oven. When lit, it routinely spit out ash and embers as if it too was choking on the pretense of grandeur. What went unchanged were the unwritten minimum standards for success and acceptance in affluent Westchester suburbia. And this was my choice. By remaining within the loose barriers of this community, I had agreed to the terms of the contract.

I took the kids to synagogue on Saturday mornings. I fought with the boys to wear neckties and the obligatory little-boy outfit of chinos and navy blazers. Sara and I argued about her dresses or hairstyle, and she always won. Once she established victory, I could put on any dress or skirt that zipped over my expanding hips. There the children played tag or hide and seek in the large lobby with other bored children, while I feigned piety in the sanctuary. I looked appropriately interested in the ancient language printed on my prayer book. Sometimes I followed the English translations and prayed that God would understand my good intentions. I faithfully drove each of them to Hebrew school three times a week so they could achieve the nonnegotiable goal of a bar or bat mitzvah at thirteen. Perhaps this was a cruel requirement for my two learning-disabled children. No matter, we were in full commitment mode, including extra Hebrew tutoring for Sara.

Outside of regular school and Hebrew school was the other social circuit of their lives, and by extension mine. Birthday parties, holiday parties, Little League, Youth Soccer, and Scouts ate up their time. Parents compared notes on their overscheduled children. Grades, teachers, sport scores, awards, and playdates were subtly compared. This was an ambitious community. Competition extended to school vacations. If it was winter, people went to Disneyland or on a Caribbean family vacation. If it was summer, they went to sleepaway camp. There was a short list of the "best" camps. Those were the camps the Jewish kids in our community went to.

Competition unsettled me. I disliked competitive sports because there was always a loser. I never really cared about grades. I believed then, and still do, in school that happiness and self-esteem are not a function of the best grades. As a child, sports meant riding a bike or roller-skating. The only time we watched a ballgame was if the Yankees made the World Series. I had no real interest in that either. Now, I sat reading whatever book to survive my time at the kids' softball games. Occasionally, another parent would nudge me to remind me my kid was "up." I was aware of my aloof attitude but unable to pretend to be enthusiastic. That was more than I could fake. Immersed in my self-imposed need to conform, I felt more and more like an imposter and began to avoid as many gatherings as I could without drawing notice. But still, we attended a few obligatory barbecues and birthday parties. We sat with the other moms and dads, two ghosts, smiling as if nothing had changed. We joined in as if we were just like them. We both knew we weren't.

I married a man more like myself than like the other dads in our community. Steve was a man with questionable confidence, programmed to work hard and to please others. The other husbands were accountants, commercial realtors, stockbrokers, and traders. They were men whose vocations were about using and making money. They thrived in the world of profit, while Steve, who cared about his family, customers, and store, existed in the shadows. The other men talked about investments and money and cars and money and vacations or their kids and money. They all seemed financially sound and self-congratulatory. They were good at easy banter and quick humor, but they seemed cocky and arrogant to me. They rarely listened to each other and exuded an air of power and control that made me bristle. I didn't realize until much later in life that what I hated most about them was how they reminded me of the men in my mother's dating years. It was visceral. I hated them then, and perhaps would always distrust wealthy men with easy charm and self-confidence.

Steve was not like them. I chose a man, who, like me, lacked self-confidence. That, I believe, was the greatest flaw in our marriage. I veered as far away from arrogant self-confidence as possible. I avoided moderation when I married Steve, as I would again in choosing the house. But unlike me, he was content with life on the sidelines. He liked being the audience. That was a comfortable seat in the arena for him. Belonging was enough for him. But to me, being on the sidelines meant second-class status. I had begun to resent his social complacency; I resented having to work harder to compensate. All his energy was diverted into saving the failing business. It was all-consuming for him. He acted at times like a wounded animal. I was too sad, resentful, and frightened to care.

How are we so shortsighted that it is not until we look back from the vantage point of the future, having survived our own plights, that we are able to so clearly see those pivotal moments that alter everything? As we live with the pain of failure or fear of change, we are lost to the potential good ahead or the ability to hope. All we know how to do is function at some basal metabolic, life-sustaining level. And this is where I found myself, for years.

In the aftermath of our fall from grace, I retreated to loneness. I avoided interaction and chose to walk alone five miles every evening. I walked back into the estate area of the Tudor we'd left. I walked in dark, in rain, and in snow. I paid homage to the real Tudors and colonials and barrel-tiled Mediterraneans. I hoped their owners loved and respected them. I lived in a self-imposed cocoon of misery. It was a singular and selfish place, and I stayed there for the next six months. But in time, the cocoon thinned, effaced, and opened; and what emerged was a thoughtful, slimmer, determined woman. I understood that I needed to begin at the place where I'd always felt secure. It was time to get back to work. I had existed at that minimal metabolic rate of existence and was ready to consider a future. For now, that meant taking a new full-time job as a school nurse. It was 1990, and a new decade was upon us. Three years had elapsed since we'd first walked through the front door of that grand, ill-fated English Tudor. I was ready to put my mistakes behind me.

Chapter Seventeen

BEYOND BALANCE

The challenge of a new job was a welcomed distraction from my nascent sense of imbalance and growing realization of the brewing identity crisis. Now that I had been a substitute nurse, I was a proven entity in the White Plains School District. I had only to meet and be interviewed by the principal of the school. The job had a better salary, perfect hours, and good benefits. But beyond all that was something more important to me, validation.

In years to come, I would realize that something life-altering happened because of that job. As I shed the "flawed wings" of misguided values, like the grand house and luxury car that had failed to bring security or self-esteem, I considered the occupational values that were still an intrinsic part of my identity. I had found a truth in nursing early on. These weren't just values I'd inherited, I had earned them. They were mine alone. Like most children, I had values that were covertly infused by my mother. I understood and absorbed her love of fine furnishings and the beautiful things other people collected. This translated to wanting those things. I understood that my religion was a valid one, albeit different. I believed in God and the intelligence of dogs and all Democrats. I believed men were somehow more important than women. These were my inherited values. Now, I considered the importance of my own interests and beliefs, my acquired and earned values.

I'd chosen nursing because of a self-confident aunt and a kind school nurse. Fate had landed us in the backyard of a large city hospital, but living in a pre-feminist world, I had limited choices. I chose nursing during that time when my brother's life hung by a thread and I considered inequities greater than income inequality. I brought these truths, and my own now unbound wings to the interview with the principal. I arrived at the interview armed with a level of self-confidence that had grown over more than a decade of nursing practice and experience. These were skills I'd acquired, earned, and valued. These were my occupational values. I would always love a good book and fine furniture. I would continue to believe in the intelligence of dogs. Those infused values stayed. But now, a changed person with an opened mind was about to be interviewed.

It was a new starting point. I never sat down and compiled a hard list of earned versus inherited values, not then or maybe ever. But I think it's something everyone should do. What I realize now is that when the "values" deck of cards was reshuffled, I held a better hand, a hand with potential to win.

The job turned out to be bigger than just about how competent I could be in an emergency. It involved the ever-changing and challenging opportunity to problem-solve and be creative, too. The wonderful hours and holidays off with my children also factored in. Working where my intent and purpose were clear would hold me here. But by far the greatest pull to stay—and I would remain there for more than a quarter century—would have to do with my allegiance to this place and this woman, who saw more potential in me than I had previously considered. I had struggled to define myself through nursing. In becoming a nurse, I'd exceeded the expectations of family and teachers. Now, the principal conducting the interview was about to challenge me to soar beyond self-imposed limitations. She offered more than a challenge. She paved a future for me without limits, and this would turn out to be one of the greatest gifts of my life.

During the interview, Principal Jeanne Vissa asked no questions about child abuse laws or asthma or peanut-allergy protocol. There were no questions about my last job or strongest nursing skills. I sat opposite the woman who seemed about my age, wearing a dated gray skirt and clunky black pumps. Everything about her dress and demeanor said school principal. A large, cluttered desk sat between us. This was decidedly not a hospital or clinic, and I was out of my comfort zone. I waited for her to speak.

"How would you like to develop a mentoring program here?" she asked. The question confused me.

"Would you like me to hold a kid-friendly first aide course or healthy-eating program?" I responded. "Or do you mean parent education?"

"No, no, not health education. I want you to develop a corporate-community school partnership program. You would work with corporate partners." She looked directly in my eyes and waited for my answer. My mind was going over any health-related connection I might be missing. I couldn't connect the dots. What did a mentoring program have to do with being the school nurse? Perhaps I was interviewing for the wrong position, or my appointment date was wrong. Was this a trick question?

But Principal Vissa had a vision I was not yet privy to. She was the principal of a newly opened and expanding elementary school. Dr. Jeanne Vissa was a different kind of principal, and she wanted a different kind of nurse. She was, in the vernacular of education, a visionary.

She waited. I considered a response. *What the hell?* I thought. I'll throw one back at her.

"Can you tell me something about the partners?" I asked, still hoping for a clue.

Her eyes narrowed a bit. Yes, she was testing me. "The Bank of New York and County Health Department." I considered a good response and decided that "willing participant" was always a good position. I would ask for clarity and details later. The involvement with the County Health Department assured me that some relevant health component was a part of what was being proposed.

"Sounds like a challenge I'd like to try," I finally answered. Jeanne Vissa was, I later discovered, building a staff of divergent thinkers and risk takers at all levels. She assumed I was in that elite league. She wanted a nurse who was looking for a creative challenge, not just a job. We were launched. She had instilled a new mindset in me, some version of a self-fulfilling prophecy. If she believed me to be creative and capable, then that is what I'd be. It was the Pygmalion effect.

From that point forward, Jeanne Vissa and I began a long, mutually respectful relationship. During the years she was principal, she recognized and developed my strongest qualities. I discovered that program development was perfectly aligned with my love of structure and goals. She came along at a vulnerable time in my life. The dream house was gone, the store was facing bankruptcy, and the children needed me less. She was brilliant and unconventional. She was an educational visionary who tapped into every resource available and questioned traditional models. She saw the potential in each student and every employee. How fortuitous that she was there just as my confidence was at a low point and my direction unclear.

One of her goals was to tap into state funding for school mentoring programs. It was 1990 and Mario Cuomo was the Democratic governor of New York. His wife, Matilda, New York's first lady, had spearheaded the ambitious program to partner schools with businesses in 1989. The objective was to provide academic and social support to at-risk students through partnerships with corporate employees. State funds had seeded the broad foundation and leadership goals. Local schools would be supported through a central administrative corps. Jeanne thought it was a great opportunity for Church Street School. She just needed a coordinator to help develop and implement the program. I wonder now if there were teachers or a social worker or school psychologist that rejected the opportunity before I arrived. It didn't matter. I was flattered and intrigued.

Jeanne was a tough taskmaster, former nun, and owner of many contradictions in style. She is best remembered for a spontaneous sleigh ride with a few students just for the fun of it and for harsh criticism of any staff member falling short of her high standards and expectations. Caught once sitting at my desk looking at a catalog, she sent me on a fool's errand to retrieve a book from her car. It was fifteen degrees and hailing ice pellets. Her car was a mess; the book impossible to find. I returned empty-handed and reflective. I was unsure of her intention, but felt at the time it was a subtle reprimand. I loved and understood her anyway. We all did. She is also remembered for the day she came to school wearing mismatched shoes. Other people have done that, but few have worn a flat shoe on one foot and two-inch heel on the other. She was able to laugh at herself as well. Her humility redeemed her. Although my contemporary, she represented the best qualities of a mother: consistent, stern, unselfish, and nurturing, with a dash of whimsy.

I rose to her standards. I welcomed nontraditional assignments. I learned about models for mentoring programs and at-risk students. I developed interview tools and standards for prospective mentors. I reviewed legal guidelines for non-district employees working in schools, and vetted the applicants. I helped teachers select at-risk students and worked with the school psychologist and social worker to establish clear objectives and benchmarks. I developed communication tools to guide the mentors and created events to celebrate our achievements. Some students were academically at risk and others needed role models and social support. I recalled my own painful elementary school years and the school nurse who threw me a life raft. I monitored their progress and problems. They met twice a week after school for two years.

Eventually, New York State confronted a budget crisis. The program ended abruptly. I am not sure if we met all quantified objectives. In my mind, success rested on the fact that none of the mentors or their students was ever absent on a mentoring day. I believe benefits are not always a quantifiable, cold metric. Surely some of those twenty-four children will recall the adults who gave them special attention.

The mentoring program was followed by nutrition programs and partnerships with other community resources. I was awarded three staff development grants. I developed and implemented a sex-abuse awareness program, as well as a puberty education program that continued and was implemented throughout the school district. For a few years, I ran the program as a business, available as an after-school program to private schools and organizations. Eventually, however, the hours conflicted with school, and it was never as enjoyable as being in my own "home" school.

I was forced to do the private programs after my regular school day ended. It was stressful rushing to another school after a long school day and then rushing home to my own school-aged children, who still needed homework prodding and "quality time" with a parent. I could juggle my daily schedule at school and my office, enabling me to wear "two hats." I enjoyed the nonstop pace of classes, events, and projects, and it was not unusual to have an extra nursing substitute assigned to my school to accommodate my programs. There was pleasure in remembering my own days as a nurse substitute. Programs were my passion, and school was my safety zone and home. Jeanne Vissa had her divergent thinker and could brag about programs unique to her school, and I had succeeded in learning how to develop, implement, and fund programs. Those skills catapulted me to the private sector.

Without benefit of a marketing campaign, but through parent networking and a short article published in a local newspaper, my puberty program was becoming known. I accepted a contract with an elite prep school.

Although it was lucrative, I never enjoyed the prep-school environment as much as public school. After school and evening hours were stressful, but it was more than that. I was keenly aware of resenting the overly confident, uniformed, not always polite students and their skinny moms, who wore riding boots and jodhpurs to collect them after school. But now it wasn't so much the feeling of being an outsider as it was disdain for their arrogance.

An intrinsic part of the program was a parent workshop, where I got a firsthand taste of the upper crust. Typically, I arrived an hour before and set out pamphlets and folders I'd either purchased or created. Slowly, the parents filtered into the beautiful cafeteria that had panoramic views of Connecticut's priciest wooded real estate. They were mostly couples and always attractive. Even the ugly people managed to be attractive. Every one of them entered the cafeteria, assessed my wardrobe and hair then the displayed materials, and dismissed both in favor of coffee and cookies.

Their attendance was not obligatory, but proof of their profound interest in their offspring. They kept me after the meeting to share their concerns, to ask delicate questions, and to warmly thank me. I always won them over. But winning them over was hard work, and I was left feeling irritated rather than validated. Both the children and parents suffered from self-congratulatory attitudes, and I suffered still from some deep-seeded insecurity that confronted me when I was with them. So, I left the money behind and retreated happily to the reality of diversity instead of disparity.

Jeanne had created a divergent and independent thinker, and it was empowering when I rejected the contract to renew. I was rejecting a salary equivalent to four hundred dollars an hour for less than six hours of time. Some would consider that foolish. But, in fact, it was especially delightful for me because of the lavish salary. Somewhere in that convoluted equation was my understanding that I had parted ways with the notion that money mattered more than anything else, like my happiness or sense of connection. It was not an amicable divorce, but it afforded a new independence. It seemed as if divergent thought led to divergent values. That reconfigured deck of values cards was now in play.

After dropping the prep-school kids and their perfect lives and perfect families, it was time to confront my own inability to see them fairly. I understood that beneath the polished veneer of luxury cars and riding lessons and ski vacations to Aspen there was also divorce, dysfunction, and despair for some. But the impenetrable coat of arrogance and condescension had rendered me indifferent to it. Awareness of my own bias was at least a start. They may have had the same vulnerabilities as other humans, but I preferred vulnerability served up raw like mine was. I preferred the kid who said his head hurt and didn't need to preface the complaint with a story about jet-lag as the cause. I didn't need that bitter reminder of disparity to perform my job efficiently. I preferred simplicity, and therefore preferred children who were unaware of social status and who had the delightful honesty and spontaneity of childhood without the affectation of affluence.

It was good enough for now to congratulate myself for choosing to part with old values and irritating people. But I hoped not to part with my sanity, or my professional ethics. Mine was the luxury of choice. But I knew, as does anyone serving or courting the public, that honing the skill of a perfectly presented public face is essential. I understood that I had a lower threshold for insensitivity and arrogance than most people. An occasional affront within the public arena was manageable, even a challenging game at times. But when the population was supersaturated with self-importance, the game became an internal, destructive, losing battle. It would be continuingly challenged by having to return to that battlefield. This was a hard part of being a grown-up.

The heart and soul of my school arrived each day in the form of yellow school busses. Eighteen big yellow busses delivered most of the seven hundred students. They came from different neighborhoods in a diverse small city of sixty thousand people just twenty-five miles north of Manhattan. The busses unloaded children from the low-income housing projects and the neighborhoods of stable co-ops and rentals scattered throughout the city. A small yellow bus delivered any homeless children staying at a shelter. A few busses or cars brought children from fine homes in more expensive areas. They came from neighborhoods of small close-set homes surrounded by chain-link fences and ambitious little gardens.

The parents were teachers, gardeners, and salespeople. There were hairdressers, nurses, and cleaning women. There were social workers and chefs. There were small-business owners and day laborers. There were lawyers and physical therapists. There were drug addicts and fast food workers. There were always a handful of parent physicians. They were black, brown, white, and Asian. They were biracial or fifth-generation pure something else. They were delightfully different and diverse. They were native English speakers, non-English speakers, and dual-language children and parents. They were a perfect cross section of America and part of a whole where I belonged as well. Somehow, I fit in well. I belonged with these people. I have always felt equity in spite of the vast differences. There has always been belonging in the collective differences in us.

This polyglot of a place offered changes and challenges in many ways. There was dysfunction, tragedy, and drama. There was the mainstream and predictable. There were parents that overprotected and some who were indifferent. There was a lot of happiness and success. It was all here. Unlike a hospital, the children and their families were ours for five or six years. Our contact was more intimate, and our impact could be more dramatic. It would be the perfect backdrop for a television series if ever anyone realized the drama and humor of the school nurse office.

In addition to endless paperwork for immunization compliance and physical exams, there was a laundry list of diseases and issues that school nurses were responsible for. The long list of disease entities could be exotic. It was not just asthma and food allergy. Yes, I had to give EpiPens for anaphylaxis, several times. But peanut allergies aside, the day-to-day differentiation of ear infection, strep throat, head lice, stomachache, and fever was simply a backdrop for the possible presentation of less-mundane issues.

I've overseen horrible cases of child abuse, juvenile arthritis, Crohn's disease, celiac, diabetes, muscular dystrophy, leukemia, hemophilia, and epilepsy. There have been two cases of Munchausen syndrome by proxy. There were rare diseases and tragedies as well. Boredom of the day to day is offset by the potential for drama, and the need to be prepared. My internal list of extraneous symptoms, medications, and care plans was soon encyclopedic. I've always been proudly defensive of the unsung wealth of knowledge owned by school nurses and outraged when it is dismissed as an easy or frivolous position. I have kept, and still keep, the details of meds, symptoms, care plans, and treatments tightly tucked in some dark little crevice in my brain. Nursing and specifically school nursing were becoming my steel core of confidence. Sometimes, though, skills and confidence were not enough.

Many years later, I'd confront one of the worst challenges of my career when one of those unassuming children presented with the simple clarity I'd become so comfortable in treating. It was the first week of school, a time of overwhelming paperwork for me and major adjustments for new and returning students. September is a time of realigning and readjustment. A fourth-grade student was sent to my office that first week. Her teacher called to say she was dizzy and was stumbling a little. I imagined a timid child overwhelmed with newness and social anxiety, and I assumed she only needed a few minutes of respite from her classroom. My plan was to have her rest and surreptitiously watch her as I worked. My guess was that I would ask her questions and take her temperature, and then she'd be ready to return. Surely, I thought, the stumbling was a dramatic guise to impress her teacher. But for Jennifer Alvarez, my assumptions were wrong.

Jennifer was not a child I knew well. She had no chronic health problems. She was the oldest of three and rarely visited the nurse. All school nurses have "frequent fliers," the kids avoiding a test or subject they hated as much as I had hated math in fourth grade, or those with families in turmoil. Sometimes, they are simply anxious about health or need a quick break from a subject they don't like. Who would know this better than I? Had Mrs. Bridgewater not been there for me, fourth grade would have been even more unbearable. Now I sat with Jenifer to ask a few assessment questions. I took her vital signs. She said she had been having headaches, but the doctor said she was okay.

As we spoke, I noticed her left eye moving oddly and not tracking. I checked her health record. No history of strabismus or vision issues. I asked her to walk across the room. She stumbled and listed to the left side. She said she was not dizzy, but her balance was off. I rechecked her eyes. She could not control the movement in her left eye. It moved randomly at times.

I called home. "Hi, Mrs. Alvarez, it's the school nurse calling. Jennifer is with me, because she seemed dizzy in class. I can't find much wrong, but I am curious about her vision. Has she seen an eye doctor for anything?"

"Yes," she replied. "I was at the eye doctor in August with her. I noticed her left eye moving around. He told me to wait a few weeks and come back if it happened again. Then, she had a few bad headaches so I took her to the emergency room. They said maybe it had to do with her vision or maybe it was a migraine. They gave her Motrin. I was thinking I would make an appointment to see the eye doctor in a few weeks."

I felt uneasy about the nonspecific appointment. I had never seen the combination of uncontrolled eye movements with loss of balance. I thought about the headache. None of it sat well. I thought about my brother's headaches so, so long ago, and where those had led.

"You know, I think you should take her to the emergency room after school and not make an appointment. I can see she is really unable to keep her balance. Her eye may have something to do with it. They can have an eye doctor and neurologist take a quick look together." She agreed to do that.

Jennifer never returned to school. First there were x-rays and MRIs and scans of all kinds. The diagnosis didn't take all that long. We weren't told at first, but as the weeks and months progressed there was a diagnosis: glioblastoma multiforme, stage four, an aggressive malignant brain tumor. Homebound instruction was planned around surgery and treatment. There was little instruction as it turned out. There were too many surgeries. First, there was excision and debulking, followed by shunts to redirect spinal fluid. There were airways and stomach tubes and many spinal taps. There was radiation and chemotherapy and later massive doses of steroids. Her classmates made cards. School families sent food and carpooled her two siblings. Friends from school distracted and cared for the siblings. Relatives from Mexico were flown in. Agencies provided assistance of all kinds. She visited school once. Her mother brought her in a wheelchair. She was bloated and bald. She was immobile in her child-sized wheelchair. Her fists were contracted, her legs atrophied. Her speech was slurred and slow.

"Hi, Jennifer," I said. "Remember me?"

Her head listed to the left and rolled forward. Her eyes looked up, and she smiled. "You're the nurse," she slurred. I wished she hadn't remembered. It made me think she had an awareness of things no ten-year-old should have to know. She died seventeen months after her diagnosis. Her classmates would go on to graduate elementary school without her.

School is supposed to be a place of mostly healthy children. Several parents would die of both natural and accidental causes over the years. Divorces and custody battles are so commonplace that there are both medical alert lists and custody alert lists. Before sending a sick child home or calling home, this list must be checked. Managing chronic health issues is often simpler than managing the psychosocial problems that seem to be ever present. Every school year brought some newly emerging drama or one continuing to play out. A collective intake of breath on the first days of school is almost audible as we ready ourselves for the unknown, but predictable, drama ahead. School and nursing have never failed to challenge me. It is where I am most confident. It is where I find complete balance between myself and a world that makes sense, even when it is cruel. It is my comfort zone. It is where my self-confidence is firm and people are respectful of each other. It is where I have never felt alone, unsure, or less. Jennifer's death, and my brother's close call with death, all the frailty and potential for pain and counterbalanced hope and happiness are shared in this place. We adjust and realign together every school year.

As I marked the years and progress of other people's children, my own children also changed and evolved. High school and college and driver's licenses and romance and adult conversations were all waiting for me, and the adults they became captivated and pleased me as nothing else ever could. These were mothering years I especially enjoyed. I never gave thought to my relationship with them. It was an unequivocal thing. It didn't require thought. It was luxurious in its simplicity. My mother, still a large presence, teetered on the cusp of old age, but still beat me at Scrabble and enjoyed her independence. It was a thin sliver of time we shared right before everything changed. Like most people, I didn't think about or notice the great shift enveloped in that short, succinct time. Most of the hours of those years were lived primarily in my school home, the Nurse's Office, also called the Health Room. For almost a decade, I enjoyed a simplicity of thought and purpose there. But things are rarely simple, least of all thought.

Looking back, I now see the simplicity of thought and purpose at work and with my children in those years, and I consider what thought dynamic could be applied to my marriage. Change had silently seeped into the fissures of our marriage, breaking the bedrock of our relationship. It seems to me now a perfect example of cognitive dissonance. That is the only way I can understand it and forgive myself.

The theory of cognitive dissonance suggests we have an inner drive to hold all of our attitudes and beliefs (values) in harmony. We want to avoid disharmony, or dissonance. We seek consistency. Dissonance can be relieved by changing the conflicting value, denying the conflict, or by reducing the importance of the conflict, telling oneself the value itself is unimportant. Simply put, we rationalize a bad situation by inventing a comfortable illusion. I was a child of divorce, a believer in the sanctity of marriage, and a woman who avoided confrontation. I believe I chose the path of least resistance and opted to negate the importance of some values. I simply ignored the importance of deep intimacy and honesty necessary in a viable marriage. I chose not to think about it. Avoidance was the easiest path. Time and schedules and responsibilities are seductive thieves. It's not difficult to move forward thoughtlessly. I had somehow spent a decade changing the rest of my life in absentminded response to everything so carefully contrived in the past. We moved forward thoughtlessly in time, through our twenty-five years of marriage. We were rounding out the end of a decade. In short order, a new millennium would be facing us, and the dissonant thoughts could be avoided no longer.

School and routines of family were safe hiding places where dissonance waited in coiled posture for an opportunity to confront reality. School was my safe haven. My school office, the Health Room, was more than a room. It was a more intimate space. Chamber better names and personalizes it. I shared the room with many children each day. There were thousands of children between the ages of five and eleven that shared the room with me. The thousands of children and their visits play out as little vignettes that I may or may not remember. Some vignettes take seconds and others play out over six years of shared space. I was witness to and participant in their growth and change. The room was magical, because it caused me to grow and change as well.

I came to think of the room, this chamber, in medical terms. It was, to me, a fifth chamber of my heart. It was not the pumping, heaving, hard-working ventricle or auricle. This fifth chamber was more subtle and thoughtful. It was responsive in its way. It processed not blood and oxygen, but all the emotions and events in my life. It had a soulful rhythm. It bore witness and provided comfort within its simple borders. I liked to believe there was room in this heart for compassion for everyone. The room was large—about eighteen by thirty feet, though I never measured it for fancy rugs or furniture. The built-in cabinets were a harsh teal color; the counters, a gray Formica. The floor had twelve-inch speckled brown vinyl tiles, perfect foils for lost baby teeth or eyeglass screws that rarely get found if dropped. They've hidden vomit and blood spills nicely. It was a forgiving choice. Two love seats, in navy upholstery, faced each other. I know where the rips were from pencils pushed into the fabric by bored students. There were throw pillows that looked like hearts and hands. I thought the head lice would prefer a warm scalp to a soft but cool pillow. There was a low, round coffee table holding puzzles and a few toys.

Of course there was artwork, too. I had children's art hanging, which was best of all. Those were framed because they were lovely and deserving. I had a favorite painting. It was a twenty-four by thirty-six-inch tempura portrait in periwinkle and yellow. The lopsided face had a crimson rosebud mouth. It rivaled any Picasso. It was gifted to me in the first year or two of my school nurse job. The painting would later be a reminder of passing time when the student was grown with a child of her own. It didn't make me sad. How could such a fabulous creation elicit sadness? The room offered none of the luxury or accoutrements found in my home. It offered a rhythm, which continued to witness my life and match it perfectly. It mirrored my heart and absorbed me into its soul. We spent our days in synchronous harmony. There was no need for cognitive dissonance or a strategy. I was grateful for this space. This space, this field of nursing, was indeed a perfect choice. The room offered comfort and security never realized in the elegant Tudor. Here, I was confident, respected, and complete in a vocation perfectly chosen, planned, and lived. I was becoming glaringly aware of the disparity in my two "homes," one a simple, functional workplace where I was most confident, and the luxury-filled other home where I waited to arrive at a similar confidence.

Summer months stripped me of that warm cocoon of confidence as effectively as it sent my down winter jacket into attic storage each June. For almost as many years as I'd been at school, I faced the financial reality of needing a paycheck in summer.

The Northern Westchester Day Camp, where wealthy children spent their days, was my summer home for many years. I started there when my boys were just four and six years old, and stayed on beyond their childhood. I stayed on in camp as I had stayed on in my marriage. I continued a blind obedience to practical issues. After all, summer was a short season in New York.

I challenged all my better angels and greatest acting skills, and collected a handsome paycheck for those efforts. But there came a time that pandering to parents was no longer an option. Just as there is no such thing as being a little bit pregnant, I could no longer be a little bit selfless. The new decade arrived with a voice too loud to stay within the boundaries of imaginary talk bubbles that had safely served me in the past. There came a time when the bloated egos and exaggerated symptoms of summer collided with defeated dissonance.

I once read that getting older is wonderful because you get to keep all the ages you've ever been. Does that mean you also get to keep your unresolved issues? I'd clung faithfully to the lonely little-girl voice that once told me I was less, but I could hide behind knowing more than other people. I listened to the child voice obediently when it told me owning more was the cornerstone of confidence and that fitting in was close to achieving a state of nirvana. But this new decade had muffled that voice. I thought that the voices from childhood were no more than high-maintenance friends I disliked but kept because they were comfortable and consistent in behavior. Now, I considered that being validated by the nouveau riche, suntanned, Range Rover–driving mindless moms of summer was meaningless. For the first time in my life, I was able to differentiate my own worth from the worth I mindlessly assigned to others.

The September of the approaching new decade, I returned with a new appreciation for the ebb and flow of school days.

I had a subjective fondness for school not unusual after two months of summer. That year the fondness was enhanced by my decision to leave camp for good. I identified with Thornton Wilder's famous play, *Our Town*. Emily, the main character in *Our Town,* returns from death to savor details she had missed in life. The poignancy of missed opportunity is the play's central theme. I was returning to school not from death, but from an awakening. Fortunately, there was time ahead to consciously experience the opportunity and detail of each day. I returned, loving my job and myself a little more.

My divorce from camp was due to irreconcilable differences, and I was newly content with the banal nonsense of Band-Aids on paper cuts and after-recess stomachaches. Waiting just beyond the mechanized routines was the next real crisis. If only the self-absorbed gluten-fearing people in places like Chappaqua and Armonk or Rye Brook could also learn to differentiate between real and perceived tragedy. Could they relate to the thought of a ten-year-old hiding an advanced pregnancy as a result of an assault by her mother's boyfriend? No more, I believe, than I could relate to hysteria over a crouton. Irreconcilable differences, yes.

A few years before I left camp, I had lost the capacity to employ the dissonance in my marriage. Manipulating my feelings seemed impossible. We were living in the fake Tudor for almost eight years before I abandoned marital dissonance and retreated to the learned behaviors of my childhood. The same trait that enabled me to survive a lonely childhood would serve again to help me escape. It was 1998, and I retreated to being alone for comfort. This time, the outcome would be different. The next two years would complete the decade and take me on a new path. Now, childhood voices were silenced. I had abandoned those needy friends and was on my own.

Chapter Eighteen

TURNING POINT

Turning fifty was a lot like entering puberty. It was an undefined time of being neither here nor there. The twenty extra pounds I'd always battled now clung tenaciously and challenged my already-faltering self-esteem. My femininity teetered precariously at the edge of a rapidly eroding cliff edge. Sometimes I managed to feel like a still-sensuous older woman. Other times, I felt like a loose-jowled, colorless, and invisible matron. The perception vacillated from day to day and was too often based on how I thought men looked at me. If I was addressed as ma'am, it was a bad day. If there was eye contact in even the most mundane daily interaction, I was still viable. It mattered to me that the dry cleaner, mailman, or pizza guy looked at me during an exchange. It confirmed my status of continued existence in a world that celebrated its belief in the holiness of hormones.

At work, the programs and activities that once rewarded me were now just daily routines. I had logged ten years at the school I still loved, but my energy was depleted. My own children weren't home all that much, more eager to be with their friends than with me. The oldest was away at college. There was one bedroom that stood empty in his absence.

My marriage had not recovered from the financial turmoil and continued inability to confront issues or have meaningful communication. We lived separate lives under the same roof. It was a roof I disliked because it wasn't slate. But most of all, what I disliked was the silence that had settled into the house. I discovered an alternative to that silence when I joined a local gym. I applauded my commitment to fighting fat. Three times a week, I drove to the gym after dinner. This was not a high-end health club. This was a bare-bones gym. There were large open areas that lacked either the high-tech appeal of exposed duct work and hanging steel pendulum lights, or the sea-green serenity of eucalyptus-scented spas. There were no Pilates classes, no Yoga Flow, and no eager trainers. It smelled vaguely of sweat and rubber-coated floor mats. This was a poor man's serious gym and was priced accordingly. I would have been uncomfortable in a more luxurious gym that offered thicker towels, group classes, and a clientele of well-toned younger, wealthy women to intimidate me.

Check-in was a simple presentation of a membership card to a bored college kid, who never attempted to match the photo on the card to the face before her. She handed back the card with a rolled-up, threadbare towel. It was late March, 5:30 p.m., dark, dreary, and cold. I was checking in and as yet unaware of it being an important day in my life. There was someone ahead of me. I waited a moment. The counter held some takeout Chinese food menus. I thought about crispy egg rolls or lo mein. A glossy white, heavy-stock, five-by-seven-inch flier with purple print caught my eye. In it a man held a bike above his head in triumph. "Never Give Up," it read.

Perhaps it was the way the ceiling spotlight hit the glossy

surface of the flier, or the ten-second delay in waiting to check in. I was attracted to the caption and the image. It advertised an event scheduled for September, six months away. The bike ride from Boston to New York was a three-day, three hundred–mile fundraiser for AIDS. A challenge was exactly what I needed. I was in! Looking back on that moment, I marvel at the complete lack of thought or curiosity given that decision. It was as reflexive as scratching an itch.

The last time I'd even attempted to ride a bike had been a clunky rental on a family vacation to Block Island. I remember going at a slow speed consistent with having a whiney six-year-old in tow, facing a steep hill. It was an on-and-off again ride, which mostly involved my feet on the ground and my crotch hovering over the cross bar. Still, I knew how to ride a bike. I remembered my speed and confidence on the red Schwinn of my childhood. I believed it was a lifetime skill that could never be lost. I folded the glossy flier up and put it in my bag. The next hour on the treadmill was a serious consideration of the bike color I might like to buy. I signed up the very next day.

And so the journey began. I became known as Wonder Woman to my friends at work. They were impressed with my ambition. My closest work friend began calling me FW, short for "Fucking Wonder." I loved the irreverent compliment. It may have been an offhand endearment, but it reinforced a belief in my ability to succeed. I embraced the new idea of a physical challenge. This would be the second time in my adult life I needed to believe in my own ability to succeed. But this wasn't a new school program formulated on theories and dependent on written skills and outreach. This was a physical challenge requiring discipline and strength, and I was overweight and fifty years old. Some of those work friends may secretly have doubted my ability or sanity. I never did.

"I'm signed up for the AIDS ride in September," I proudly announced to the manager of a large and well-stocked cycle shop. Of course, his assumption was that I was an A- or B-level rider. Those are the cyclists capable of logging in forty or fifty miles per week and able to average speeds close to twenty miles an hour. Those were the riders who welcomed, rather than feared, hills. He also assumed existing ownership of a bike and a basic knowledge of bike language, technology, and equipment. He assumed I knew all of these things. In fact, I only knew the color I preferred.

He looked at me approvingly. "Cool, great ride. Have you started training? When was your last metric?" He threw these questions at me in rapid-fire excitement. *Metric?* I thought. That sounded ominously like math to me. It seemed impossible, but math still summoned fear in me, all these years after fourth grade. I feigned understanding and admitted to not riding for several years. Actually, I'd never ridden a fancy road bike and had never considered measuring speed or distance in anything but my car.

"I basically think I'd like a new bike," I told him. There was no old bike. The accoutrements of cycling were expensive. Brands and logos and every kind of status symbol flood the cycling marketplace. Elite riders are as recognizable by their clothing and bikes as they are by their speed or endurance. Road bikes are the Ivy League of the cycling world. Dirt bikes, hybrids, cruisers, and mountain bikes all have their place in Middle America, but there are only road bikes at the Tour de France. I understood that the AIDS ride was a road-bike event. As it turned out, the event was dominated by road bikes but peppered with imaginative human-powered wheels in many forms.

But I, the woman with a keen eye and appreciation for the finer things in life, was already lusting for the performance and status of a better bike. Here was a whole new venue of excess to explore. I began to learn the finer points of craftsmanship. I compared carbon and steel frames with titanium frames. I learned about Shimano brakes and other components. I learned about gears and grades. I was measured as if I were a wealthy businessman buying a custom-tailored suit. There were rigid-soled bike shoes in loud colors that were more exciting than any Ferragamo. There were long- and short-sleeved bike shirts that clung efficiently and unfortunately to my flabby midsection. I loved the jerseys and jackets that featured the names of olive oil and racing-gear sponsors. Yes, I loved the suggestion that corporate sponsors endorsed my ambition!

With enough natural padding in my bottom, I bought spandex bike pants without the padded-seat option. I selected an aerodynamic helmet that looked both futuristic and safe. I was ready for the star of the show, the bike. And then, I fell in love with Celeste. It was love at first sight. A Bianchi, an Italian beauty of honorable lineage. Her color was celeste green, and she would carry her given name as she became mine to love. She had twenty-three gears and weighed just eighteen pounds and would deliver me to victory across the finish line. I rationalized her two-thousand-dollar final cost as a solid long-term investment and guarantee of success. And now, Celeste, my sleek green sister would carry me away to greener pastures, or at least just away.

Celeste lived on a wall in the garage for her first month at home. It was still too cold outside for this new activity. I visited her every day and spun a pedal now and then as if it was a roulette wheel. I kept the physical bond intact. Meanwhile, I studied training guides and ride information. I waited.

A warm-enough day finally arrived the first week of April. It was a Sunday morning, and at 8:00 a.m. few cars would be on the road. I put on the long black spandex tights and a cobalt-blue long-sleeved jersey emblazoned with Italian words in front and back. I chose canary-yellow bike socks with red chili peppers at the ankle. They went nicely with the red and cobalt bike shoes I'd chosen. The shoes were outfitted with metal clips on the sole. I loved the hard noise of metal on concrete when I walked. This was serious stuff. Fifteen pounds of equally serious fat on my bottom was extra insulation I reasoned. Somehow, I believed that sitting on a bike was an all-forgiving posture for fat-bottomed women. Each metallic strike against the cement garage floor bolstered my ego. I strutted around the safe interior a few times, and stretched my calves and quads like a pro. I imagined I'd be sweating after the first few hills. Anticipating the potential for dehydration I filled my matching green Bianchi water bottles and placed them in their frames. I removed the band from my high ponytail, coiled my hair—my signature hairdo—and placed it at the nape of my neck to assure a proper fit for my helmet. I was suited up and psyched up and ready. "Let's go, Celeste, we're off!"

We emerged from the garage, leather-palmed hand to green taped hand grips. I pumped my fists against the grips. It was the equivalent of a bobsled racer giving that final slap before pushing off an ice-covered track. We walked to the end of my thirty-foot-long driveway. Best to mount the bike at the curb this first time out, I reasoned. I swung my right leg over the seat and thought about engaging the shoe clips as the bike rolled forward. There was the sound of metal on metal as the male and female parts tried valiantly to merge and lock in place. *Clank, clank, tap, clank-tap, twist-tap, slide-tap, clank, clank,* it was hopeless. There was no love affair between these parts. I tried the left foot next with the same result. Fortunately, we were on a gentle downgrade. Simple gravity kept us moving forward. I opted to move the pedals by resting some part of the shoe on the four-inch nub of the bike clip and willed them to obey in a circular motion. The pedals complied but the forward and backward play in each stroke were reminders of the inefficiency of the accommodation. *For now,* I thought, *this is good enough.* I'd practice clipping in and out later.

I conquered an almost-smooth pedal stroke and arrived safely at the end of the large cul-de-sac. There were another twelve homes set back the same thirty feet as my own fake Tudor. They were an ambitious mix of almost new colonials, cube-like contemporaries, and ranch homes pretending to be quaint English stables. There were no sidewalks and no people in sight. Cars sat in driveways.

The cul-de-sac may have been a perfect choice had the road not dipped at a fifteen-degree angle. I started the ride at the low end and now faced a hill I'd never noticed existed in the three years I'd lived there. This suddenly looked like a formidable hill. I drew a deep breath and gripped harder. I began the battle with my stronger right leg.

I pumped hard and moved forward less than a foot. I pumped with the left sliding-away pedal. I seemed to be losing speed. Perhaps speed was a poor choice of words. I was losing forward movement. Now, there was a decided sway from left to right. Celeste and I were slow dancing. We moved and swayed and rocked slower still. Celeste decided to lean over as if she were doing a graceful, tango-like dip.

Come on, I thought. *Not now, Celeste, this is our maiden voyage.* Celeste was a high-strung thoroughbred, obviously insulted by the novice who had mounted her. If she were a horse, she might have thrown me. Instead, she simply banked deeply and deposited me on the pavement as if unloading a distasteful burden. My left shoulder hit first, followed by my left knee and wrist. It seemed to happen in slow motion. There were superficial scrapes on my knee and wrist, injuries requiring nothing more than cleaning and a Band-Aid. I quickly glanced around to see if there were witnesses, and was most relieved to see none. Not even one, lurking behind a kitchen curtain. My new black spandex had a jagged horizontal rip at the knee. *Serves me right,* I thought, *for wearing spandex.* I inspected Celeste for surface bruises and found none. She had fared better than I had. I brushed myself off quickly and walked us back home. Celeste was placed back on her wall hook. I didn't even look at her as I removed the still-full water bottles. No gentle tap or casual wheel spin this time.

I brought the water bottles to the sink and emptied them. I looked up at the clock. I had been out only ten minutes. Standing at the sink, I allowed my previous thoughts of gliding gracefully to the finish line be replaced by the reality of a fat-bottomed fifty year old in shredded spandex feeling foolish.

Chapter Nineteen

LEAVING LONENESS

The transition from loneness to shared experience that took place between April 4, 1998, and the victorious finish just five months later was as insidious as it was profound. I can remember abandoning the very first training ride that met on 72nd Street and Riverside Drive. We were to meet at the base of the Eleanor Roosevelt statue. That seemed a good omen to me. I always loved that first lady. She was big, bold, outspoken, homely, and a champion of women's rights. But then I imagined a group of more attractive thirty-year-olds, trim and confident riders assembled and stretching at her feet. It occurred to me that both Eleanor and I would fade anonymously into the background as unimportant. I reconsidered driving a car topped with a bike that was tied down with over-stretched bungee cords that might snap at any moment on the West Side Highway and imagined swerving cars and cursing drivers, a crushed and mangled Celeste dying an undignified death in her prime. I opted for an extra hill and busier street near home.

There was another ride scheduled for Central Park the following week. I'd do that for sure. I pushed away thoughts of collisions with carriages drawn by horses wearing garish feathered headgear. In deference to safety, I packed a fanny pack with emergency reach numbers. If something did happen, my family needed to know. It was strange to live with such frail tethering to them. They never asked, and I never offered where I rode off to. Had I withdrawn that much? When had we become so independent of one another? It occurred to me that families might age the same way individuals do—different in how it looks and functions subtly until it's unrecognizable from its former self. There comes that day of reckoning when you see an older woman's face in the mirror and recognize it as your own. The day I buckled my emergency reach numbers to my waist was a similar revelation. I had high school–aged children who needed me less and a husband who didn't know who I had become. Still, I would manage to be home for dinner, until the day I wasn't.

That training ride on April 4th was an especially cold day. It was too cool to enjoy being outside. I brought Celeste when she still wore her ugly pedals and assumed a few miles in the heart of the city would be easy enough. Only a handful of riders showed up at the Boathouse, our meeting place. The volunteer leader gathered us in a tight circle and applauded our enthusiasm. He wore bike shorts and had enormously overdeveloped legs that looked like they belonged on a heavy baroque dining table. They looked powerful. He wore a hooded sweatshirt, carried a khaki backpack, and had a nice-looking Trek bike. There were three thirty-something women. They wore biking gear and had decent bikes. I was older and had a better bike. I hoped they registered that detail. The rest of the group was made up of men of different ages. They looked serious yet aloof. You could tell by their posture and relationship to their bikes that the bikes had become extensions of their bodies. They were seasoned riders. Another man stood slightly away from the group. He had an older English Raleigh road bike. When I was a kid, we called them English racers. I thought then that Americans didn't race on bikes. He was my age, maybe younger. He wore sweatpants and sweatshirt in classic gray. Serious riders don't wear loose sweatpants. He was obviously not a serious rider.

I thought he looked familiar. He looked vaguely like a man I had seen at the gym on a treadmill. Standing in the cold just waiting was unpleasant. I shifted from foot to foot and rubbed my hands together to keep warm. I leaned Celeste against the huge rock outcropping that faced the boathouse. The three women were in a tight conversation. The men patiently waited and exchanged a word or two with each other. The cold was getting to me. I decided a quick trip inside for coffee was a necessity. I asked the only person who had made eye contact and seemed alone if he would watch Celeste for a few minutes while I warmed up. He smiled. He had a lovely smile and warm brown eyes. He said he was also freezing and suggested he come with me and that we bring the bikes with us. Two bikes and two people left the group.

Apparently, the glossy white pamphlet on the counter of the gym was effective because that's where he'd found out about the ride, too. "Do you know if anyone else from our gym signed up?" I asked. But he had no idea. "Basically, I go there most evenings to escape from home and just work out and then I leave. I'm not even sure why I signed up."

"Why did you sign up?" he asked. He looked directly at me, and into my eyes. I liked his eye contact. Before the question, I had only noticed that he was not much taller than I am and was dressed wrong for the ride. Now, his eye contact and direct question piqued my interest. He waited for my answer and watched my face.

"I guess I needed to remind myself that I was still alive," I blurted out without thinking. I smiled, hoping it would make the remark seem more flippant than serious.

"You too?" he laughed. "Well, if you've fallen off the bike yet that would remind you that you're alive." I was happy to share the details of my overambitious first ride with him. Enough time had passed that I could now laugh at myself. At least now I didn't fall over in slow motion like a recently sprayed cockroach.

"Sounds like a case of existential angst to me," he said. His analysis of my story seemed spot on. I reached back in my memory to recall that meant an urgency to act in the face of discomfort. I couldn't decide if this man was a very deep thinker or simply testing my ability for good banter. I was hooked either way.

"Yeah, existential angst. Do you think that angst will keep me going three hundred miles or do you recommend a few PowerBars?"

"I recommend a cup of chili and glass of wine for now. Good for what ails you. We can lock the bikes up on that fence and call it our first official rest stop." It was a monumental moment. Deciding to abandon the group that day was, perhaps, the beginning of abandoning other rules of conventional behavior. We exchanged names and discussed the next scheduled training ride. His name was Nick.

Training rides were soon a shared experience. We followed the training schedule provided by the ride organizers and now, as formal training partners, joined the larger group for all future outings. We eventually got to know other riders. Many of them assumed we were a married couple. We routinely loaded our two green bikes onto a single bike rack for training destinations. The bikes bobbled along highways and country roads on the back of the car while we enjoyed the anticipated challenges of hills and distances in unknown places. We consumed hundreds of PowerBars on those rides and both loved lemon the most. He always reminded me to drink water on hot days. He challenged me on steep hills. "Come on, only ten more strokes and you're done. There's a guy behind me that thinks you're a shit rider. Show him who you are." He already understood my need not to be dismissed. Sometimes it was a bribe. "If you get to the top before I do, I'll buy you a box of Good & Plenty." (He already knew my favorite candy). He was a better hill rider than I but always stayed behind me to encourage. He was a human whip. At rest stops, he remained as funny and provocative and full of banter as during our first encounter in Central Park.

We never stopped talking. When our legs rested, our thoughts and minds took over. Any random thought that passed casually through our minds while riding was recalled to be shared.

"Did you see that amazing hemlock about three miles back near the high school? It has to be at least a hundred years old."

"My ass feels like I've been sitting on a beehive."

"Did you happen to notice the big guy wearing hot-pink bike shoes . . . love to know where he found those."

"Do you think I've earned a slice of white pizza yet?"

We often read the same book or saw the same movies. We'd mince and dice the deeper meanings and social significance. *Angela's Ashes* and *Good Will Hunting* kept us engaged for hours of conversation. I couldn't always follow his complex train of thought. He was definitely more philosophical and had a better background in history and literature than I. I was better in contemporary fiction and vocabulary. We complemented each other perfectly. We both admitted that math would never be my strong suit.

The unspoken thoughts and words were more significant. These were germinating separately and painfully. I was keenly aware of the silence in my marriage. I had adjusted to loneness but now understood a facet of my marriage that remained undeveloped and unlived. The simple pleasure of shared discussions and provocative thought energized me. I was reminded of the younger me with that long ago boyfriend, Steve Davidson. I contemplated my own responsibility for the deficit. Had I been content to distract myself with the acquisition of objects I cherished, as if they knew me best? Had I been too eager for stability when I ignored my mother's reminder all those years ago about sharing my love of books and art? Had I not been aggressive enough in coaching and developing these traits in someone so anxious for my happiness? At this point, did I have the energy to remediate or the will to return to the status quo?

I began a journal, intending to track my cycling and training progress. My intention was never to reflect on or acknowledge a blossoming romance. It was never meant to be shared. Silence in my new partner's marriage was not the enemy. Nick had told me on that very first day at the boathouse that the gym was his escape. On the rides that ensued, I learned that in his marriage, silence was often welcome respite from the anger and vacillating moods of a wife who had become enamored with a rabbi she regarded as her spiritual mentor. Nick felt discounted and angry. He escaped at first to the gym, then to the bike, and then to training for a three hundred–mile ride. She remained indifferent. He escaped eventually to be with me.

We should have guessed sooner what would happen. Looking back, it seemed clear from the beginning and the first words spoken. It was, I'm sure, existential angst that brought us together and then moved us along. We each wanted an outlet and a change. There was an urgency for change we hadn't even identified. We would come to acknowledge that we had undertaken a monumental change that couldn't be measured in miles.

Had it not been unseasonably cold, we might never have spoken. It was, to me, a more cosmic event. Our meeting was something unexplainable in the universe that set me back in time to retrieve lost milestones that were rightfully mine. It was a disruption to the forward force of a time and space continuum that sent me back, in a time warp, many years to know what it may have been like at sixteen or eighteen or twenty had I not been so afraid and insecure. The new force that had my legs and feet moving in simple circular movement altered time and thought.

Chapter Twenty

EXISTENTIAL DECISIONS

I didn't write in the journal every day or after every ride. I began innocently enough to track my progress on a journey I wasn't sure I'd ever complete. Regardless, at some point the words began to document more than miles. At some point, the angst pent up inside of me was transferred via pen to paper. Somewhere in those journals I began to consider a different life. I began to understand my own strength and how to nourish my soul.

The earliest entries document tangible progress, like the exchange of bike pedals for clips that bonded to bike shoes with clip receptors. With a slight outward rotation of my heel, I was free. Otherwise, I was literally married to the bike for better or worse. I entered my weight loss, down ten pounds then twelve, and at some point I must have weighed comfortably under one hundred and forty pounds because I no longer recorded my weight after that. I documented difficult rides and the places we took them. I knew I'd want to recall those details.

There was the first level, B or better (advanced riders), that met in Central Park and rode across the George Washington Bridge. The challenge was the hills ascending the famous Palisades once we crossed over to New Jersey. The ride leader told us we would be at three thousand vertical feet on one hill. I was cautiously optimistic. I knew that Nick would be behind me, shouting empty threats and flattering falsehoods: "Show that asshole that just shouted that you can do it!" he'd scream from behind. It worked. There was a spectacular view of the city skyline on that ride, but I never looked. There were hairpin turns around ninety-degree corners that ensconced the cables of the bridge's suspension. Those corners snagged my self-confidence as surely as if I'd been garroted by a steel cable. I twisted out of the clips just in time to meet head on with a glass wall. I took the next three cables with dampened confidence and greater caution, walking Celeste around them. I consoled myself by thinking I'd never wanted to be an acrobat or circus act, which is how those hairpin turns felt.

On another ride, we rode sixty miles from Eleanor to Nyack. It was my first long ride and included steep hills in the riverfront town of Piermont. Again, I journaled about the hills and miles, but now the entries recounted elements of a budding romance having little to do with gears, wind force, or vertical feet. I wrote of feeling as if the bikes were like horses in a fable. They were stallions we mounted. I wrote about the sensation of wind on my face and of riding away with him. The romantic images lacked the details of place or time. They could have been illustrations in a child's book that featured curls of mist and rolling purple hills and puffy white clouds that had little to do with reality. Had I regressed to having the dreams of a twelve-year-old, or was this what romantic love was like?

In Nyack, we stopped at a rest stop with our group of twenty.

The colorful bikes and clothing were all collected in front of a delightful bakery named The Runciple Spoon. We were just two more ageless, faceless people in a group. Only we were different, I knew, because we had arrived on stallions that rendered time effete. That night, my journal entry was poet Edward Lear's "The Owl and the Pussycat." Lear's word "runcible" is a nonsense word he coined. But the poem and its content held great significance, especially the last two lines.

They dined on mince and slices of quince,
Which they ate with a runciple spoon;
And hand in hand, on the edge of the sand,
They danced in the light of the moon.

At some point, my journal entries offered very few facts and were more a rambling account of my growing affection and awareness of a need for a man who was not my husband. I often reflected on the nature of our conversations in an effort to justify their importance. Surely they were not substantive. While riding, we were only able to speak to each other at traffic lights or rest stops. It was bicycle foreplay. I'd want to ask if he'd noticed an unusual cloud formation or a field of buttercups that looked like it had been digitally created. But the helmets and the wind and need to listen to traffic prevented the exchange. So I held the thought. We both saved things we'd share later. It was delayed pleasure and a pattern we savored. The minute the bikes were rested against a tree there was a rush of words and thoughts.

"Did you see the great blue heron in that marshy grove about two miles back?" he'd ask.

I'd ask if he noticed the sweet scent of pine needles when we'd ridden through a long stretch of road flanked by very large Norwegian pines.

Each of us was so attuned to the beauty in nature. Each of us was silently registering our good fortune in finding another person who understood the need to celebrate that beauty. Soon, the comfort level and pleasure in the rides and shared thoughts would overwhelm the importance of the original mission. We both worked hard on fundraising letters that would earn the $3,000 we had committed to the AIDS charity sponsoring the event. We achieved our targets before deadline. We were getting stronger in the endurance and skills needed for the actual ride. But there was something more than the ride we had yet to admit to. We were falling in love. I'd think about why I was newly aware of being happy. I told myself it was just nostalgia for childhood days with my mother's friend Elaine. I remembered how happy I felt on that trusty red Schwinn on rides with her. As a child, I first fell in love with nature because of her patient lessons. But I knew this was not just happy reminiscence. This was something more.

By late July, we were on target. There was no great challenge expected on another preparatory ride. It was flat terrain, under thirty miles, and the destination was the beach at Rye Playland, an amusement park and treasured childhood destination. It was not supposed to challenge me but would prove to be the biggest challenge in my adult life.

We left the small group of riders at the one rest stop on Boston Post Road. We were at a small inlet near Mamaroneck Harbor, enjoying the scenery of a few swans and mallards too much to leave when the group took off. We were happy to be alone, and lazily got back on the bikes a half hour later. Once we got to our destination, we locked the bikes together on the boardwalk and sat facing the beach.

The air was scented with suntan lotion, French fries, and greasy hot dogs. The smells of summer at Playland and I suppose hundreds of similar places. But this had been my special place as a child. We never went more than once or twice a season, and it was always a luxury. I began to tell Nick about my favorite rides as a child. He listened as I relived the Magic Carpet ride, the Old Saw Mill boat ride, and the fun house. My brother and I were delighted by small electric shocks that sent us flying off a revolving disc we sat on. I watched in awe as my brother navigated successfully through a large revolving barrel that threatened to land him on his rear end. I felt transported in time, but something else was happening, too. I became aware of the joy of that memory and the joy of the present shared moment. My past and present merged into a total sense of well-being. It was one of those rare moments in time when you are aware of happiness that is priceless and perfect, if only momentary.

We sat quietly and did not speak for a few minutes. He held my hand in the quiet. Gulls flew above and watched as we kissed.

Only in hindsight do I grasp the significance of that moment with forgiveness. We were so tentative when our hands touched and in that kiss. We were adolescents suddenly aware of an opportunity and also aware of the consequences of indulging ourselves. We were unprepared for more natural instincts. While we had shared our innermost thoughts, the ability to connect physically had remained untapped. The intrinsic need to fulfill that desire had been gestating as long as we had denied it. The world had tilted once again. I remembered how often I'd gotten lost on the beach or boardwalk as a child. I seemed always to be dreaming as I walked and ended up in the lost-child area. I was never afraid when that happened. But today, I was afraid.

We hadn't planned on needing each other. We both assumed

that lusting phase of life had passed. I'm not really certain it ever existed for me. I was too busy hiding from men or planning other things to think about it. My energy was always diverted into career and motherhood and acquiring things that validated me. When there were rare moments of solitude, I'd enjoy loneness in the form of reading or painting or writing or simply enjoying my surroundings. I could satisfy my need for political or intellectual discussion with coworkers, friends, or my mother or brother. I was fundamentally secure in these primary relationships. But still, I'd had the unconditional love and respect of a husband of almost twenty-eight years. He was the first man I ever trusted and had proven worthy of that sacred trust. He denied me nothing. My unreasonable purchases and lofty dreams were endorsed by him and perhaps his means of compensating for what he may have known he could not provide. A sensitive man, he probably interpreted my increasing silence and avoidance of intimacy as unhappiness. I knew my happiness mattered to him. When had I become indifferent to his needs, so selfish?

In fact, Steven's tenderness was heartbreaking. He left for work before me most of our years together. I have always slept wrapped under several blankets. In any season, including the hottest summer nights, I am comforted by the weight of blankets over me. Only my right foot is deliberately exposed and peaks out, turtle like, as if to monitor the safety of my environment. Each and every morning, he would kiss me good-bye and gently cover that exposed foot with the blankets. This endearment best symbolizes the problem. I needed to have my right foot uncovered as much as I needed to share my thoughts and ideas. Covering the foot and indulging my every whim were not what I craved. The gesture told me I was cared for and safe, but it also confirmed that he didn't understand my needs, and therefore didn't understand me.

How come he never knew that I disliked lilies and waited anxiously for them to wilt and die after he lovingly brought home expensive florist arrangements? How could he know when I feigned gratitude and chose to spare both his feelings and the truth? But now I was confused. Had I been kind and committed or just the protagonist in my role as loving and ethical wife and mother? I had worked hard to win that role. I read the script and played the part convincingly for many years. But the emerging reality of the ethical conflict and an unknown future offered no fast solution. There was only the reality of immediate need and the dawning awareness that my libido did, in fact, exist.

Chapter Twenty-One

CRUELLA STRIKES

I called in sick at work, and we met at the gym lot. It was now June and beautifully warm. I wore the casual black linen slacks and aqua hand-knit top that I would have worn to work. We each carried small tote bags. We weren't going to workout; we were going to the Gramercy Park Hotel. God knows why he chose that hotel. It's an elegant old hotel on 22nd and Lexington with rare, iron-gated private green space available only to area residents of the toney neighborhood. The hotel is billed as an elegant boutique hotel in a desirable residential neighborhood. It's also expensive. Maybe he believed its elegance might diminish our own insecurity and bolster our ability to act upon inelegant intentions.

We arrived at 11:00 a.m. We did not hold hands. Perhaps we sensed that would set off suspensions of infidelity at the front desk. The lobby was heavy with wood and velvet and a marble fireplace. The porter looked at my bag and asked to carry it. I was sure it had a huge scarlet S on it. In fact, it contained only a short silk full slip in a creamy beige. It was sexy and understated. I also carried two votive candles and a pair of carnival glass candle tumblers that would shed soft golden light. I had verbena-scented body lotion, too.

The room was depressingly dark for a sunny June afternoon. The lone window faced another building. There was a sad attempt at a kitchenette in the corner. The pipes under the sink were exposed. It reminded me of a single-room occupancy for poor people. And then, dead center, dominating the room and all its ugliness, was a queen-size bed covered in a burgundy and beige, heavy tapestry bedspread. The bed dared us to approach. It was the Cruella Deville of beds. We avoided touching it and awkwardly undressed standing at opposite sides of Cruella. It seemed like a performance. We were changing into costume, like actors. It was not even 1:00 p.m. Why were we in underwear in a Gothic chamber? What was the hurry? And yet, we were there to consummate our love and be transported to the next level.

We faced Cruella and lay down tentatively on our backs. The ceiling fixture was a crystal flush mount. The crystals had a dull film, which disturbed me. I got up and lit the candles. He got up and searched for appropriate music on the small radio. He was rewarded with static. A moment later, I got up again to find my scented lotion. Then he got up to retrieve a gift he'd brought, a miniature Waterford crystal clock to symbolize our time ahead. Finally, there were no tasks left, save one. We lay down and faced one another. I rubbed lotion on his arms and legs. We kissed. We declared our love. We fondled and caressed each other. We fumbled and fondled more. We were sexual illiterates. We were thirteen-year-olds trying out forbidden fruit. We expressed feelings of guilt and betrayal about our spouses, and then we held each other and gave up.

He may as well have been in a confession booth at church. I am sure erections are few and far between there. I was as uncomfortable as the average woman trying on a bathing suit in fluorescent light. Childhood ghosts joined us in bed. My father's infidelities took up residence on my side of the bed. I thought of the married men my mother dated when I was growing up. Nick's Catholic school education and conversion to Judaism for marriage pushed into his thoughts, he later told me. It wasn't difficult for him to imagine his parents holding their heads in disbelief at where he was now. The bed was crowded with guilt and ghosts. We agreed to abandon Cruella for lunch and a walk on Third Avenue. After that, we checked out of the hotel. The desk clerk looked us boldly in the eye. Did he think this was the fastest tryst ever, or did he imagine I was being paid by the hour? In fact, we were relieved to have failed at infidelity, and that shared relief served to strengthen our bond.

We called each other at 7:30 every morning, when we could speak privately. He was already at his office by then. Sometimes he slept there. We planned next rides and decided to sign on for the Montauk Century, a hundred-mile ride. We thought it might make sense to stay there overnight. I stayed up thinking about him and couldn't sleep. I pictured us on bikes, struggling and sweating up a hill. Then, when I allowed my mind more freedom, I thought about us in bed. I thought about that a lot. I thought about sleeping and waking next to him. I thought about sex. I thought Montauk was a good plan.

It's been said that there are no accidental revelations. People who write letters and keep journals or carelessly leave email messages undeleted expect to be caught. Credit card receipts, new underwear, and sudden weight loss or a change in grooming habits are also telltale signs of marital deceit. My journals entries became longer and changed from documenting weight loss and miles logged to proclamations of love and plans for time together. When I missed Nick, I wrote about it. When we shared a special moment, I wrote about it. Sometimes it read like poetry. I could have a random memory of an amazing ride or funny anecdote and feel compelled to get up at first morning light to enter the thought. I was preserving and extending our time together by writing about it. I wrote often and hid my journal in a small drawer of my bedside table. I considered it a private place inhabited by discarded treasures like bookmarks, random hair clips, and inkless pens. Things left there had anonymity and privacy.

Sometimes I went to spin classes, and other times I met Nick in his office instead. We accidentally overcame our sexual inhibitions one morning when I stopped by his office to see if he had slept there. He answered my tapping on the window, and in the pale morning light opened the door and invited me in to wait while he dressed. He had messy hair and morning breath. He wore only a pair of old gym shorts. There was no plan. There was no bed, music, or candlelight. It was just us, thrilled to be alone. We held each other for a long time and didn't speak. It was as if the room and our ability to reason faded away simultaneously. Passion found its way into a most unlikely room. After all our carefully laid plans for the luxury hotel, we finally made love on the floor of a hard, dull gray, commercially carpeted waiting room. The spontaneity adding all the fuel and honesty we needed. The journal entry of that date featured a simple drawing of a heart.

On one beautiful May weekend, Nick was away on a long-scheduled college tour to Boston with his eldest daughter. He was looking forward to being alone with her. Things at his home had deteriorated. His wife knew there was another woman. Our phone calls and poorly hidden love notes had been discovered. Her vitriol and outbursts drove him further away, and ironically to sleep in the office that served as a clandestine retreat for us. Now that he was living primarily in his office, it sported a lumpy air mattress and a well-worn blanket. We faced a daily dilemma. Would we meet at the gym or at the office? When the office was the choice, it often meant abandoning a scheduled class. Spontaneity reigned.

In contrast to the spontaneity of our time together, Nick's homelife had become a predictable course of angry outbursts and accusations. This pattern began long before we'd met. His discovery of an undeleted e-mail conversation between his wife and a friend devastated him. He read her romantic ruminations and daydreams about their rabbi with disbelief. He had begun to feel displaced by the rabbi's frequent, informal visits to their home and shared dinners. She hung on the rabbi's words and craved his advice. She spent any free time at the synagogue volunteering. There were other congregants who offered up casual gossip filled with innuendo about the "closeness" of the pair to him, not sparing his pride or her reputation. He told me he felt no choice but to draw a "line in the sand." Either they would leave that synagogue or end the marriage. She firmly denied an affair. In fact, there was never proof or an admission by either of infidelity. The author Aldous Huxley said it best: "There are things known, and there are things unknown, and in between are the doors of perception." His pride and perception became the power that drove him to demand a decision. If she would not consider admitting to something going on with the rabbi, he would not consider marriage counseling. The window was inches from slamming irrevocably shut when he signed on for the AIDS ride. By the time we met, there was not even a tiny fissure of space.

And now, he was in Boston, newly alone with his eldest daughter and enjoying an opportunity to reassure her of his love and unwavering commitment to her. We had still not articulated the need for an exit plan. These were our days of magical thinking. We were straddling a dangerous wall that divided propriety from passion.

Chapter Twenty-Two

MATH MATTERS

Boston was a turning point for both of us. That weekend happened to be the weekend Steven read my journal. I got up on Saturday morning, showered, and headed off for an early spin class. I quietly left the house while everyone else was sleeping. As soon as Steven woke up, he turned over in bed and reached across with a single purpose in mind. He pulled open the small drawer of that bedside table and easily located my journal. As I pumped my legs at spin class, lost in the music, he read and was stricken with the most painful reality of his life. The woman he loved and trusted and had shared three decades with was somehow lost.

I was halfway through the class when I heard my name announced on the loudspeaker. I was being summoned to the front desk. My first thought was of Nick. Had there been an accident or a scene in Boston? Maybe he had left and was surprising me. I unclipped my bike shoes and nervously walked toward the front desk. As soon as I saw Steven standing there I knew immediately what had happened. He stood perfectly still but the rage and emotion in his face gave an impression of vibrating, pulsing heat around him. His fists were curled, his arms wriggled in some helpless weird way. He held my journal in one uncontrolled hand. He held it up and out at me. He looked into my eyes for confirmation.

In all of our lives, no moment was as filled with pain as that one. Denial was not an option. There was everything to say, but words could not capture his exquisite pain, or my own for inflicting it on him. That moment would be a deep scar I would own for my life. It marked a defining moment in my life. I'd like to believe it was inevitable and the only way I could have moved forward. After all, I had changed and discovered fulfillment I hadn't known possible. I was no longer the woman he had loved and cherished. That woman was lost to him. None of this was his fault. It was no longer enough to have everything I thought I'd wanted but to ignore the silent world that rendered it all unimportant now. I wanted out, and I knew I both had to and that I could.

Is that the meaning of existential angst then, when you know you have to flee to survive? I considered the selfishness and the pain. I reflected on the impact on children, family, extended family, the giant ripple effect I could prevent. I reflected on concrete issues, the income problem I'd face and all the material losses. I would need to sell jewelry and art to hire a lawyer. And then there was the social stigma. Neighbors would avoid us. Friends would judge and choose sides. Simply put, I understood that my decision would mean a deconstructed life. I didn't return to the class. I was nauseous and frightened. I knew that the days of magical thinking were past. I sat for a very long time on a bench, recovering my composure. There was a simple concrete decision to be made. Should I go home and find Steve or call Nick in Boston for advice? Neither choice could stabilize a now spinning room and queasy stomach. I returned to the home

I lived in but no longer believed could shelter me. The house was empty when I arrived.

I weighed and measured and calculated endlessly. I contemplated what challenging the rules meant. I sat with pencil and paper at work and at home, writing my thoughts as if seeing them grounded on paper would offer clarity. After just a few weeks, I understood that clarity would also not come from living together as if nothing had changed. We went to a marriage counselor, where Steve's willingness to change and to be more communicative was heartbreaking. I knew there was nothing he would deny me. But I also knew the limitations that were tightly bound to his offers. And so I struggled endlessly to be ethical and kind and practical as I also considered if I had a legitimate right to my self-indulgence.

At some point in time, I simplified my thoughts and made a list of yeas and nays as if it were a parliamentary decision. I created columns and tried to quantify my decision. The math was heavily weighted by ethics and social pressure. The stay column grew. I tried to convince myself that this was all just a matter of math. If I continued to make lists, then there would be a winning column and a losing column. And yet, I hated math, and sports also, for just that reason. Every win is tinged with sadness for a loss. I knew there was no answer in quantifying life. I calculated that I had spent 9,125 days considering if there could be more to life. When I thought of the next 9,125 days working on a change I believed might not be possible, I acquiesced. I wanted to abandon the numbers and live unencumbered by elaborate equations.

We fell into a pattern of being absent from home when possible and having limited conversation when together. It was almost as if the decision were made by default. The children adapted to the culture of silence. We all understood that life was about to change drastically. As we considered the practical issues of separate lives, the children were reassured that their parents would always be an enduring, loving, and unified presence in their lives. Now fourteen, nineteen, and twenty-one, they were aware of our decision to live separately in the near future. Steven and I put together a plan that offered the least disruption. It included staying within a few miles of the current neighborhood and the ability to be with either parent at any time. Since two were already in college, it was less complicated. Their primary residence would remain with me during the transition, and later, the new small Cape would be home for our reconfigured family.

Steven's newly rented luxury co-op, not far away, was a spacious two-bedroom, two-bathroom space and home to much of our furniture. I was painfully aware of this disjointed reality for them, and us. Neither home held all the components of life as they knew it. I believe they adjusted well and understood the sad but complex nature of our marriage. I also welcomed their expressed concern for their father. We had raised sensitive and loving children. And now I hoped they would be supportive of him and forgiving of me. With that hope, I could begin to live out a new life.

I embraced the honesty of living moments and events in the framework of my new reality. I was focused on the training rides that had become more ambitious as we moved closer to September. By July, the training guide suggested a minimum competency of one-hundred-mile and seventy-five-mile rides back to back. On one mailing, a list of sponsored rides and groups was sent to facilitate joining up. There was one group meeting in New Paltz hosted by the owner of a quaint bed and breakfast. The owner, Don Leff, had done the ride the year before.

Now seventy, he was taking this year off, but staying close to the event by organizing and hosting training rides through the rolling beauty of the Catskill Mountains. Nick and I were as excited about the stay at a bed and breakfast as we were anxious about the miles to be conquered.

We quickly replied to the RSVP, understanding that most training rides had groups of twelve to eighteen. There were only five rooms to be had at the quaint old farmhouse owned by Don and his wife, Audrey. We wanted to be one of those lucky few guests. Now, both the rides and our lives were becoming more clearly defined and purposeful. There were other ambitious rides that Nick and I took on. We rode from Peekskill to Cold Spring along a road that hugged the Hudson River. It was thirty-six miles that at times left the river edge and climbed for more than a mile from 415 feet to over a thousand feet. My quads burned and my chest felt like it might burst at times. This was deemed a level-three hill, which is not as challenging as a level two or one. We had seen the route map and elevations planned for Boston to New York. It had many level-one hills in Connecticut. The hardest would be in Storrs, close to the campus of the University of Connecticut. After completing that monster hill, we would be pitching a tent and trying to sleep wrapped in foil blankets. I needed to stop whining and be positive. I was determined. At times, my determination was met with defeat.

The weekend of the back-to-back rides at New Paltz was only a month away. I needed to be comfortable with single one hundred–mile rides. That needed to be a firm base, since the actual ride would be three days in a row of almost one hundred miles a day. We signed up for the hundred-mile Montauk Century, which would fall four weeks before the New Paltz weekend. I was cocky and confident with the belief that Long Island is mostly flat and, barring stiff winds, the ride would be an easy victory. There was a stiff wind that day. It was also close to ninety degrees that June weekend.

Along the ride, there were many local cheerleaders and businesses that supported the riders with cheers, water, cowbells, and even cannoli. And here was the unexpected adversary, my appetite! Yes, I drank some water and made sure to use the port-o-san. But the Italian pastries, so delicious, offered an opportunity for gluttony and carbs that diverted my circulation from my legs to the work of digestion in my stomach. I pumped on in the heat until the nausea and weakness could not be ignored.

The day ended in the emergency room of a community hospital, hooked up to an intravenous solution that cured my dehydration and cocky attitude. I slept in the back seat of Nick's car and arrived home feeling very much like a limp pile of dirty laundry. I had learned an important lesson about hydration. I had a new respect for the frailty of the human body. I also came to terms with not actually being a "fucking wonder woman." I would remember that on the next big challenge. We were now looking forward to that back-to-back ride in New Paltz. Humbled by the defeat in Montauk, I looked forward to meeting that seventy year old who had successfully done the ride.

Chapter Twenty-Three

LEDA

July crept up almost unexpectedly. Suddenly, it seemed, the big weekend in New Paltz was here. We drove up the crunching gravel driveway, bikes tightly corded to the trunk. An older, slightly built, dark-haired man was waving his arms wildly in greeting. In spite of his slightly stooped posture, his animation made him look like an excited teenager. He followed our car up the driveway and continued waving and smiling until the motor was off.

"Hi guys, Don here. Gosh am I happy to see you." His spirited greeting seemed the equivalent of a too-firm handshake or a happy puppy frenetically jumping and wagging its tail. In fact, he was trailed by a mellower Golden Retriever that partially hid a timid black-and-white Shih Tzu. The dogs demurred to their pack leader. We would soon learn that Audrey's Farmhouse was unique in many ways, including being dog friendly.

"Wow, Don," I said, "this is a lovely surprise." It was not only the warm greeting, which validated "us" as a newly minted entity, but the sight of the 1740 pre-Revolutionary farmhouse that thrilled me. I took in the metal roof, original gray shakes, and rippled glass windows. We stood under a huge oak tree that may only have been a century younger than the house. I continued to take in the charming details of this house. I would always be that child who savored and collected details. "C'mon, let's get these bikes off the car, and I'll show you my new bike." Don and Nick made quick work of getting our bikes unloaded, and Don launched into a show-and-tell of his bike, a titanium Kestrel. I only knew of a kestrel as a bird. Now I understood it was also an expensive bike.

"I just can't wait to meet the rest of our group tomorrow. There will be eighteen of us," he went on, still as energized as he was when we first pulled in the driveway. He filled us in on details of the ride, which included detailed cue sheets (ride maps) and weather conditions. He had planned well for a weekend that was as special to him as to us. He led us into the house, and we stood in a kitchen where the lingering fragrance of a savory breakfast and coffee still hung in the air. The southwest exposure of the expansive multi-paned kitchen window brought bright sunshine, which reflected off the table setting of cobalt-blue glasses and pewter flatware resting on a rough-hewn farm table.

The dramatic view beyond those colors was of the Gunks—the Shawangunk Ridge that looked like a sheared-off side of mountain, bleached white. It was an impressive sight, and well-known as a destination for serious rock climbing. We would tackle the ascending mountains on bikes from a less treacherous but equally challenging route. Moments later, Don's wife, Audrey, entered the kitchen, flanked by Shawnee the Golden Retriever, named after the Shawangunk Mountain Range, and little Kiva, the Shih Tzu named after the sacred altars built into the Navajo Mountains in the southwest. Audrey's soft-spoken, measured speech was in sharp contrast to her husband's hyperalert, assertive style. She was a sixty-something, delicately boned blonde, with rich and engaging deep brown eyes. She was simply lovely. Audrey led us on a quick tour of the home that bore her name.

The large main room featured original rough-hewn ceiling beams that held weathered baskets and dried field flowers. An enormous stone hearth dominated the room. The honey-colored, wide-planked pine floors were pegged with original nails. The walls were painted in butter-cream yellow milk paint. I loved all the original details and Audrey's ability to add furnishings that were as comfortable as they were consistent with the period.

"You see that very small door under the staircase?" she asked us. "That was actually hidden under paneling for many years. We are told that the history of the house was not just a farmhouse but served as a link in the Underground Railroad." She showed us a heavy iron padlock that had been found many years before in the room below."

"Feel the weight," she said as she handed off the object. "Can you just imagine how important this was?" she asked. I could. Next, she handed us our own room key. "You guys will be in the Cathedral Room. Breakfast is between eight and ten. If you prefer to be alone, there is a small room off the library set for two. You may not be ready for people before coffee," she added.

Without knowing us, she seemed to perceive our preference for privacy. Was it our constant hand-holding and a projected undercurrent of romantic urgency? Although almost a generation older than we were, I imagined that Audrey and Don might have shared a similar story and need for each other. I noticed their constant eye contact and an attentiveness missing in many older couples. This thought was soon interrupted by the sound of voices. Other guests were arriving. I looked out the window and noticed several bikes lined up on the lawn. Don was now outside eagerly greeting other riders.

Nick pocketed the room key, and then, with Audrey, we joined the newly arriving guests that were gathering under that giant oak. Other bikes were leaning against the tree. Don seemed to already know the others well. There was lots of back slapping, laughter, and bike talk. I noticed that Don always had a hand on other men's shoulders and his eyes covertly on the women. He was a man with maneuvers. He was used to being the host and in command of any situation. His eyes and level of awareness were sharp, finely honed. A cunning crow, he missed no detail. A likeable, attractive cunning crow of a man. He introduced us to the group and I quickly forgot their names. They were seasoned and serious cyclists with good bikes. The array of bikes now assembled featured brands like Trek, Specialized, and Cannondale. There was another Bianchi in silver and an impressive, mean-looking, sleek, black Italian bike whose brand I can't remember.

There was a thirty-something stocky gay couple that Don addressed with reverence. They were not pretty girls, so they escaped the covert glances, but they apparently ranked highly as riders and good company. A frizzy red-haired woman and her bearded, balding husband were off to the side stretching. I had the feeling stretching was a form of foreplay for them. The others were thirty- and forty-year-old singles who seemed to revere Don. They had ridden with him during last year's event and had bonded for life like geese. We gathered on the lawn, exchanged pleasantries, and began filtering back into the farmhouse. Now, we could finally venture up to the Cathedral Room to settle into what would be a private sanctuary.

Key in hand, we walked back through the main room and kitchen to a previously unnoticed door which hid a narrow, crooked, wooden staircase. We ascended cautiously, the staircase hinting at disappointment ahead. The room wasn't large. A very steep gable formed its ceiling. The same battered, rough-hewn beams ran up the sides of the steeple and joined at a center beam.

Why had Don and Audrey named this the Cathedral Room? Weren't cathedrals places of grandeur? We later learned that it had been a hayloft. And only later would we consider the room sacred ground, worthy in our minds of grandeur. In this room, the bed took up most of the floor space. The feathered mattress and pure-white down comforter and pillows were heavenly soft. Two sprigs of freshly gathered lavender tied in thin twine lay across the pillows. Simple white *point d'esprit* curtains covered small windows facing solidly south and west in this corner room. An old red maple chest and padded rocker completed the furnishings. The dresser held a small bottle of Courvoisier cognac flanked by two chubby, footed glasses and an etched tumbler with an already-used candle melted inside. A small candlestick lamp with a plain white linen shade was turned off. There was a simplicity and soft light that reminded me of a Wyeth painting, perhaps of his Helga series. How often I was grateful for those childhood years of learning art that continued to enhance my life.

We flopped into the bed and sunk down. We took matching deep breaths and absorbed the room.

"Do you want a drink before dinner?" I asked.

"No, not yet, look at the color of that sky, the clouds are lit in gold. This is an amazing room. No, let's have dinner down the block and have that drink later."

"There's no rush you know." The greatest luxury of all was time.

We returned to the room several hours later full and lazy. By then, the room was dimly lit from an almost-full moon. We sank into the down comforter in the nearly dark room and again floated gently down into what felt like a nest. We were weightless in spite of too much dinner. There was silence in our room, so apart from other guest rooms. This hayloft was the highest point in the farmhouse and once sat above a chicken coop. The bit of height and unobstructed views of rolling fields to the south and white-faced cliffs to the west created the sensation of being in an actual nest in a tree. We were safely above any possible danger. We were two birds in a downy nest. The heavy beams of the eaves looked almost like branches above our nest. The brandy, feathered bed, and lofty height led me to a heavenly half-dream state.

In perfect, sweet safe silence we dozed off for a short time. From time to time I was aware of him touching my face or whispering, and when he got out of bed at some point, it was his absence that woke me. He sat quietly at the window, gazing off, and I joined him there.

"Hey, Wonder Woman, would you like a sip of brandy about now?" He lit what was left of the candle and poured the glasses to half full.

He took a last look at the landscape and joined me in bed. We were still on top of the incredibly deep, soft comforter. While he poured, I undressed and turned down the comforter. He undressed and slipped into bed after handing me the drinks. Could it be that the bed itself was as deep and dense with feathers as the comforter? Neither of us had experienced this luxury before. We sipped the brandy and moved closer to each other. There was no sense of empty space within the layers. Every possible space filled magically with feathers. Feathers seemed to be floating with us in weightless warmth. We moved slowly even closer. We kissed gently as to not alter the sensation of slowly floating. We encircled limbs so that we could float together. We began to circle and fly together. Our bodies now joined perfectly, we soared. We dipped in gentle rhythm above treetops and clouds. We looked into each other's eyes from time to time to affirm our reality.

From that night on, we referred to the magic in the Cathedral Room as Leda's dream. Only Greek mythology was capable of such enduring beauty. In that Greek myth, Zeus, in the form of a swan, seduces Leda. The erotic overtones in art and poetry have been enjoyed and interpreted through centuries. Rubens and Michelangelo have painted the myth we lived. My favorite poem about Leda was crafted by Hilda Doolittle in 1919. Hers was the first feminist interpretation. The last portion of the poem reads:

Ah, kingly kiss—
no more regret
nor old deep memories
to mar the bliss;
where the low sedge is thick,
the gold day-lily
outspreads and rests
beneath soft fluttering
of red swan wings
and the warm quivering
of the red swan's breast.

Bright sunlight woke us the next morning. We were ready to return to reality and the original purpose of this weekend. The reality of bright-colored bike shirts and the distribution of cue sheets for the ride were in stark contrast to our nest.

Don eyed us with a knowing glance and small grin. He seemed attuned to our mellow mood. A larger group now gathered on the lawn. Everyone was in high spirits and eager to ride. Don reviewed the ride and planned stopping points. He mentioned the need to drink in the same breath that informed us there would be no access to bathrooms for much of the ride. I tucked that thought away. Helmets and gloves on, we mounted bikes and quickly formed a colorful queue starting downhill toward New Paltz. Today's ride of seventy-one miles went from New Paltz to the Ashokan Reservoir. I was happy for the cue sheet, which noted every turn, marker, and pitfall. At least we wouldn't get lost. I still wasn't sure I could complete seventy-one miles at 5,200 vertical feet. The ride, as described by Don, sounded beautiful. We would view three watersheds, a spillover near the Esopus River, and be at the highest summit in the Hudson Valley. We could see over and across the Shawangunk Ridge and then return. It sounded wonderful, but I remembered we weren't going by car. I would be pushing myself and Celeste up those cliffs with my legs. *Oh my God.*

I was still a novice. Grades and vertical feet and difficulty indexes were not yet a part of my vocabulary. What I would soon understand well is that a grade of zero is, of course, a nice flat road. A grade of 2 percent is not very steep. It will reduce the forward force a bit and can absorb about 50 percent of a rider's energy. A grade of 6 percent cuts speed in half and absorbs 80 percent of a rider's energy. That leaves just 20 percent to forge on and keep the legs moving. A grade of 10 percent is only for frequent and fit riders. For most riders, it means succumbing to a walk up the hill. Rides are also described in terms of vertical feet and ratio of grade to distance. I would soon become familiar with these terms, intimately familiar.

There were several 6 percent grades that day. There had to be to climb the elevation. I never had to walk a hill. My dignity and pride often are my greatest climbing buddies. If there is a younger, confident male rider behind me, I am motivated to suck it up and pedal hard. The most dreaded words to a sensitive rider are, "On your left." This signals a faster, passing rider. It's a courtesy, but also an indictment. Nick knows this weakness of mine. He often prods me on with real or fictitious male show-offs behind me, and it works every time. For that ride, we mostly enjoyed the sight of cornfields and cornflowers and grazing cows on 2 percent grades.

We passed through wooded areas that Don suggested were perfect for bathroom use. I needed to pee. I hesitated. The frizzy redhead asked if I wanted to join her down a small path to relative privacy in a small thicket. We walked about fifty feet and decided that was a good spot.

"Do you have any tissues on you?" I asked.

"No, I guess we have to use leaves." We glanced around at some brambly bushes, moldy leaves, and a questionable patch of poison ivy. Bare-assed and squatting side by side, I considered my options. The thought of wet, pee-soaked spandex was unbearable.

"Do you have any money on you?" I asked.

"Yes, I do, I have a five-dollar bill in my back pocket." There was no hesitation. She pulled the bill from her back pocket and ripped it in half, and we laughed at how expensive that little relief was. We remained bike friends on that ride, the next day's ride, and on several more occasional weekends shared at Audrey's.

I learned from Don how to execute a perfect "air-blow." Runny noses plague me. It's not just a problem in cool weather, but with exertion on a steep hill. Carrying tissues is a silly luxury. Expert cyclists, gymnasts, skaters, or skiers are minimalists when it comes to gear. Carrying a wad of tissues or balled up handkerchief is just not done, and wiping snot on sleeves or gloves is disgusting. Don demonstrated the technique to me on that ride. You simply turn your head as far to the side as safely possible. While moving forward, take a deep breath, accelerate a bit, and blow out as fast and hard as possible. If you do it right, it misses hitting you or anyone else.

When we approached the last hill of that day, which led blissfully to the farmhouse, I was exhausted and the next-to-last rider in the group. As always, Nick rode behind me, even if he could have been ahead. Don looked back to check the group, his flock. He yelled in his loudest voice back at us, at me, "Remember, you have to finish strong. The most important thing is looking great when you get to the end! You must always look good and finish strong!" I believed this philosophy applied to lots of things in his life.

The next day, we remounted after a luxurious breakfast. The day's ride of just forty-two miles should have been easy in comparison, but my legs were still fatigued. Cue sheets in hand, we rode past more farms and fields. We passed apple orchards with visible fruit, a reminder of approaching seasons and change. There was a sense of camaraderie. We were spent by the time we returned that afternoon. Mission accomplished, we opted to leave Audrey's and spend an hour or two in New Paltz. There was no question that we would return. Don and Audrey felt like family. We'd soon begin to think of the farmhouse as our first home together, the Cathedral Room a cherished memory we'd return to.

Downtown New Paltz was a time warp. The sixties never left Main Street. What was I doing in the sixties? I reflected. While Janice Joplin belted out her songs and tie-dye was the uniform, where had I been? I had been struggling through high school and night school, then starting nursing school. I had been traveling on the number-four train every day to New York Hospital and doodling in charcoal with Steve Davidson. We had affected the look without living the culture. I had been disconnected, and, I believe, in denial. I had escaped the culture of sex and drugs, but missed out on learning how to make decisions in considering those choices. I lived in a parallel world and avoided the rebellion that may have altered my later choices.

Those young-adult years of testing limits and of confronting fears were stymied by my need for security.

Now, three decades later, I thought about myself at sixteen or eighteen or twenty as I sat with Nick in a vegetarian café with SUNY college students, who were trying to appear irreverent in style and behavior. We felt that we belonged there. We were more irreverent by definition. My time of confrontation and rebellion came later in life and was recent. I had challenged every rule I'd believed in and lived by in a marriage I thought was forever. We were more irreverent than any kid with contrived dreadlocks and pierced lips. I loved New Paltz. I could go there, gather up some missed youthful piece of my life, and leave it, embracing how I'd changed.

August was a month of committed training and continued conviction to being together. We tried to ride as often as possible. We revisited Montauk so I could claim conquering a century ride. It was better without dehydration. Ironically, it rained heavily for a good portion of the ride, and water poured through the vents of my helmet and down my face. My hands were wet, and I constantly dried them uselessly on my slick rain jacket. That thin nylon jacket kept the rain out and the sweat in. We were drenched. We continued the water theme when we completed the ride and returned to our room at the Montauk Inn. There, we shared a long hot bath in an oversized tub. We added essential oils of lavender and rosemary and lit a eucalyptus-scented candle. We turned off the lights and sat back in the dark, back to chest, like a bobsled team. We didn't speak. In the quiet, we listened to a slow drip from the faucet and waves outside the room. The sounds hypnotized us. We floated in scented silence.

There was a ride to Silvermine and New Canaan, Connecticut. There we stayed in a room that reminded me again of a Wyeth painting. It was all shades of gray and cream with thin light and a simple four-poster bed. We spent as much time within the framework of the bed as on the road. Sex or silence often took a back seat to long, thoughtful discussions about the impact of our irreverence and an unknown future. We understood and cared deeply about that ripple effect.

We returned to Audrey's when we could. Once, we stopped by unexpectedly on a weekday as Don and Audrey were sitting for lunch. There were no guests to be tended to. They had two plates set on simple mats at the kitchen table where they could observe the view. Don lit two candles, kissed Audrey's cheek, and then sat down to eat. In that moment, I believed in lasting love, and we imagined our own future.

Chapter Twenty-Four

BOSTON

The final plans for Boston to New York were made. There were so many details. We listed and packed suggested supplies. They included rain gear, sleeping bags, and appropriate bike clothes. We were to share a tent for two nights. This was a far cry from featherbeds and soaking tubs. We arranged for bike shipping and for a hotel in Boston. We studied train schedules to bring us there and parking lots for a three-day stay in New York for the car. On a weekday, the week before the ride, we brought the bikes to the lower west side of the city to be registered, tagged, and transported to Boston. They were traveling with more than two hundred other bikes in a huge truck. They would arrive before we did. I remember watching the bikes as they were walked up the ramp into the truck. It reminded me of my children's first day of school, a necessary, sad-happy milestone. We would be reunited with the bikes in Boston soon enough. We would retrieve them and begin the ride on September 16, 1998.

In Boston, we joined a new family of 1,600. This family was not just large but unusual in the disproportionate numbers of gay men. We had been so focused on training and fundraising before arriving in Boston that we had lost track of an important part of our goal: fundraising for AIDS. The heart and soul of that goal was about to be revealed by the participants of this ride.

I wonder now who, besides the gay community, even remembers the fear and misery that ushered in the beginning of the AIDS crisis. In the twenty-five-year period between 1980, when the first awareness of a new disease emerged, and 2005, the incidence and death rates grew exponentially. In 2005 alone, 950,000 new cases were diagnosed and almost 530,000 people died. The memory of that suffering should have been permanently imbedded. But like most historical crises, the sharp edges softened in time. Today, the annual death rate has dropped to under 6,000 and effective antiviral drugs extend and improve quality of life. As a nurse, my memories are mostly of public fear of the disease and of the gay community as the source of its origins. The AIDS rides that took place across the country over seven years raised over one hundred million dollars.

As we looked around, we saw many riders like us. They rode recreationally, not competitively. Some identified with the cause, and I imagine some suffered from existential angst for a host of possible reasons. There were some riders that rode with the pain of personal loss. The riders were all ages and had all kinds of bikes. Sometimes the bikes were not good choices for a long road journey. Some riders wore signs pinned to their backs featuring photos of dead or dying loved ones, the faces and ages of the loved ones painfully youthful. On the longest and steepest hills, the photos reignited my energy.

The obviously gay cyclists, God love them, brought their creativity and outrageous humor to the ride, and lent a spirit of fun to the grueling parts. Their helmets were pure whimsy. There were stegosaurus spikes running from forehead to neck, propellers spinning, and flowers growing on helmets. There were Raggedy Ann pigtails and Rapunzel braids growing from air vents. They wore hot-pink and purple or rainbow-colored bike shoes. They dressed as superheroes and cartoon characters. It was not unusual to see a red cape flying behind a rider as he descended a hill. Their levity added comic relief when we most needed it, though I suspect that relief was needed more by them.

Our huge group first assembled at 8:00 a.m. on the grounds of a Northeastern University campus field. I can't remember the names of specific streets that surrounded the field. The field sat about thirty feet lower than street level. A concrete wall with chain-link fence above it created a border. We were packed like sardines and start times were not staggered. We would leave together in a massive wave of wheels, handlebars, and brightly clothed people. I was overwhelmed by the size of the crowd, loud music, and thoughts of the effort ahead. I held Celeste upright with one hand and gripped Nick's free hand with the other. We waited like this for at least an hour. We could hear muffled announcements on a bullhorn. The messages were difficult to hear and then became drowned out by words we could decipher.

"SINNERS, REPENT!"

"SINNERS, REPENT!"

"AIDS is God's wrath!"

A small and loud group above carried signs with Biblical references and numbers corresponding to scripture. Their posters bobbed up and down, and their voices grew louder. It took a few minutes for their intent to register. The atmosphere around me changed from celebratory to sour. They were a smaller group, but determined to disrupt. They were not God-fearing, simply homophobic.

"Faggot, faggot, faggot!" they chanted. Hateful, hurtful chants that sounded familiar, like those you'd hear at a sport's event. These were the ugliest people I had ever seen or heard. We were horrified. I hoped that only the riders closest witnessed this.

Finally, an even louder sound drowned them out, the deep blast of an air horn signaling that somewhere on this field a ribbon had been cut, and we were off.

That first half hour was frightening. I longed for safe space. We rode just inches apart from one another. We were shoulder to shoulder, hand grip touching hand grip. This looked like the Tour de France. My breath quickened; I felt nauseous. This was not the start I had envisioned.

I had not wanted to be in a Peloton. I was no pro. "Nick, I'm scared, we're all too close. I can't ride like this." He quickly looked at me and nodded, affirming the danger.

"Wonder Woman, take a breath. We're all going so slow that if we fall it will feel like a bounce castle." That reality and joke moved me forward. The voice of reason. Eventually the crowd did thin. There was never a time that anyone was in single file. Nick would alternate between being next to me for conversation or behind me for inspiration. On one long grueling hill, he dutifully kept me going. When a harsh male voice in obvious annoyance yelled out, "On your left!" giving me a dirty look as he passed, Nick went into defensive mode. "On *your* left buddy!" He dogged him and taunted him up the hill. He stayed close behind and would periodically shout, "On *your* left!"

Road rage exists in bike form, although that was our only experience of it on this ride. Mostly it was sidewalk cheering from people in neighborhoods we passed and event volunteers dressed as clowns or chickens entertaining us if the route got boring. There was the ever-present sag wagon, complete with bike repair and first-aid items. There was never a dull moment. When I wasn't preoccupied with a struggle, I was entertained. We were a caravan of cyclists and clowns on a serious mission.

Beside the sag wagons was a truck that carried riders' tagged personal belongings. They were driven ahead for delivery to the campsites. Two pink plastic flamingos were riding in that truck. They were ours. Without even knowing how well our own idea of fun would be received, we'd risked tacky lawn ornaments to mark our tent. Little did we know we had the perfect audience. The staked, plastic, bright-pink birds flanked our tent entry. Our names were painted across their long necks. They even made it back to Manhattan and eventually lived behind a mature woody rosemary bush that survived New York winters facing south.

Rest stops were at fifteen to twenty mile intervals. Elite riders quickly peed, rehydrated, and left to maintain all-important time goals. We enjoyed the camaraderie and fun too much to do that. We often met the same gay couple at rest stops, recognizable by their Mickey Mouse ears and a big polka-dot Minnie bow between a set of ears on their helmets. Their timing and ability was similar to ours. They also often held hands as we did. I imagine these men had waged their own battles over the sanctity of loving each other.

I became a Port-o-San connoisseur. Rows of them were eagerly used by everyone. It wasn't just their cleanliness or deodorizers that differed. Toilet paper holders and the presence of enough toilet paper were important. Some had mirrors glued to the inside of the door. Personally, I questioned the satisfaction of watching yourself void. There was often good graffiti or a personal message on an inside wall. The Port-o-San could be a place of inspirational phrases. At one stop, I was impressed. Feeling compelled to offer a rating, I told a tired man waiting his turn, "That is the best Port-o-San yet. It has a wall pocket to put your things in. I felt like I was in Bloomingdale's with a purse holder for my bag."

"Oh, honey, so sorry to tell you, but that's a urinal, and I think your bike gloves are wet."

Day one was the longest and most difficult day. We rode ninety-six miles. There were fifty miles climbing to an elevation of eight hundred feet. The longest, hardest part of the day was a seven mile climb to nine hundred feet in Storrs, Connecticut. I know there was either a level-eight or level-ten grade to one long, long hill. I tried valiantly. I told Nick to ride ahead when it was obvious I was holding him back and making it harder for him. "I'll meet you at the top, don't worry. Have an extra Clif Bar while you're waiting." My quads burned and ached. They threatened to quit. From the side of the shady country road, volunteers shouted encouragement. "Last hill, you can do it, last hill in Storrs!"

Fucking liars, I thought. I knew that wasn't true. Someone on the last hill said the same thing, and now I knew they were empty words. My chest felt like it would burst and expel the contents of my withered purple lungs and bloated heart to the ground. I tried counting pedal strokes, a technique that always helped. I looked around at other riders. Everyone was riding in slow motion. It became clear that some people were walking their bikes along the sides of the road. A new lane had formed for walkers. They looked like hopeless prisoners in a chain gang. Nausea was setting in. I managed to stay balanced and get my water bottle out of its frame.

No one was speaking anymore. It was silent. The energy

needed for speech was a priceless luxury at this point. The walker lane became more populated. I saw Minnie and Mickey walking in that lane. There were no smart-assed spunky male riders saying, "On your left." I was alone with little to motivate me to stay upright and connected as a single unit to Celeste. I noticed the sun was getting lower through the tall pines that flanked the hill. Now I was worried about riding in the dark and having to pitch the tent at night.

I told Celeste it was time to walk. I joined the ranks of the slow-lane walking dead and trudged my way to the top. Nick stood anxiously at the left side waiting for me. I imagined he'd stopped, realizing I'd be among the walkers. He knew which gate my flight was arriving at. He offered a kiss and a Clif Bar.

We arrived on the campus of UConn as the sun was setting. The field was filled with small triangular blue-green tents. Row upon row of metal bike stands held dusty bikes. The seats had all been covered in plastic grocery bags to protect them from night showers and morning dew. Music was playing from a PA system. Larger, more permanent tents with rolled up sides held signs that offered massage. A long, ugly, metal trailer that had once been attached to a truck held a sign that read SHOWERS. *How was that possible?* I thought. Along the sides of the vast field, barbecued burgers and hot dogs were sending smoke signals to exhausted, hungry soldiers. This looked like a scene from *M*A*S*H*, but the mood was festive. Surviving this day warranted celebration. We located our tagged personal belongings and found an empty space to pitch our tent—a place to call home for the night.

First, we unpacked the flamingos and staked them in. That the tent somehow rose from the ground in the correct shape was a miracle I take credit for. Years of mom weekends at my daughter's camp had taught me a few important survival skills.

We ate, showered in the trailer, and fell into the two-person tent. The only luxury items were two, still-wrapped silver foil squares that would open to human-sized baking sheets. It was September and nights were chilly. We fell asleep immediately and awoke before sunrise the next morning, slightly disoriented and very stiff. We looked at each other, two huge Hershey kisses inside a small tent, and laughed.

Day two's destination was Seaside Park in Bridgeport, Connecticut. The ride hugged the coastline of Connecticut. It was scenic, but still featured thirty-seven hills. Total mileage day two was 88.9 miles, only a small improvement. After the monster hill in Storrs, I was fearful. Fortunately, no hills were as evil as the Storrs's monster, and walking wasn't necessary. We managed to stay mid-pack and arrive at the campsite well before sunset. The sweetest surprise of all was arriving to find a pitched tent with two pink flamingos waiting to welcome us home. An anonymous friend had been at work. Minnie and Mickey? The atmosphere was joyous. We had all completed the longest and most difficult part of the ride. Tomorrow we would ride into New York and then, unbelievably, into Manhattan. We were almost home.

We were running on adrenalin day three. There were still over seventy miles to contend with, but fewer and lower hills. The strangest portion of day three for me was passing from Connecticut into New York via Westchester County. We went down Boston Post Road through Rye and Port Chester and New Rochelle. We passed the Neptune Diner and the McDonald's we ate in when my kids were small. We passed car dealerships and supermarkets that brought me back to being in my thirties and forties. *Who am I now?* I thought. I was troubled by feeling detached from the past. I felt sad and momentarily disoriented, past and present colliding.

We rode though the Bronx, nowhere near the neighborhoods I grew up in. Still, it was the Bronx, the place that first formed me. I felt strangely reconnected to origins that made me sad again. I assumed the passing sadness was just fatigue. We were about to leave Westchester.

The Bronx became Inwood and Manhattan. Now the ride would be easiest of all. The highest point in Manhattan rises only 265 feet above sea level. The only challenge now would be city traffic and crowds. *This is just how it began,* I thought. Again, a momentary feeling of melancholy passed over me. Fatigue? And then the sight of an actual end appeared. As we came down Broadway to 11th Avenue toward 38th Street, we could see metal parade barriers along the streets. There were volunteers distributing long-sleeved victory T-shirts. Across the front was a huge banner with the ride logo and the words, NEVER GIVE UP. On the shirts, a rider held his bike above his head in victory. Soon, most riders mimicked the logo and held bikes high while friends and family recorded the moment.

Behind the barriers still separating riders from spectators was a huge crowd. There were balloons and welcome-home posters and children riding on shoulders. There were whistles and hand clapping and names of loved ones being shouted into the crowd. Nick and I became spectators now. There would be no family or friends or handmade posters for us. We had not and could not include our families in this monumental accomplishment. This moment was a stark reminder of the irrevocable choice we had made. It marked the beginning of painful wrenching from a past that would remind us of the sacrifice we were making.

We walked our bikes to the garage and secured them to the back of the car as we had done countless times in the past five months. As we drove home in silence, I closed my eyes. Nick reached over and touched my hand from time to time. We were together. Where was home now?

Chapter Twenty-Five

HOMESTRETCH

"You have to finish good. It's all about looking good at the finish line." Don's words were not resounding well for matters off the bike. Steve had moved out. We had lawyers that worked quickly to dissolve twenty-eight years of shared life equitably. There is little equity in divorce. The equity is actually in the division of pain rather than assets and possessions. The sale of the ill-fated Tudor substitute was unresolved. I was anxious to sell it. There was no emotional connection to this house. The time spent there was marked by loneliness, failure, and guilt.

"Hey, guess what? It looks like I may be homeless if the new mortgage company doesn't get back to me this week," I joked to Nick. I'd found a cute little Cape house that would be a home in my name only, but it was taking forever to get final approval. This was a cliffhanger. We'd sold the Tudor to an obnoxious young couple with one child. They loved the showy facade and proximity to the synagogue. They loved the price they were paying, which was under market value. Death and divorce yield wonderful buying opportunities when available.

The biggest challenge I faced was how to pare down three decades worth of possessions and necessities that had grown to live in 3,500-square feet to fit into 1,400-square feet.

"Do you want the Fiestaware or the Franciscan dishes?" I asked. Steve had already moved out. The marriage counselor had become his friend and advocate. She found him a sublet in a wonderful condo on City Island. She and her husband were right next door. That kindness saved him from desperation and ultimately set him on a path to new peace. My mother also rallied to support him during this painful transition. He had been a kind and loving son-in-law for almost three decades. They cared deeply about each other, but her constant presence in our lives, ironically, served to both undermine the marriage and to create a duality of primary relationships. She was my companion when he devoted all those long hours to the store, and she was mother and friend to both of us. Now, she created a more formal definition of these roles. As she supported and reassured him of her continued presence in his life, she also accepted and eventually welcomed Nick into my life. She understood now, as she always had, that her daughter was acknowledging greater unmet needs. She became a liaison and family goodwill ambassador. We were all grateful for this.

Good communication between all of us made setting up two homes easier. I could ask those practical questions about dishes or furniture and move us along in our new lives. As to those dishes, "It doesn't matter. I can get new stuff," he said, wanting to make it all easier. Always helpful, he was considerate and self-sacrificing to the end. I wallowed in well-deserved guilt every time we spoke. I focused on the task at hand. I distracted myself with reviewing and reflecting on the destination of the details of our accumulated lives. No small task. I was grateful for his newly discovered ability to function independently and efficiently. There was an efficient exodus from our collective lives. His dignity and my resolve enabled us to navigate to separate futures, our children reassured that their parents were strong and unquestionably present for them now and forever.

Chapter Twenty-Six

MOVING ON

Nick and I also ventured separately and tentatively into the practical issues of new lives. He moved into a small apartment in Pelham, a neighboring suburb. Like me, he had left his parents' home to marry. This was his first apartment alone. We shopped for sheets and dishes and pantry items. He'd left his home and marriage to stay mostly in his office with only some clothing. Shortly after his move, a package arrived from his elderly parents, who lived in Florida. He was relieved that they had been quietly nonjudgmental about his decision, expressing only concern for his well-being and relationship with his daughters. The package included treasures from his past and practical items. There was an old alarm clock in a light wood frame that had awakened him all through high school and felt instantly like an old friend. His father, a chef, also sent a favorite pasta pot and cooking utensils. These, he knew, were gifts from the heart, and he was moved to tears for the memories and unconditional love these gifts conveyed.

While Nick adjusted to his new apartment, I still had a few long weeks left at home as I waited for the closing date the obnoxious young buyers of the Tudor had agreed upon. The practical issues of this move meant less space in spite of a guaranteed bedroom for each of us. Mine would be an eleven-by-fourteen dormer with two small windows facing precariously close to the cookie-cutter Cape twenty feet away. The houses in this tract averaged fifteen hundred square feet. My new car, a Volkswagen Beetle, would look more at home in this driveway than the Mercedes we'd returned. Everything was downsized, it seemed. With no basement and only a crawl-space attic, there was no room for a "to be determined" category of possessions. It was now or never. I needed to go through everything I owned and to decide the destiny of my possessions.

All the treasures I had sought, stalked, collected, and loved now confronted me, I thought each deserved the dignity and thought of re-homing them carefully. Before I wrapped anything in tissue or Bubble Wrap, I forced myself to recall the origins and significance of each object in my life. I thought the ritual would make parting easier. I remembered the words of a friend who professionally appraised fine art and antiques. "Beth, what must it feel like to own a Chagall?" I mused one afternoon as she discussed a recent appraisal of a Chagall for a client.

"The Chagall, like all treasures, owns people for a while." This thought was comforting. I plodded forward, surrounded by boxes, wrap, and markers. The things that did own me were an odd collection. With Beth's words in mind, I easily sold things with names like Lalique and Royal Copenhagen. I disposed of most furniture, save the Baker and antique pieces, which I happily gave to Steve for his condo. A tiger maple chest on chest that was my own childhood storage, a piece my mother had purchased secondhand right after I was born, came along for my daughter's room. The hand-stamped brass drawer pulls and classic form were ageless. Its value, if any, was lost when

I stripped the original finish and stained it antique white. My intention was to make it look shabby chic, a misguided effort. In any case, I consider it the first piece of furniture in my life. It was also a concrete link to my mother. Not surprising was a need to hold onto things from my earliest years. I wondered if they were reminders of the insecurities of my childhood, and therefore served to reassure me of my ability to persevere.

The Roseville pottery collection belonged in that category, too. The very first piece was given to me by my mother as a prank wedding gift. It was a dusty-rose simple vase with pale gardenias and misty green leaves. She'd purchased it for twenty-five cents, and it had always been somewhere in my childhood home. I thought it was ugly. When we'd moved to the apartment near the elevated train, I took that vase to the trash in the basement twice during clean-ups. Each time, my mother missed it and retrieved it. She finally stuck it in the rear of an upper kitchen cabinet for its own safety and to appease me. Later, it appeared, beautifully wrapped as a wedding present to me when I married Steven. It became the first piece in what became a large collection of Roseville pottery. I'm sure there is some lesson there about evolving taste and sentimentality.

I packed a tiny porcelain dog that was given to me by Mary, my mother's Scrabble friend. At some point she must have noticed my fixation with that shelf as I waited patiently for a long game to end. It was another token of childhood. A miniature Waterford mantle clock that was not from the distant past was packed. It was a piece of a promised future. The ill-fated tryst to the Gramercy Park Hotel is a sweet and funny memory, and the clock a reminder of both time past and racing forward.

The only other piece of furniture that stayed, as if bonded to me, was the French provincial chair of my earliest memory. The chair has been recovered several times, and would continue to be a piece I'd contemplate reattiring. Staring at it for even just a second will conjure up the memory of my father in that chair. It's something I won't do often, because it serves little purpose to imagine a different outcome. I will remember his crossed leg and funny shoes of woven brown leather. I will remember a foot swinging and his hand on my head. The chair will stay, as will the memory.

Finally, there were the photos to consider. What to do with wedding albums and another dozen leather-bound albums of birthday parties and dance recitals and vacations? There were three bar mitzvah albums that are almost embarrassing for their cost and the cost of the celebrations that marked that rite of passage. Collectively, these visual records belonged to all of us. These were precious images of first birthdays, haircuts, days of school, and days of life—precious, joyous times that we lived as a family. I would spend many self-indulgent and sad moments with those photos. The sadness mixed with gratitude for the love bestowed and priceless gift of children we both cherish. The children and grandchildren are the greatest legacy of our marriage and lives.

With whom did these belong? There were loose photos that had ended up in shoeboxes and Tupperware. I carefully packed them in extra heavy boxes and labeled them. They would come with me. That wasn't a selfish decision. I knew I would have a small crawl space to store them and could grab them in a fire if I had to. I designated myself as the temporary guardian of photographs. They were there for the asking if anyone wanted them. My children and later my grandchildren will think photos are transient images on a cell phone to be scrolled through quickly. The images I've kept will be of a different era. The century-old sepia-toned photos that stayed with me will never generate much interest, but who knows if that will always be the case. People take interest in their histories at different moments in their lives, but who would expect anyone to look at a faded black-and-white photo with a wavy white border?

My two favorite photos are in small gold frames. One is a photo of me at five, in overalls and striped Polo shirt. I am peeking out from the side of my grandfather's '57 Chevy. The car is two-toned black and white. I have short bangs and a mischievous expression. I remember being happy, teasing my grandfather, and mugging for the photo. The other is of my brother and me sitting together on a small pony. The pony is brown and white and has a silver star decorating its bridle. The star is in a circle that we thought was a sheriff's badge. My mother paid a dollar for us to sit on the pony and get the photo. Those little opportunities sometimes happened in our first Bronx neighborhood. My brother has a copy of the same photo in his home. Like mine, it would follow him through life. I know why we love the photo, because we shared it all and understand each other in a special way. The photo is perfect because that small pony reminds us of our shared ride through life.

I treasure the oldest sepia-toned photos of my great-grandparents and their extended family. They have hung on some wall of every home I've lived in. Hopefully, my children will want to follow that tradition even if they don't know the stories of these people as I do. Those stories will end with me, I imagine. I find that both sad and comforting. I believe that, after two generations, we become historical ephemera ourselves. The indiscretions, questionable decisions, and sad events are forgotten. In time, there is a softening of the edges and fading of the memory to pale sepia.

In contrast, the photos of our wedding day, a very warm April day in 2000, show bright blue skies and the rolling green Block Island hills. There are colorful kites and loved ones gathered around us. It had been exactly two years since the unseasonably cold day in April in Central Park when we abandoned a first ride because it was, fortunately, too cold. All these photos capture happy moments in time, but remind me that they are just that, fleeting moments. They remind me that, no matter how fast you pedal up a hill or how you look at the finish line, time moves past you. The camera captures the moment, and then time moves forward and leaves you behind.

Epilogue

SUMMER IN LEDA'S HOUSE

I wonder if bike years are counted like dog years? Stella, my eight-year-old dachshund would be fifty-six of our years if that were the case. If Celeste were a dog, she'd be 112. Now I'm thinking I have too much time on my hands. Why am I thinking about dog years and bike years? After all, Celeste is not a living creature. Perhaps this is what happens when you have your first full summer off in fifty years. This must mean I'm old. I've worked since age fourteen. First it was summer jobs with Steve Davidson at Montefiore. Then it was full-time nursing with a few unscheduled weeks to savor. Then it was home care, then school nursing with all those years of camp nursing in summer.

I ride Celeste eight miles around the Titicus Reservoir every morning. I do a few nice hills, enjoy the views, and congratulate myself for continuing to ride with confidence and for living on the periphery of this beautiful reservoir with a bike route.

Nick and I bought this antique treasure once the children

were all independent. It's almost 175 years old and our few years here have been uniquely ours. The 1845 house reminded us of Audrey's. Actually, it bears little structural or geographic similarity to Audrey's. It's not as old, and not a farmhouse. There are no views of sheared cliffs or fields. Downtown New Paltz is an hour away. We have an antique metal sleigh bed and a feathered mattress. Our bed faces a lovely stream and woods. It's not the Cathedral Room, but it is ours to enjoy every day. It's ours alone. We are special here and aware of every moment shared. We are grateful for gifts that can never be quantified.

We are still in love, content with our shared lives, though I confess to residual traces of insecurity and anger from childhood that sneak into that happiness. I originally imagined my first summer off since childhood would undo those small remnants of my inner child, but I'm not sure I want that now. I kind of like the vestiges of that Bronx edge. It keeps my juices flowing. So what if I never yield to a Mercedes or BMW at a four-way intersection? I've made strides. I often give the benefit of doubt to smug young women wearing spandex midday. Maybe they work part time. Maybe they are political activists or volunteers. Best of all, I mostly do not give them much thought at all. That's real progress.

It is strange to have a summer off. My grandchildren are with their parents on vacation in Maine or Cape Cod. The others are happily paired or married and working through summer. Nick's youngest is struggling through nursing school. She is a little like me, so I'm rooting for her. She is tenacious.

It's just us this summer. It's just me not working. The house is so much like a B&B, perfect for summer. There's a front porch, big backyard, a garden, and a hammock. There's a bike route at the end of the driveway and a rowboat in the reservoir.

Celeste has a new companion in our small garage. It was

time to retire Nick's secondhand bike, so a new silver Specialized bike hangs above Celeste in the double rack nearby. It's a younger, faster bike. Nick still rides behind me on hills. I still need to hear him taunt me lovingly all the way to the top.

The summer will not be all rest. We are taking two weeks to ride the rolling hills on Block Island. We are taking a long overdue fundraising bike challenge the last week of summer. It is one hundred miles in Maine to benefit Parkinson's research. It's been over sixteen years since we rode Boston to New York. We haven't trained, and we are out of shape. We are sixteen years older. There's a good chance I will ride the sag wagon or walk a hill. However I ride, I know it will be with him by my side. We will share every moment and detail together. I'm planning on looking good at the finish line either way. You need to look good at the finish line.

ACKNOWLEDGMENTS

I was fortunate to discover Brooke Warner and She Writes Press when writing and publishing this book became a goal. Brooke patiently guided and taught me how to reign in rants, ruminate, and reflect with purpose and develop a memoir that yielded a good story and self-discovery. I am forever grateful to have found myself in the supportive family of She Writes Press.

To my loving husband, Nick, who read each word many times and relived the moments with dedicated interest and enthusiastic support, I treasure our constant sharing and the rare silence of thoughtful pauses. You know and love me so specially. *"Sempre il mio principe."*

To my brother, Stephen Payne, somehow we are still sharing, still connected, and somehow . . . old! Mom would be pleased. I am.

To Mark, Scott, and Sara, you are the most precious possessions of my heart. I hope this memoir brings understanding, insight, and then a few good stories that carry on into the future. I love you.

For Hattie, Charlotte, Joseph, Nico, and Oliver, the next generation of people we share and love.

ABOUT THE AUTHOR

Dave C. Smith Photography

Barbara Santarelli, RN, BS, HCA, has been an employed nurse for more than four decades and an elementary school nurse for the past twenty-five years. She's authored articles about sex education for teens, and credits her long and varied nursing career to her cryptic sense of humor and persistent optimism. Twice married (currently to husband Nick), Santarelli is a mother, grandmother, avid reader, and cyclist who considers Stella, her nine-pound Dachsund, and Celeste, her road bike, to be members of her extended family.

SELECTED TITLES FROM SHE WRITES PRESS

She Writes Press is an independent publishing company founded to serve women writers everywhere. Visit us at **www.shewritespress.com**.

Blue Apple Switchback: A Memoir by Carrie Highley. $16.95, 978-1-63152-037-2. At age forty, Carrie Highley finally decided to take on the biggest switchback of her life: upon her bicycle, and with the help of her mentor's wisdom, she shed everything she was taught to believe as a young lady growing up in the South—and made a choice to be true to herself and everyone else around her.

Miracle at Midlife: A Transatlantic Romance by Roni Beth Tower. $16.95, 978-1-63152-123-2. An inspiring memoir chronicling the sudden, unexpected, and life-changing two-year courtship between a divorced American lawyer living on a houseboat in the center of Paris and an empty-nested clinical psychologist living in Connecticut.

Renewable: One Woman's Search for Simplicity, Faithfulness, and Hope by Eileen Flanagan. $16.95, 978-1-63152-968-9. At age forty-nine, Eileen Flanagan had an aching feeling that she wasn't living up to her youthful ideals or potential, so she started trying to change the world—and in doing so, she found the courage to change her life.

The Full Catastrophe: A Memoir by Karen Elizabeth Lee. $16.95, 978-1-63152-024-2. The story of a well educated, professional woman who, after marrying the wrong kind of man—twice—finally resurrects her life.

The Sportscaster's Daughter: A Memoir by Cindi Michael. $16.95, 978-1-63152-107-2. Despite being disowned by her father—sportscaster George Michael, said to be the man who inspired ESPN's *SportsCenter*—Cindi Michael manages financially and heals emotionally, ultimately finding confidence from within.

There Was a Fire Here: A Memoir by Risa Nye. $16.95, 978-1-63152-045-7. After a devastating firestorm destroys Risa Nye's Oakland, California home and neighborhood, she has to dig deep to discover her inner strength and resilience.